socialism
today

progress

GEORGI SMIRNOV

SOVIET MAN
The Making
of a Socialist Type
# of Personality

PROGRESS PUBLISHERS
MOSCOW

Translated from the Russian by Robert Daglish

СМИРНОВ ГЕОРГИЙ ЛУКИЧ
СОВЕТСКИЙ ЧЕЛОВЕК.
ФОРМИРОВАНИЕ СОЦИАЛИСТИЧЕСКОГО ТИПА ЛИЧНОСТИ

На английском языке

First printing 1973

Printed in the Union of Soviet Socialist Republics

CONTENTS

6

INTRODUCTION

The emergence in the USSR and other socialist countries of a new type of personality is a fact of outstanding historical importance, acknowledged throughout the world by both the friends and enemies of communism. The shaping and development of this new type of personality is a result of the revolutionary transition to a new form of society, of the building of socialism and communism. What effect have these changes wrought on man's position, on his intellectual and moral character, on his life style? What are the essential common features that allow us to speak of a new type of personality? How are they related to the moral experience man has accumulated in the course of centuries? Within the general framework of the socialist type of personality to what extent do people still differ in their activity and behaviour? It is natural that we should ask ourselves these questions, particularly the last, since it is connected with the whole idea of personal freedom.

In other words, what we are talking about is the progress of personality in a socialist society, the development of the individual in a context of changing social relations, since, as Lenin said, "the materialist sociologist, taking the definite social relations of people as the object of his inquiry, by that very fact also studies real *individuals*, from whose actions these relations are formed."[1] "All history consists of

---

[1] V. I. Lenin, *Collected Works*, Vol. 1, p. 406.

the actions of individuals, and it is the task of social science
to explain these actions. . . ."[1]

Marxism states that to change a man's character one must
change the conditions of his existence. The doctrine of scientific communism on the revolutionary remaking of society,
the emancipation of the working people from capitalist
exploitation and oppression of all kinds serves this very
purpose. Moreover, no Communist can imagine the attainment of happiness for all without happiness for the individual, since he thinks of communism as an association in which
"the free development of each is the condition for the free
development of all".[2]

The emergence of this new kind of person in the socialist
countries concerns the interests of people of all classes, every
section of society throughout the world. The new people and
new relations between them are the alternative to the bourgeois and every other kind of society based on exploitation. The Great October Revolution in Russia and the subsequent socialist revolutions have repudiated the old, seemingly
unshakeable order of things that has existed for centuries
with the blessing of both religion and official morality, and
it makes a direct difference to the warring classes in countries where the old order still exists whether the successes of
socialism are acknowledged or not. If a new man has been
brought into being and possesses outstanding moral and
ideological qualities, this must mean that the building of
socialism serves the interests of the working people, that the
Communists have the truth of history on their side.

The history of Soviet man as a socialist type of person,
despite his individuality and even uniqueness, contains
certain essential features of a general nature that relate to
the solution of the complex social problems involved in the
formation of a new type of man in all countries of the world.

It is this that has made the "Soviet phenomenon" the
subject of universal attention. A people that has been able
to cast aside the age-old canons and forms of life of exploitative society, that has created fundamentally different

---

[1] V. I. Lenin, *Collected Works*, Vol. 1, p. 397.
[2] K. Marx and F. Engels, *Selected Works*, in three volumes, Vol. 1,
Moscow, 1969, p. 127.

economic and political conditions, that has adopted the communist view of the world as its own and displayed unprecedentedly high moral qualities and ideological and political unity—such a people could not fail to attract tremen- dous interest in its way of life, in its actions and thoughts. For everyone with any ability to think it is becoming increasingly clear that behind the bold refashioning of the whole structure of society, behind the unsurpassed military victories, behind the astonishingly rapid rate of economic advance, behind the sputniks and the luniks, behind man's breakthrough into outer space, behind the splendid, high- spirited art—behind all this there have been people. And these people have displayed exceptional devotion to the new socialist system, tremendous determination and courage, organisation and discipline in defending it, and have at the same time shown themselves to possess such attractive human qualities as kindness, responsiveness, spontaneity and modesty. The Western observer cannot fail to notice all these things and draw his own conclusions.

One finds evidence of this in the great number of ques- tions that Soviet people are asked when abroad, in the numerous studies of various aspects of Soviet life. Films are made about Soviet people. Novels, philosophical and polit- ical treatises are written about them. Learned discussions are held on the subject. People argue about them in the intimate circle of their friends and think about them when alone.

The Soviet man is a great source and generator of ideas in the modern world. This is one of the most characteristic features of the ideological situation that has been developing ever since the first working people's socialist state came into being.

In the bourgeois world two opposite attitudes towards the socialist changes in the USSR, towards the Soviet man, his ideas and way of life, emerged from the very start. On the one hand, among workers, among fair-minded people gener- ally there was approval and enthusiastic support; on the other, in the circles of imperialist reaction there was hatred and a desire to destroy the new society.

The imperialist bourgeoisie built up a barrier of lies, slander and misinformation around the Soviet people. One smear campaign was followed in quick succession by another. The ideals, policy and practical measures of the Communist Party and the Soviet state, the behaviour of Soviet people were twisted out of recognition and interpreted in the most fantastic ways. No bourgeois propagandist ever attributed more terrifying qualities and deeds to anyone than were attributed to the Bolsheviks. Soviet people were alleged to be doing the most absurd things imaginable. Colossal efforts were made, above all, to distort the image of the revolutionary and the Soviet person in general, to create a bogey with which to frighten ordinary folk.

But this, quite deliberate line of imperialist propaganda, dictated by the logic of defence of the class interests of imperialism, has come into ever wider conflict with the logic of facts, the logic of history. The successful building of socialism in the USSR, the Soviet Union's victory over Hitler Germany, the successes of the Soviet economy, science and culture, the consolidation of the social and state system have had the effect they were bound to have on people's attitude abroad. One of the highlights in this process has been the Soviet pioneering of outer space, which has triggered off a whole series of acknowledgements of Soviet achievement in all fields, from economics to ideology and culture.

These successes in consolidating and developing the socialist way of life, in producing a new kind of person have provided the international working class with an example that inspires them in their struggle against imperialism. As for the imperialist bourgeoisie itself, a process is taking place that could be called the splitting of the bourgeois consciousness. One part of the bourgeoisie still clings to its position of global, absolute refusal to acknowledge Soviet achievement, to the position of preventive war and the physical destruction of socialism, while another part, under pressure of circumstances, is compelled to admit the viability of socialism and is gravitating towards positions of peaceful coexistence of the two systems.

So a path has been travelled from downright, absolute denial of everything socialist to acknowledgement of the strength and viability of socialism, the prestige and influence of its ideas; from attempts at overt military and economic strangling of Soviet power to a search for constructive solutions of the acute problems of peaceful coexistence with that power, to conceptions of a "counterforce" and "flexible reaction"; from the assumption of the total absurdity of a state of workers and peasants to the notion of a "single industrial society". Such are the historical parameters in which the influence of socialism on the strategy and tactics of imperialism has expressed itself.

This is not to say that imperialism's opposition to socialism has weakened in either the political or the ideological and theoretical field. The ideologists of imperialism are trying to give their own peculiar explanation of Soviet people's devotion to the ideas of communism, to the socialist system. More and more books that present a deformed and twisted picture of the Soviet man flood the bookstalls.

The questions of the individual, and of individual freedom, today increasingly form the centre of the ideological and theoretical contest between socialism and capitalism. The increased interest in these problems of late is due to their growing significance in this struggle. The question of man as an individual, of the nature of humanism, is treated on a level with such questions as the class structure of society, the class struggle, the state, and so on.

Since the middle of the 20th century mankind has had to face up to such problems as how to eliminate unemployment and poverty, how to avoid a nuclear holocaust, how to liberate all people from colonial oppression. Scientific and technological advance presents opportunities for solving these problems, but the stumbling block is the obsolete system of imperialism that stands stubbornly in the way.

Capitalism by its very nature continues to intensify the exploitation of the working people, along with racial and national discrimination. At the same time, in defending itself from the onslaught of the working people, the advancing forces of socialism, the imperialists speculate widely on the ideas of freedom of the individual and humanism, and unblushingly proclaim such ideas as the notion that man is congenitally asocial by nature, that there is eternal conflict between the individual and other people.

Marxists-Leninists see the solution to the problems of the individual in the abolition of capitalist exploitation and the building of socialism and communism, the building of a society in which man who creates all values is himself the highest value. The Communists have started and are pursuing a tremendous creative journey. Their road is not an easy one and cannot be without its mistakes and setbacks, but progress has on the whole been successful and much has been done to create the best possible conditions of life and work for the whole mass of the people with the declared aim of extending the real rights and freedoms of the individual. So much has been achieved, in fact, that no solution or even fruitful discussion of the problems of the development of the individual and society is possible without reference to Marxism-Leninism, to the Soviet experience and the experience of other socialist countries.

CHAPTER ONE

THE MARXIST-LENINIST CONCEPTION OF MAN AS AN INDIVIDUAL

A new human personality has taken shape in the course of great revolutionary changes, in the process of building socialist society. Since socialism is the first society in history to have been consciously fashioned by man, in accordance with definite ideological and theoretical principles, our analysis of the process by which this socialist type of person has acquired its characteristic features should be preceded by a general description of the Marxist-Leninist conception of the individual, and of the Marxist-Leninist approach to the question of the relationship between society and the individual, as well as of the special features of communist humanism.

The problem of the individual and society has for long been the subject of intense ideological and theoretical controversy. Throughout the history of social thought man's attention has been concentrated on such questions as the social consequences of his activity, the relationship between ability and social status, between rights and duties, freedom and responsibility, self-respect and respect for others, individuality and collectivity, good and evil, happiness and unhappiness, death and immortality. Any solution to these problems is bound to touch upon the interrelationship between general and personal interests, moral standards and principles, the ideals of various classes.

The abstract approach to the problem of the individual, the desire to consider "man in general", "the individual in general", the assumption that man is inherently asocial, selfish by nature, the élitist or aristocratic interpretations of the whole concept of the individual, or the religious-ethical approach—all these to a greater or lesser dergee characterise the various pre-Marxian, bourgeois conceptions of the individual. Bourgeois ideologists since they are always in one way or another engaged in justifying or defending the capitalist system concentrate their attention mainly on "outstanding" and "critically-minded" individuals.

Karl Marx, the ideologist of the revolutionary proletariat, took an entirely different approach to the problem of the individual. Unlike the bourgeois humanist, with his abstract reflections on the good of man in general or philanthropic notions of compassion for the weak and lowly, Marx addresses himself directly to the man of toil, to the working class, and seeks the solution in the history of society itself, in its revolutionary renewal. From this it follows that consistent juxtaposition of the Marxist-Leninist treatment of the problem of the individual to the bourgeois approach is essential to a real understanding of the real processes of the individual's development in socialist society, and also to the ideological and theoretical struggle that is being waged over these questions between socialist and bourgeois ideologists.

1. PRACTICAL REVOLUTIONARY CHARACTER OF COMMUNIST HUMANISM

Marxist-Leninist literature has produced a fairly comprehensive definition of what communist humanism actually implies. Nonetheless it is on this question that the theory of scientific communism is subjected to constant attacks by imperialist propaganda. This is where one encounters, particularly of late, most of the speculative ideas of the advocates of Right and "Left" revisionism. The purpose of these attacks is to distort, either openly or by implication, the historical continuity between Marxism and previous socio-political thought, and the fundamental opposition between the communist and the bourgeois ideologies.

Some critics maintain that the Marxists in general have no theory of the individual, that they ignore the problems of humanism and the individual as a philosophical category; it is alleged that Marxists acknowledge nothing but material needs, underestimate man's spiritual life, the importance of passion, mood and emotion and refuse to recognise creative freedom and individual liberty.

Such assertions are in glaring contradiction to the elementary facts, as can easily be shown. All the early works of Marx and Engels, including Marx's *Economic and Philosophic Manuscripts*, are permeated with the idea of liberating and humanising the individual. This idea is quite definitely formulated in the Communists' first programme, *The Manifesto of the Communist Party*, in which Marx and Engels gave their classical formula: "In place of the old bourgeois society, with its classes and class antagonisms we shall have an association, in which the free development of each is the condition for the free development of all."[1] In *Capital* it is clearly and unambiguously stated that "the development of human energy" will be an "end in itself" of communist society.[2]

Some of our adversaries maintain that Lenin underestimated the problem of the individual. But here, too, they evade (or deliberately ignore) the essence of Lenin's contribution to science, the general direction, the ethos of all his activity. Lenin could not have underestimated the significance of the problem of the individual for a number of reasons. First, because he, like Marx and Engels, saw the goal of the revolution and the building of communism in the all-round development of the working man and made more than one statement to this effect. Secondly, when preparing for the revolution and building up his militant party of the proletariat as an organisation of revolutionaries, he could not have failed to give theoretical and practical attention to the questions of what qualities should characterise the personality of a revolutionary. Thirdly, and lastly, from the moment the Soviets took power Lenin persistently and systematically, in addition to his tremendous work in directing defence and economic construction, concerned himself with the problems of educating a new type of person. He elucidated communist morality, laid down the principles of political education and Party propaganda, worked out the funda-

---

[1] K. Marx and F. Engels, *Selected Works*, Vol. 1, p. 127.
[2] K. Marx, *Capital*, Vol. III, Moscow, 1959, p. 800.

mentals of polytechnical education in the schools, and much else. He himself firmly rejected the charges that Marxism paid too little attention to the problems of man as an individual. Such allegations, he wrote, were "idealist nonsense", acknowledgement of which would demolish Marxism "*completely,* from the very beginning, from its fundamental philosophical premises."[1]

The idea that Marx and Engels were humanists only in their youth and abandoned humanism on becoming proletarian revolutionaries is widespread among bourgeois sociologists and philosophers. This clearly springs from the desire to counterpoise the ideas of humanism that captivated Marx and Engels in their youth to the doctrine of class struggle, of proletarian revolution and the building of socialism and communism which they evolved later.

Certainly Marx and Engels were humanists and democrats from the start. It may be asserted that it was their love of man, their concern for the working people that impelled them to study the processes of social development, to seek effective, realistic ways and means of solving the age-old problem of the liberation of man. Throughout their lives the ideas of humanism inspired their creative efforts and gave them indomitable energy. Lenin said that Marx and Engels "became socialists after being *democrats,* and the democratic feeling of *hatred* for political despotism was exceedingly strong in them."[2]

Marxism-Leninism culled from the humanist trends of the past the ideas of freedom and all-round development of the individual, the defence of human dignity, the need for humane social relations. But humanism was never a purely homogeneous phenomenon. Humanism burgeoned from the struggle of the emergent bourgeoisie against feudalism. It found its expression in a passionate protest against oppression and tyranny. The mass of the working people took an active part in this struggle, but they and the bourgeoisie, though joined in protest, displayed different attitudes to the ways and means of putting humanist ideals into practice, particularly to the question of the nature of property and

[1] V. I. Lenin, *Collected Works,* Vol. 14, p. 318.
[2] Ibid., Vol. 2, p. 26.

to social system. The interpretation of these problems by various thinkers depended on what economic interests of what social groups they represented. Hence the need for a class approach to the study of the history and content of humanism.

In the work of the humanists of the Renaissance (Dante, Petrarch, Leonardo da Vinci, Erasmus, Rabelais, Copernicus, Shakespeare, etc.) we often find sharp criticism of the feudal system and its world view. Their ideal was that man should be liberated from feudal and religious servitude; they proclaimed man as an individual combining intellectual prowess with physical perfection. Social relations would be humanised once the fetters of feudalism were broken and the hierarchy of the feudal estates abolished.

The humanist ideas of the Renaissance were taken up by the 18th-century advocates of Enlightenment, who proclaimed the slogans of liberty, equality and fraternity. Humanist attitudes were characteristic of individual bourgeois intellectuals in the 19th century and are still to be found among them. Bourgeois humanists believed and still believe that their ideals can be realised in a world based on the rule of private property. Hence the irreconcilable conflict between humane ideals and the property-owner's individualism that characterises the bourgeois conception of humanism.

Another trend of humanism was represented by the utopian socialists (Thomas More, Tommaso Campanella, Jean Meslier, Henri Saint-Simon, Charles Fourier, Robert Owen and others). In Engels's words, they "anticipated innumerable things the correctness of which is now being scientifically proved by us."[1] In Russia, utopian socialism was brilliantly represented by the great Russian humanists and revolutionaries Herzen, Belinsky, Dobrolyubov and Chernyshevsky, who exercised a direct influence on the formation of socialist views in Russia.

Despite the historical limitations of their views the utopian socialists expressed the aspirations of the oppressed masses and, if not always consistently, developed many of the ideas that we treasure today and that we are translating into reality. The idea that property should be owned in common,

---

[1] K. Marx and F. Engels, *Selected Works*, Vol. 2, p. 169.

that every member of society should perform some kind of work, that the opposition between town and country and physical and mental work should be eliminated, that distribution of goods should be in accordance with work and needs, have become part and parcel not only of the theory of scientific communism but, above all, of the world view of millions of working people, and inspire them to fight for the communist remaking of the world. Thomas More, for instance, saw man as the highest of all values. He was indignant that man himself should be "... in much less estimation than the gold itself."[1] "Thus, I do fully persuade myself," wrote More, "that no equal and just distribution of things can be made, nor that perfect wealth shall ever be among men, unless this property be exiled and banished. But so long as it shall continue, so long shall remain among the most and best part of men, the heavy and inevitable burthen of poverty and wretchedness."[2]

Although historically the concept of humanism was related to the bourgeois ideological trend of the Age of the Renaissance, we may rightly claim that utopian socialism was head and shoulders above the abstract humanism of the bourgeoisie, since from the very outset it implied the demand for a radical transformation of social relations in the interests of the working man.

Thus, the communist ideology does not deny the great and good achievements of man in either the theory or the practice of social relations. On the contrary, Marx's teaching, Lenin wrote, "emerged as the direct and immediate *continuation* of the teachings of the greatest representatives of philosophy, political economy and socialism".[3] It organically comprises the ideas of the freedom and dignity of the individual, the ideas of collectivism and the idea of the liberation of man by means of revolution. The communist ideology fully accepts such lofty manifestations of the human spirit as creative labour, love, friendship, the splendid creations of art. What is more, it may be said that the communist ideology would probably never have come into being if mankind

---

[1] Thomas More, *Utopia*, Boston, 1878, p. 279.
[2] *Ibid.*, p. 222.
[3] V. I. Lenin, *Collected Works*, Vol. 19, p. 23.

had not created all the wonderful things for which it is worth taking up arms against the destructive forces of a dying system, and if there had not been in society forces ready and capable of undertaking the struggle. Mankind finds in communism a new and more effective form for its further development. But just because the communist ideology embraces all that is most humane, it is incompatible with everything that oppresses, insults and seeks to belittle human dignity.

In Marxist humanism there is nothing resembling sectarianism in the sense of a narrow hidebound doctrine standing apart from the mainstream of the development of world civilisation. Lenin stressed that Marx's genius lay in the fact that he gave answers to the questions posed by advanced human thought.

But Marxists-Leninists reject the abstract approach to the analysis of social phenomena and scientific concepts. In class society these phenomena and concepts have a concrete socioeconomic and political and, hence, class content. There is bourgeois democracy and there is proletarian democracy, there is freedom that is reserved for the exploiters and there is freedom for the working people, there is formal equality before the law in capitalist society and there is real, actual equality under socialism; in any national culture in bourgeois society there is the culture of the exploiting classes and the culture of the exploited. The same applies to the ideas of humanism. There is no such thing as humanism in general; there is bourgeois humanism and there is communist humanism.[1]

---

[1] A few years ago the Chinese propagandists were sharply opposed to "presenting communism as humanism". It was quite out of the question, so they asserted, to talk of Marxist humanism, of the humanism of the working class. Anyone who spoke of the humanist character of communism was merely preaching bourgeois ideology. The Chinese theoreticians argue as follows. Because bourgeois ideologists, presenting themselves as humanists, defend private property and attack the socialist revolution, because the ideas of bourgeois humanism aim at creating favourable conditions only for the upper crust of society and do not touch the foundations of capitalist social relations, humanism must be thrown overboard lock, stock and barrel. Anyone who is in favour of humanism is in favour of bourgeois humanism, therefore, he is against the socialist revolution, that is to say, he is an accomplice of the imperialists.

As a brilliant and fearless thinker and revolutionary, Marx could not be content with abstract moralising about the benefits of virtue. He saw that bourgeois humanism and the various educational projects of bourgeois philanthropists would not stand the test of history. In defending private property, the founders of humanism and its continuers among the bourgeoisie, always were and still are supporters of individualism and opponents of collectivism. Hence the inconsistency and contradictoriness of bourgeois humanism, and its inability to defend the interests of the people.

The development of capitalism, the proletariat's entry into the struggle, a profound dissatisfaction with bourgeois life and a sense of protest against exploitation and oppression

---

Attacking the humanist character of the communist ideology, the leaders of the Chinese Communist Party divorce Marxism-Leninism from the general progress of world social thought and juxtapose Marxism-Leninism to the democratic trends in the history of society. Thus they oppose the Leninist understanding of the continuity between Marxism and the history of social thought that preceded it. They seek to replace the science of communism with a sectarian, eclectic concoction of ideas that answers their political ambitions.

The slogans of liberty, equality and fraternity had been proclaimed long before Marxism came into existence. They were the watchword of freedom for the bourgeoisie. But the Marxists have set themselves the task of establishing freedom for the working people, making work obligatory for everyone and, on this basis, achieving equality and fraternity among all the working members of society. Human brotherhood, when proclaimed by the workers, as Marx pointed out, is the truth and not just a phrase. In a May Day appeal to the workers, Lenin wrote in 1905: "All workers are brothers, and their solid union is the only guarantee of the well-being and happiness of all working and oppressed mankind. On the First of May this union of the workers of all countries, international Social-Democracy, reviews its forces and gathers its strength for a further unremitting and unswerving struggle for freedom, equality, and fraternity." (V. I. Lenin, *Collected Works*, Vol. 8, p. 348.) Marxists-Leninists give these slogans genuine substance and put them into practice by revolutionary means. They set themselves the task of establishing freedom for the working people, equality for all members of society in conditions of socialism and communism, obligatory work for all able-bodied people, and general brotherhood on this basis. Revealing the humanist character of the historic mission of communism, the Programme of the CPSU states: "Communism accomplishes the historic mission of delivering all men from social inequality, from every form of oppression and exploitation, from the horrors of war and proclaims *Peace, Labour, Freedom, Equality, Fraternity and Happiness* for all peoples of the earth." (*The Road to Communism*, Moscow, p. 450.)

led Marx and Engels to seek ways of emancipating the working people. Through objective, scientific analysis they established that the development of society is a natural historical, law-governed process of the replacement of socio-economic formations, that the transition from one such forma-tion to another comes about as a result of social revolution. Marx and Engels revealed the basic contradictions of capital-ism, contradictions that lead inevitably to its destruction, to the victory of proletarian revolution, of socialism and com-munism.

Thanks to them, the humanist ideas of the emancipation and development of the individual were placed on a scientific basis and acquired a real prospect of realisation. Naturally the Marxist understanding of the essence of man was dia-metrically opposed to the bourgeois view, this being true both of Marxism's interpretation of the role of the social environment, of economic relations in the formation of personal characteristics and its understanding of what methods would prove effective in changing the conditions of life and the character of man.

From the outset of their scientific and revolutionary acti-vity Marx and Engels were against the abstract, idealist understanding of the essence of man and roundly criticised the idealism of Strauss, Stirner and Bauer, and also the views of Feuerbach. In criticising Feuerbach for his abstract approach to the understanding of the essence of man, Marx and Engels wrote that Feuerbach considered people outside any definite social context of conditions of life which makes people what they really are. He saw the human essence only as the "species", as an internal, mute universality linking a multitude of individuals by exclusively natural ties.[1]

Unlike Feuerbach, Marx and Engels regarded people as real individuals closely connected with one another, mainly by their productive activity. For Marx "man is a *corporeal*, living, real, sensuous, objective being full of natural vigour".[2] The essential distinction between man and the animals is his ability to work. Man has become man since he began

---

[1] K. Marx and F. Engels, *The German Ideology*, Moscow, 1964, p. 58.

[2] K. Marx, *Economic and Philosophic Manuscripts of 1844*, Moscow, 1961, p. 156.

to produce instruments of labour and, with their help, material goods. Marx and Engels regard the production of goods required to satisfy people's needs, in other words, the production of material life itself, as the first historical act. For man "production is his active species life".[1]

Marx's substantiation of the definitive role of production relations in social life was undoubtedly a major scientific achievement. This made it possible to see the history of society as a natural historical, i.e., law-governed, objective process. Marx "did so by singling out the economic sphere from the various spheres of social life, by singling out *production relations* from all social relations as being basic, primary, determining all other relations."[2]

The deepest, most fundamental motives of human conduct were thus laid bare. "In the history of society... the actors are all endowed with consciousness, are men acting with deliberation or passion, working towards definite goals; nothing happens without a conscious purpose, without an intended aim."[3] And further: "to ascertain the driving causes which here in the minds of acting masses and their leaders—the so-called great men—are reflected as conscious motives, clearly or unclearly, directly or in ideological, even glorified, form—that is the only path which can put us on the track of the laws holding sway both in history as a whole, and at particular periods and in particular lands."[4] Economic interests are the motivating factors. "...All class struggles for emancipation, despite their necessarily political form—for every class struggle is a political struggle—turn ultimately on the question of economic emancipation."[5]

From the standpoint of Marxism, however, it is not enough to consider only the social environment. One must also take into account the class structure of society and the class struggle. Engels wrote: "...It is not a question so much of the motives of single individuals, however eminent, as of those motives which set in motion great masses, whole peo-

---

[1] K. Marx, *Economic and Philosophic Manuscripts of 1844*, p. 76.
[2] V. I. Lenin, *Collected Works*, Vol. 1, p. 138.
[3] K. Marx and F. Engels, *Selected Works*, Vol. 3, pp. 365-66.
[4] Ibid., p. 367.
[5] Ibid., p. 369.

ples, and again whole classes of the people in each people."[1] Marx's and Engels's discovery lay in the fact that "the actions of 'living individuals' within the bounds of each such socio-economic formation, actions infinitely varied and apparently not lending themselves to any systematisation, were generalised and reduced to the actions of groups of individuals differing from each other in the part they played in the system of production relations, in the conditions of production, and, consequently, in their conditions of life, and in the interests determined by these conditions—in a word, to the actions of *classes*, the struggle between which determined the development of society."[2]

The theory of the class struggle was the thing that first elevated sociology to the level of a science.

Taking concrete examples, Lenin gives models of Marxist analysis of the interaction between the socio-class structure and the conduct of the individual. The Narodnik describes the wretched plight of the individual craftsman and his exploitation by the buyer-up and out of sympathy for him proposes that his independence can be maintained by creating an *artel* (workshop). This proposal fully accords with the Narodniks' moral ideas but, as Lenin pointed out, it does not take into consideration the whole organisation of the social economy. In the context of the capitalist economy any kind of *artel* can be only a tiny palliative that at best will raise a group of individual craftsmen to the ranks of the petty bourgeoisie.

Considering the position of this same individual craftsman, Lenin pointed out the inevitability of the exploitation of the small producer under capitalism, the antagonistic contradiction between the interests of the haves and have-nots which constitutes the substance of the scientific concept of the class struggle. The development of the class struggle inevitably ruins the individual craftsman or small producer as an "independent" worker and throws him on to the hired labour market. "And, consequently, the interests of the producer do not, in any way, lie in reconciling these contradictory elements, but, on the contrary, in developing the

---

[1] K. Marx and F. Engels, *Selected Works*, Vol. 3, p. 367.
[2] V. I. Lenin, *Collected Works*, Vol. 1, p. 411.

contradiction and in developing the consciousness of this contradiction."[1]

Materialist monism, applied as a means of explaining the motion of social life, points to economic interests as the determining factor in the system of ideological motives and ultimately the prime mover of all interests. The connection between the individual and the social group indicates the concrete form within whose framework the mechanism of interaction between the individual and the mass operates. In other words, we are thus confronted with the basic, decisive factors of the social environment that determine the conduct of the individual.

The Marxist-Leninist conception of the individual is crowned by the theory of the proletarian, socialist revolution, which endows communist humanism with its greatest historical value and distinguishes it in principle from abstract, bourgeois humanism. Let us note some of the basic humanist aspects of the theory of the socialist revolution.

First, the socialist revolution substitutes socialist ownership for private ownership of the means of production and establishes the power of the working people. Its aim is to use all material and spiritual wealth for the free and all-round development of the abilities of the working man, for his active participation in social and political life.

Second, the need for the replacement of capitalism by socialism and communism is in Marxism-Leninism inferred entirely from the economic movement of society. The socialist revolution comes about through the inevitable operation of objective laws, i.e., through history itself.

Third, the socialist revolution is carried out by the masses of the people led by the proletariat and directed by the Communist Party, i.e., as a result of and by means of the purposeful, conscious preparation of the forces of the revolutionary vanguard.

Fourth, revolution is the only realistic way of transforming millions of workers and peasants, crushed by arduous toil and poverty, into conscious workers purposefully creating the most favourable conditions for their own existence. "Both for the production on a mass scale of this communist

---

[1] V. I. Lenin, *Collected Works*, Vol. 1, p. 407.

consciousness, and for the success of the cause itself, the alteration of men on a mass scale is necessary, an alteration which can only take place in a practical movement, a *revolution*."[1] In other words, man emerges as the transformer of his own being and his own essence.

Fifth, the proletarian revolution involves some form of compulsion, regardless of whether methods of armed struggle are used or the aim is achieved by peaceful means. Force is not a part of the Marxist ideal. But socialism can be reached only through the use of force because capitalist oppression is maintained by force. The Communists recognise its inevitability and work out their policy in accordance with the laws of the class struggle. The Communists stand for revolution by force, for the compulsory confiscation of the means of production from the big capitalists, because otherwise the humanist aims of communism cannot be achieved.

The socialist revolutions that have already been carried out are undoubtedly the most humane actions ever performed by mankind because the way for them was prepared by the whole course of social development, because their aim is to abolish the parasitic classes and they are, consequently, carried out in the interests of the working people. Revolutionary struggle is the broad movement of the masses, who have become aware of the need for social change. Lenin called revolutions big days for the workers.

Thus the basic aspects of the Marxist-Leninist humanist conception may be summed up as follows: (1) the essence of man may be understood and explained only through analysis of the social environment, above all the production, economic relations, which determine the activity and behaviour of classes and hence also the social qualities of types of individual, (2) the liberation of the working man, his development as an individual can be effected only on the basis of the emancipation of the working class and all working people by substituting social ownership for private ownership of the means of production, the transformation of all members of society into working people and the utilisation of social wealth for the development of the abili-

---

[1] K. Marx and F. Engels, *The German Ideology*, p. 86.

ties and talents of the working man; and (3) only through
the socialist revolution do the working people achieve the
"humanisation of circumstances" and change themselves
accordingly.

Such an approach to the problem of the emancipation
of the individual naturally rejects the vague, suspect humanism of the liberal bourgeois. Relentlessly exposing the
hypocrisy and deception of this bourgeois humanism, Maxim
Gorky wrote: "The humanism of the bourgeoisie has existed
comfortably side by side with slave-owning, the slave trade,
the 'right of the first night', the religious inquisitions, the
mass extermination of the Albigenses of Toulouse, the burning
of Giordano Bruno, Jean Hus and tens of thousands of
nameless 'heretics', 'witches', craftsmen and peasants who
were attracted by the echoes of primitive communism that
survived in the Bible and the Gospel. . . .

"In general the bourgeoisie has never tried to make life
easier for the mass of the workers except by charity which
lowers the dignity of those who toil. . . . Having stolen their
millions and billions, the 'lords of life' spend a few
wretched pence on schools, hospitals and homes for invalids.

"Proletarian humanism makes its aim to liberate the
proletariat of the whole world from the shameful, bloody,
insane oppression of the capitalists, to teach people not
to regard themselves as objects to be bought and sold, raw
material for the fabrication of the gold and luxury of the
middle class. . . .

"The humanism of the proletariat demands inextinguish-
able hatred of philistines, of the power of the capitalist,
its lackeys, parasites, fascists, executioners and betrayers of
the working class—hatred of all that causes suffering, of
all that lives by the sufferings of hundreds of millions of
people."[1]

It would be wrong, of course, not to see the sincere
humanist intentions of some sections of the bourgeois intelligentsia of the West in which concern for the fate of
mankind is clearly manifest. Such concern is vividly
expressed in the work of Bertrand Russell, Ernest Heming-

---

[1] Maxim Gorky, *Collected Works*, Vol. 27, Moscow, 1957, p. 464
(in Russian).

way, Jean-Paul Sartre, Hewlett Johnson, Erich Maria Remarque and others. These people have a deep sense of the inhumanity of capitalism. They see that the world of economic enslavement, social oppression and profit is incompatible with humanity, that in all respects monopoly capital acts as a force inimical to man. One cannot fail to value their protest, to respect their appeal for humanity. Marxists-Leninists see progressive intellectuals as allies of the working class in the struggle for peace, democracy and social progress. But at the same time they are still a long way from the true path of struggle for realisation of the ideals of humanism. Their ideals are ambivalent and their good intentions go no further than occasional reforms that leave capitalism intact and consequently do little to change the position of the masses. From the standpoint of "abstract humanism" the abolition of private property is always an unjustifiable act of force, the denial of freedom, suppression of the individual. Unlike abstract bourgeois humanism, proletarian humanism is a humanism of revolutionary action. This is the reason for the irreconcilable disputes concerning the problems of humanism and the individual that are waged between the Marxists and their opponents.

The service rendered by Marx, Engels and Lenin to history and the world consists in their having been able to see in the working class the force that can transform capitalism into socialism, and in their elaboration of the theory of the socialist revolution, the dictatorship of the proletariat and the building of communism, in which the ideals of freedom and the all-round development of man acquire completely concrete and realistic expression, related to the development of production and society as a whole.

2. EFFECT OF SOCIAL CONDITIONS ON HUMAN BEHAVIOUR

The question of the interaction between the social environment and the individual has a special theoretical and practical significance. By examining it we are able to concretise the notion of the diametrically opposed approaches of Marxism-Leninism and bourgeois theory to the understanding of the essence of man, and thus obtain a deeper conception of the sources of the individual's spiritual world, the conditions and motives of his activity and behaviour. Here we discover what fundamentally shapes the typological peculiarities of the individual and the laws and tendencies of the mutation of typological patterns.

Social Environment as the Basic Factor in Shaping the Essential Man

The significance of the environment in shaping the individual was recognised by pre-Marxian materialism and is also recognised by some contemporary trends in bourgeois sociology (behaviourism, structural-functional analysis). But in doing so these trends either overlook the active element in the individual or consider the reflection of numerous environmental factors in the consciousness of individuals without actually selecting those which are fundamental and definitive.

As soon as he is born, man finds himself in quite definite conditions that took shape before he came into the world. When in the course of time he becomes an active individual and begins to make conscious choices he still cannot isolate himself from society. He belongs to a social group and is bound to it by common economic interests, he accepts its ideology and morality. He belongs to a certain nation and his native language and culture are those of that nation. Man either earns the means of his existence by his own labour or acquires them by exploiting the labour of others. When he works he fulfils a definite role in the system of the social organisation of labour and enters into corresponding relations with other workers. Man lives in a state which obliges him in one way or another to observe the laws of that state. He may belong to some political party and be in a certain relationship to that party. He is a member of a family and acts as a parent, son, daughter, brother, sister, grandson, and so on. In short, throughout his life man lives in close contact with his fellows, in a collective, in society, with which every person is connected by countless threads.

It is the economic, socio-political, cultural and ideological conditions of life that make up man's social environment in the broadest sense of the term. Every individual and every generation, Marx wrote, finds as something given, as the real basis of their life activity a definite "mass of productive forces, capital funds and conditions which, on the one hand, is indeed modified by the new generation but also, on the other, prescribes for it its conditions of life and gives it a definite development, a special character."[1]

Man's conditions of life and his connections with other people, collectives and groups, create around him a constant although extremely mobile complex of factors which determines his activity and behaviour. These factors are the people with whom each individual comes into daily contact, the world of the things that surround him and, finally, the culture which he absorbs. The environment is the immediate source from which he draws his thoughts, knowledge, experience, moods and, therefore, the motives of any particular actions. Consciousness can never be anything else but conscious being.[2] Consequently man's character and behaviour are determined by the social conditions in which he lives. "...The real intellectual wealth of the individual depends entirely on the wealth of his real connections."[3]

But it is not merely a matter of what a man takes from his environment. How the environment exerts its formative influence upon him is also very important.

The extent to which elements of the environment are absorbed depends on the position a person occupies in the system of social relations, in the process of social activity and, consequently, on the level of his own activity. The influence of the environment must be examined through the prism of material conditions, the spiritual values of society and its political organisation, as follows:

(a) production, economic relations predetermine the division of people into classes and, hence, the character of their activity, the sources and level of their material well-being, in short, the material conditions and stimuli of conduct;

(b) thanks to being a member of a particular class or social group an individual acquires through the system of family upbringing and school education certain notions of

---

[1] K. Marx and F. Engels, *The German Ideology*, p. 50.
[2] Ibid., p. 37.
[3] Ibid., p. 49.

the rules of behaviour, the meaning of good and evil, traditions, habits, aspirations, aims in life, and so on, that is to say, notions of the spiritual values, all of which act as spiritual and moral stimuli;

(c) in the political sphere, the state, which in antagonistic socio-economic formations, defends the interests of the ruling class, and in socialist society, the interests of the whole people, sees to it that people act as it requires, if necessary, by means of compulsion.

All this taken together conditions man's assimilation of social experience, the formation of his individual qualities, and his mode of action, which differ widely in different societies and different classes and groups.

Thanks to the singling out of economic interests as the definitive motives of conduct of the masses, thanks to the classification of individuals into social groups (classes), the very development of the individual emerges not as an accident affecting only the psychological sphere, but as a social phenomenon completely subordinated to certain definite laws, to the laws that determine the development of society as a whole. As for the individual himself, its first and basic law is the definitive role of the social environment in respect of his qualities and behaviour. From this comes the social content of the individual and the essence of man in general. In his *Theses on Feuerbach* Marx points out that "the human essence is no abstraction inherent in each single individual. In its reality it is the ensemble of the social relations."[1] In other words, man's essence consists in the essence of the social phenomena that he assimilates in the process of his vital activity, and that is expressed in his behaviour. Consequently, the essential tendencies, the growing points and the nodes of tension, the critical situations and explosions in social life find their "plenipotentiaries" in the shape of concrete individuals and social types.

This gives rise to a natural question. If environment plays the definitive role in shaping a person's character, why do extremely different persons, often with opposite views and aspirations, emerge from one and the same set of conditions? The course of one particular person's life, however,

---

[1] K. Marx and F. Engels, *Selected Works,* Vol. 1, p. 14.

does not disprove but rather confirms the thesis that man's character is conditioned by the social environment. In reality, no two individuals ever share exactly the same conditions of life. There are bound to be differences in intercourse, experience and knowledge, and it is these that effect the formation of various motives, and then the actions, of people living in what seem to be similar circumstances. The life of each individual is a unique record of the acquisition of knowledge and experience. One must also take into consideration differences of a natural biological and psychological character, which in identical circumstances may exert a different influence on the behaviour of individuals. But even allowing for all this, historical experience has shown convincingly enough on the mass scale that similar social conditions generate similar aspirations, common patterns of human behaviour, while a change in the social environment brings about corresponding changes in personal qualities.

This is where the microenvironment, or the individual's immediate environment, comes in. If we consider only the basic elements of a social system, we can never understand the distinctive features and variety of individual's spiritual world as law-governed social phenomena. It is the microenvironment, the combination of the general and the particular, that supplies the factors, the conditions which mould the unique individuality of any given person.

The proposition that the social environment plays a definitive role in the social content of man's essence does not rule out active participation by the individual in his own development, does not remove the peculiarities that arise from his distinctive biological and psychological features. As a social animal, man is distinguished from the rest of the animal world by his capacity for conscious activity. But a person can be a consciously active being only in close contact with society, assimilating its riches and its laws and realising his needs and aspirations in society and with its help. In this interaction the determining role belongs, however, to the social environment.

When the question is posed in this way, we see the essence of man in all its concreteness and totality. It gives due prominence to the optimistic idea of the possibility of the revolutionary transformation of the world and the success of education. "If man is shaped by his surroundings, his surroundings must be made human."[1]

Man in the System of Social Relations

To obtain a more concrete idea of the effect of the social environment on man and the interaction between society and the individual we must take a closer look at the way in which the individual becomes involved in the system of social relations, and how different social relations predetermine the individual's status in society, his role and the direction of his activity. It is wrong to juxtapose the individual in general to society in general, as though society is something external and exists alongside the individual. Every person is involved in the system of social relations as an active being and acts as a specific, individual bearer of a certain socially significant content.

The most general division of social relations is expressed in material and ideological relations. Production, economic relations, while directly reflecting the demands of the productive forces, exert a definite influence on other spheres of social relations, on the whole pattern of society. This process has two stages: the formation of classes with their specific interests in the process of the development of social relations, and the formation, on the basis of production, economic relations, of superstructural forms—the state, law, ideology, by means of which these interests are realised and protected. It is in the sphere of production relations that the main and fundamental relations between people are shaped: relations of ownership of the means of production, the division of labour and distribution of the articles of consumption.

Unlike ownership of the means of production and the forms of distribution, where relations are formed concerning the objects of the material world, the products of labour, the division of labour and the exchange of activity affect the actual performance of man. The division of labour is a complex category embracing organisational technological

---

[1] K. Marx and F. Engels, *The Holy Family*, Moscow, 1956, p. 176.

division of labour, organisational technological relations and elements of a socio-economic nature. Man's position in production, his place and role in society as a worker depends to a decisive degree on the division of labour.

The appearance of instruments of labour and their development inevitably gives rise to branches of work, to different trades, that is, it determines the division of labour as its general condition. Thus, the division of work into trades, branches and separate functions and the consequent exchange of activity within separate enterprises, and also between industries, are technically conditioned. "Labour," Marx said, "is organised, is divided in different ways, according to the instruments it has at its disposal."[1]

This may be described as the organisational technological division of labour. The interaction between people determined directly by machines and the technological process, by the organisational needs of the process of labour, may be described as production-technical or organisational technological relations. They are present not only in material but also in intellectual production.

However "any production is the impropriation by the individual of the objects of nature in the framework of a definite social form and by means of that form"[2]. This means that the distribution of the basic forms of activity, of functions between classes depends on who owns the means of production. As Marx observes, "...The characters who appear on the economic stage are but the personifications of the economic relations that exist between them."[3]

To clarify the distinction between the production-technical and socio-economic aspects of the division of labour and exchange, let us take the example of the factory. At all factories the relations between the management and the technical administration, on the one hand, and the workers, on the other, are determined by the technical equipment and the technological process. Moreover, at all factories, whether they are socialist or capitalist, *these* relations are approximately the same: the workers of various

---

[1] K. Marx, *The Poverty of Philosophy*, Moscow, p. 149.
[2] K. Marx, *Capital*, Vol. I, p. 85.
[3] K. Marx and F. Engels, *Works*, 2nd Russ. ed., Vol. 12, p. 713.

trades and various degrees of skill perform functions predetermined by the technical peculiarities of the factory. If, on the other hand, we consider the socio-economic, and then the political and moral relations, we find that these are determined by whether the factory is a capitalist or socialist enterprise. The relations between people, the worker's attitude to the factory's interests, the political and moral character of the personnel become sharply differentiated.

Thus, the position and role of the social groups in production, the forms of the division of labour, the character and forms of relations between people in the process of the exchange of activity—such is the essence of the aspect of production relations that we are considering.

Socialism destroys not all the relations that have been formed in capitalist production, but primarily those that spring from the character of property and express exploitative relations. As society approaches communism, the new social relations make it possible to build a material and technical base that is qualitatively different from the material and technical base of present-day capitalism. Hence the need for the builders of the new society to pay close attention to those aspects of the development of the worker's personality that are directly conditioned by the machinery he operates.

Production, economic relations determine the division of society into classes and, consequently, the class structure of society, the content of social relations. In the broad sense, all relations in society, economic, political, class and national, may be called social relations. But it is customary to define social relations in the narrow sense, i.e., relations between groups—classes, nations, families, various kinds of associations—and also the relations between the individual, on the one hand, and society and any social group, on the other. The specific nature of these relations consists in the character of the interaction between the groups, i.e., either in exploitation, in class struggle (in an exploitative society), or in friendship and mutual assistance (in a socialist society). To put it differently, social relations comprise the relations that concern the pattern of society, the distribution of people in groups and the mutual relations between these social groups. Social relations are a kind of focus in which economic, political, moral and legal relations are brought together.

The status of classes and other groups, the needs of their development are expressed in the form of interests. The interests of classes are a generalised expression of their economic position, the primary foundation of the existence of ideas and political organisations, of the whole superstructure. The interests of classes have a decisive influence in forming the interests of the individual. "...Personality is conditioned and determined by quite definite class relationships."[1]

The content of ideas and political institutions is designed either to preserve existing relations or to destroy them, depending on whether they correspond to certain class interests. A system of political views and theories expressing the interests of a class or any other social group is an ideology, and the relations that evolve between people on the basis of ideological principles are ideological relations. So, if there are fundamental interests that divide or unite people in the sphere of economic relations, they find their expression in ideological relations, in the field of politics, principles, legal and moral standards, philosophy, art and religion.

Ideological relations comprise political, moral, legal, aesthetic and religious relations. The basic question of political relations is the question of state power. The state is created to secure the economic interests of the ruling classes. The basic question of political relations—which class shall hold state power—is decided by who in society owns the means of production. Consequently, political relations are the continuation and concentrated expression, the generalisation and culmination of the relations that evolve in the sphere of the economy. In the political sphere, the individual manifests his relationship to the state and state policy, to the interests and activity of political parties, in short, takes up certain civic positions.

The rules and standards of human behaviour that regulate relations between people in general and between individuals,

---

[1] K. Marx and F. Engels, *The German Ideology*, p. 93.

on the one hand, and society, the collective, on the other, constitute in sum the morality which appraises human conduct and defines it in such categories as good, evil, conscience, justice, and so on. Consequently, the relations between people expressing their mutual obligations and the obligations of individuals to society, to a particular class or collective are moral relations. Where a state exists, a considerable part of these rules is set out in the form of laws, whose observation is ensured by the coercive powers of the state. The part of these relations that is regulated by law makes up the legal relations. Such vitally important conditions of the development of the individual as freedom and responsibility, rights and duties are regulated in the sphere of moral and legal relations.

So, the general position concerning the determining role of the environment in respect of the individual emerges as a concrete distribution of people into classes and other social groups, specific to each given socio-economic formation. Man's social content is revealed as the sum total of the various differences in people's position, in the roles they perform, in the character of their interests, and ultimately as a definite pattern of socially significant qualities comprising the features of this or that social type of individual. The revolutionary replacement of socio-economic formations which occurs under the pressure of development of the productive forces always signifies a change in the class structure of society and at the same time in people's conditions of life, their interests and aspirations, in the pattern of social types. The slave and the slave-owner, the serf and the feudal lord, the proletarian and the capitalist—such are the basic class types of individual found in antagonistic formations. The individual, however, is the concrete bearer of social relations, a social type combining the general and the particular, the concentration of an enormous diversity of performed roles and motives of behaviour.

Active Participation of the Individual

While stressing the formative role of the social environment, we have also noted the active part a man plays in forming his own personality. Not only the personality but all material and spiritual values, and society itself, are the result of human activity, and this activity itself is the generic attribute of the human essence. "...Just as society itself produces *man as man,* so is society produced by him."[1] We find the same thought in Lenin. The environment serves not only as the material, but also as the object of the individual's spiritual life, and the individuals not only depend on social relations, they also form them.[2] "But when I investigate *actual* social relations and their *actual* development, I am in fact examining the product of the activities of living individuals."[3]

Stressing the significance of belonging to one's own particular group is certainly no indication, Lenin thinks, that the individual is but the passive product of circumstances. Rather it points to an active attitude towards one's own and the general interests. "Far from assuming fatalism, determinism in fact provides a basis for reasonable action."[4]

A person assimilates social experience and realises his own essence by fulfilling one or another social role in the process of activity. Only by fulfilling this role does he become involved in the system of social relations and act as a bearer and creator, as a focus of the given combination of social relations. In contrast to the school of structural-functional analysis, specifically the work of Talcott Parsons, who believes that the social system is formed out of roles or role expectations, on which collective norms and values are built, Marxism-Leninism maintains that to understand what is actually meant by personality one must begin from society as a whole, from the basis of society—the production relations.

One cannot elucidate the social meaning of personality by pointing out merely the role structure of a type. One must consider at least three elements: (1) the position of the individual in the system of social relations, i.e., his belonging to a certain class, to a social group within that class and the relations this involves with the means of

---

[1] K. Marx, *Economic and Philosophic Manuscripts of 1844,* p. 103.
[2] V. I. Lenin, *Collected Works,* Vol. 1, p. 405.
[3] Ibid., p. 408.
[4] Ibid., p. 420.

production, with the sources of existence, his place in the system of the social organisation of labour; (2) the real forms of a person's activity in life, or, in other words, the totality of social roles which he performs, as predetermined by his place in society, and as society presents them (known among sociologists as role expectation); (3) the ethos of the individual, i.e., the system of needs, interests, beliefs and ideals acting as motives of individual conduct and determining the specific attitude of the individual to the performance of his roles. In other words, the role behaviour of the individual, i.e., his actions in this or that capacity, may be understood only in the framework of a more general social system, the framework of classes from which specific social structures, the social content of the individual, are derived, and to which they are related.

In this connection we would stress the fundamental significance of the Soviet Marxists' criticism of the behaviourist and functionalist conceptions of behaviour.

The position of Lundberg, Schrag and Larsen, for example, is typical of behaviourism. In what they call an effort to shake off traditional sociological subjectivism, they organise their empirical studies of concrete models of behaviour on the basis of various environmental factors. In taking this approach, however, they understand as objective factors that which cannot be reduced to "subjective elements", i.e., to "understanding" or "mood". In a criticism of this approach to the study of human behaviour, G. M. Andreyeva rightly emphasises that in defining personality one cannot ignore the set of factors related to its internal, subjective world. But behaviourism's chief failing is that for all the apparent "objectivity" of its approach to reality, it does not elucidate the objective conditions of existence of the personality.

G. M. Andreyeva notes that the weakness of this one-sided interpretation of the "objective" in sociology is particularly apparent when one tries to relate the behaviour of the individual and the social activity of society. Unlike psychology, for which the description of behaviour and its mechanism is an object of investigation, sociology must explain various types of behaviour. Comparing the positivist, functionalist and Marxist approaches to the study of man, she writes that whereas "for socio-psychological research in

its 'classical' version behaviour is the legitimate and fundamental target of research, for the sociologist it is only the
external pattern of the extremely complex processes that
make up the life of society. The behaviour of the individual
does not explain how the actual social reality evolves; rather
it must be explained in connection with that reality. In the
same way the individual's behaviour does not explain his
essence, but is, on the contrary, the manifestation of that
essence. The actual nature of the individual must be inferred from the objective conditions of his existence."[1]

The functional analysis school (Talcott Parsons, Robert
Merton) was a kind of reaction against the behaviourist
propounding of the problem. In contrast to behaviourism the
advocates of functional analysis maintain that the individual
must be studied not merely in himself but also as a member
of the group on which he is oriented and to which he himself belongs (reference group). It is certainly a fact that
people belonging to one group quite often choose to be
guided in their behaviour by the criteria of another group,
to which they do not belong.

In this respect the school of functional analysis has taken
a step forward. It has a definite practical value when it
comes to working out the technology and method of mea-
suring the behaviour of the individual and the group. Behaviour is treated as something motivated in a definite way
and not merely as the reaction to an external stimulus. But all
the same, situations are interpreted as a result of the individual's own subjective orientations and thus the positive
elements in the functional analysis school are considerably
reduced by this subjectivist approach.[2]

Hence, according to "functional analysis" or, as the
school is also called, "social action theory", people's relations are based not on their knowing one another, but on
their attributing certain qualities to one another. Instead of
the concept of cognition of the object (individual or thing),
we are offered the concept of the formation of the meaning

[1] G. M. Andreyeva, "Man as the Object of Sociological Research",
from *The Individual Under Socialism,* Moscow, 1968, pp. 112, 113, 117
(in Russian).
[2] N. V. Novikov, *Criticism of the Contemporary Bourgeois "Science
of Social Behaviour",* pp. 26-73 (in Russian).

of these objects. The "appraising being", which is concerned
not with real objects but with their "meaning"—such is the
model of the personality in Parsons's voluntarist conception.[1]

Parsons maintains that the basic character of the structure
of the personality evolves in the process of socialisation on
the basis of the structure of the system of social objects, but
he has in mind only the immediate groups (family, school,
etc.) in which a man moves.[2] Moreover, he ignores the
decisive role of the system of production, of economic relations, on the basis of which and depending on which all
these groups are formed.

Thus, neither behaviourism (behaviour as the reaction to
a stimulus from the external environment) nor functionalism
(behaviour motivated by the consciousness of the individual)
take us beyond the bounds of behaviour as such, which, as
we have already said, needs to be explained. People's behaviour results from the influence exerted by many social
forces. The concrete "appears ... as a summing-up, a result,
and not as the starting point, although it is the real point of
origin, and thus also the point of origin of perception and
imagination."[3]

Characterising this feature of the Marxist approach to
the study of man, Andreyeva stresses that the behaviour of
individuals loses its independent significance and merges
with the more general object of social analysis—man considered in all the complexity of his interrelationships with
society. "The sociological analysis of man is not, therefore,
part of the investigation of society itself, it is another side
of one and the same question. The picture of man in sociological research must also be a 'picture' of society. The
analysis of the general objective laws of social development
also emerges not simply as a 'component' of sociological
analysis, but as the basis and prerequisite of a series of
empirical social inquiries."[4]

The task of the sociologist is meaningful analysis of the

---

[1] N. V. Novikov, *op. cit.*, p. 35.

[2] *Sociology Today*, Moscow, Progress Publishers, 1965, pp. 58-59
(in Russian).

[3] K. Marx, *A Contribution to the Critique of Political Economy*,
Moscow, 1971, p. 206.

[4] G. M. Andreyeva, op. cit., p. 120.

individual. As Marx said, "the essence of a 'particular individual' is not his beard, his blood, not his abstract physical nature, but his *social quality*. . . ."[1]

3. THE INDIVIDUAL AS THE SUBJECT OF SOCIAL ACTION

Analysis of the interaction between the social environment and the individual may be made still more concrete by examining the actual concept of the personality, its structure and direction, the problems of classifying individuals into types, in short, all that directly reveals the individual as the subject of social action. ". . .My *own* existence *is* social activity,"[2] Marx observed.

The Concept of Personality

Definitions of personality are numerous (some specialists put the figure at up to fifty), but there are two basic, diametrically opposed approaches to the interpretation of its essence. According to the first point of view, only those can become individuals ("personalities") who possess original qualities—depth of feeling, originality of thought. According to the other view, every person is an individual, a personality, by virtue of the fact that he possesses certain socially significant features.

We hold that the notion of individuals as a chosen category of people is unscientific. It deprives us of objective criteria and the possibility of dealing theoretically with the problem, does not correspond to the historical emergence of this concept and, finally, runs counter to the democratic nature of the communist teaching.

The character of man's vital activity in society presupposes both isolation from and intercourse with other people. Man is a social animal, "not only a social animal, but an animal that can be individualised only within society."[3] A

---

[1] K. Marx and F. Engels, *Works*, 2nd Russ. ed., Vol. 1, p. 242.

[2] K. Marx, *Economic and Philosophic Manuscripts of 1844*, p. 104.

[3] K. Marx, *A Contribution to the Critique of Political Economy*, p. 189.

man's life is inconceivable without intercourse with other people, but at the same time he requires a certain degree of privacy. The interconnection between these two sides of man's vital activity conditions the individual's assimilation of generally significant attributes and, consequently, generates a need to endow man with a personal character, necessitates the concept of the personality.

The content of every person's consciousness is determined by what he can assimilate from his environment in proportion to his activity and abilities. In the process of his mastering of social experience and making it his own, this experience undergoes an inevitable change. According to his physical capacity and the time available to him, man can assimilate only a certain amount of knowledge, standards and principles. He assimilates these selectively, adapting them to the positions he has previously elaborated or in accordance with the interests he has acquired through belonging to a social group (reference group orientation). In other words, the objective world assimilated by the individual, the subject, as a result of his unique path of cognition and experience is transformed into a special combination of knowledge, experience and beliefs peculiar to the given individual which characterises this person as an individual and gives him his own special image.

It is here that one is tempted to accept as the personality only this uniqueness and to reduce the concept of the personality to a certain totality of outstanding features. But to designate a certain combination of qualities the concept of the individual as a specific, separate human being is quite sufficient. The concept of personality, however, implies a general yardstick of man's social nature. Every person, while he is the product of a definite social environment, is at the same time a unique and inimitable expression of the content of that environment, of the universal that exists in the life, primarily in the group, to which he belongs. The world of needs and interests, feelings and thoughts inherent in every individual person characterises him, on the one hand, as a part of society and expresses what he has in common with many other people; on the other hand, this world characterises his own particular condition and distinguishes him as something autonomous and original. Every person is a unity of the general and the particular. The general is present in the individual, expresses itself, is personified through the individual, and it is this that we see as something original, and that allows us to single it out as personality, as a special "face" or "image".

The very history of the emergence of the concept of "personality" tells us the same thing. The original meaning of the term "persona" in the Greek theatre was that of a mask which the actor wore to appear on the stage. Later the term was extended to mean the actor himself and the part he played. But the point is that the mask represented a particular type from real life. Thus, even in those days we find a tendency to distinguish by means of the mask of a particular character that which is generally significant and familiar in life, that concerns many people. This was one of the things that gave the Greek tragedy its profound human appeal. Consequently, the concept of personality found its way into the language as a response to a need that had developed in the course of time to designate the typical, the socially significant in the make-up and behaviour of people. But generally significant features are not the privilege of an élite; they are the natural attribute of every person, although they may be expressed more or less strikingly.

Finally, if one assumes that only a few people may be accounted individuals ("personalities") one encounters the insoluble problem of what criteria are to be used for categorising people as individuals. From one point of view, a particular person may possess original qualities and is, therefore, to be regarded as a personality; whereas from another standpoint his qualities may seem quite ordinary and he is not to be regarded as a personality at all. In other words, we find ourselves in the realm of subjectivism and arbitrariness. When we regard every person as a personality we have in mind the indisputable fact that the individual, for all his originality and uniqueness, is the bearer of certain common features that have objective existence, and this gives us our objective criterion. Only on this assumption can personality become an object of scientific inquiry. "The problem of personality can be solved," wrote A. S. Makarenko, "if we see personality in every person. If, on the other hand, personality is projected only in certain people, according to some special means of selection, there is no problem of personality."[1]

The history of scientific cognition, and particularly that of artistic creativity, has vastly expanded our notion of the human character, of types of personality and has confirmed the idea that personality is the individual expression of socially significant qualities, the combination of socially significant features, the individual form of the existence of social relations, the measure of a man's sociality. The more deeply and extensively a man assimilates the world around him, the more striking are his personal qualities, the more outstanding his personality. And similarly, the richer and more complex a man's inner world, the more profoundly does he express the essence of social relations. Universality and distinctiveness are indissoluble elements in the concept of personality. Personality can be a measure of sociality, i.e., of the universal, only by remaining a particular phenomenon, because the purpose of measure is to register differences in the universal.

Thus, personality may be described as "the concrete expression of the essence of man, i.e., the integration in a given individual of socially significant features related to the essence of the given society."[2] But such integration is to be distinguished from any concrete sum total of qualities. Personality is the social image of every individual and requires concrete characterisation. The qualities of the personality may be more or less striking, profound, original, but every person must inevitably possess them because of his being involved in the system of social relations.

When the question is propounded in this way, we are able to take a correct approach to the comparison of the concept of personality with the concept of man. "Man" and "personality" are concepts of similar dimensions. There are as many personalities in the world as there are normal adults. But these two concepts differ in content. The concept of "man" is concerned with nature and society, it includes

---

[1] A. S. Makarenko, *Selected Pedagogical Works,* Vol. 4, Moscow, 1949, p. 210 (in Russian).
[2] *Sociology in the USSR,* Vol. 2, p. 492 (in Russian).

his physiological and biological structure, and also his social side. But whereas the concept of man deals with the general features of the human race—biological organisation, consciousness, language and work—the concept of personality deals with the social characteristics possessed by a separate type of person and expressed in a particular, individual form. The concept of personality is a social concept.

Needless to say, this position gives no grounds for ignoring the demands and qualities of man connected with his biological origin. Every person possesses an aggregate of physical and psychological organisation, of primary needs whose satisfaction involves a wide sphere of consciousness, emotions, interests and aspirations. The influence exerted by man's physiological and biological organisation on his behaviour is very considerable and is the subject of special research. This influence must be taken into consideration whenever the individual's interests and aspirations are being discussed. But science has long since established that, important though natural factors may be, social conditions and the social ethos of people's consciousness have the decisive effect on the conduct of the masses and, through them, on the behaviour of individuals.

Social Structure of the Personality and Its Ethos

Any study of personality is inconceivable without a study of its structure. Only by revealing this structure can we arrive at an understanding of its elements, their interconnection and the personality as a whole. The various forms of man's being and activity predetermine the existence of a certain number of structures or, perhaps, structural layers—organic, psychological and social. We are mainly interested here in the social structure of the personality.

In a certain sense personality is always a subjective reflection of the external world. The assimilation of the materials of the social environment builds up into a specific system, into special forms of individual consciousness, which cannot be identified with the social consciousness.

The social consciousness develops in definite forms (political, philosophical, scientific, moral, legal, artistic, religious). Each form of social consciousness has its specific content stemming from the object which it reflects, and also its specific means of reflection and internal structure. The social consciousness exists in the form of psychology (feelings, moods, emotions, skills, sense of purpose, habits, etc.), and in the form of ideological systems (theories, principles, declarations, constitutions, programmes, slogans, and so on). The social consciousness is objectivised and preserved in books, historical documents, in the fine arts, in music, in visual and sound recordings, in oral composition, in customs and traditions and in material objects.

The social consciousness is objective in relation to every individual person; it is the part of the social environment from which the individual consciousness draws its vital material. In relation to the individual social consciousness takes the form of the sum total of knowledge and experience, political, legal, moral and other principles, standards, appraisals and traditions, goals and ideals that society (state, party, family) through education and upbringing and system of propaganda seeks to instil in its members. The state maintains established principles and standards also by means of compulsion.

Naturally, the individual consciousness is far smaller in volume than the social consciousness. At the same time the individual consciousness differs from social consciousness in its mode of reflection, its "conservation" of information. In order to characterise the individual consciousness one must have a special system of concepts that differs from the system of concepts expressing the state of the social consciousness. It must be a system of concepts that adequately reflects the particularity of the individual perception of the world.

The particularity of the individual's inner spiritual world lies in the psychological processes, the qualities and conditions by means of which a person assimilates the external world and acts upon it. These include the cognitive processes (feeling and perception, memory, thought and imagination), both emotional and will-directed. The effect of this reflective activity is registered in the qualities of the personality—needs, interests, knowledge, beliefs, ideals, abilities, etc. When we speak of the formation of a person's scientific world view or his communist morality, we always have in mind the fact of the transformation of general principles into the beliefs of separate individuals. But when analysing the process of transformation of the categories of the social consciousness into categories of the individual consciousness we cannot equate the system of sciences comprising the scientific world view, the system of morality of the given society, with the knowledge and beliefs of individuals, since the knowledge and beliefs that a person assimilates from the world around him function in the individual consciousness differently from the way they function when they are objectivised in scientific literature and works of art.

The individual's immediate motive of action is always fairly unambiguous. The individual is guided by definite meanings[1] and pursues a definite goal dictated by the need, the interests (personal or social) registered in his precepts. These meanings which the individual assimilates as bunches of precepts make him always more or less inclined to take this or that decision. A system of precepts, a system of meanings gives us the value orientation of the individual as the concrete manifestation of the individual's relation to the facts of reality.

The individual's value orientation is defined as "a relatively stable system of precepts evolved as a result of man's ability to objectivise, based on emotions, knowledge, beliefs, inclinations and abilities, that is, on the integration of preceding social and individual experience.... Conditioned by objective causes and connections, the individual's value orientation is a manifestation of the universal that makes up the social type characteristic of a certain level of social

---

[1] The Soviet psychologist A. N. Leontyev explains "meaning" as follows. Meaning is that which "is revealed in an object or phenomenon objectively—in the system of objective connections, relationships and interactions. Meaning is reflected, registered in language and thus acquires permanence. In this form, in the form of linguistic meaning, it makes up the content of social consciousness; as the content of the social consciousness, it also becomes the 'real consciousness' of individuals, objectivising in itself the subjective meaning of what the reflected has for them" (A. N. Leontyev, *Problems of the Development of Mentality*, Moscow, 1959, p. 223, in Russian). Thus, meaning belongs primarily to the world of objective historical phenomena, but it also exists as a fact of individual consciousness. It is the form in which the individual person assimilates generalised and reflected human experience.

development. As an element of the structure of the personality, value orientation is a manifestation of the particular that characterises individuality. . . ."[1] A man's value orientation reveals his understanding of the world, moral principles and ideological beliefs.

The value orientation, however, has its limits and does not cover the whole complex of spiritual activity. There is a system of such orientations, and this system must be described and designated. The individual's value orientations are concrete and located in various forms of social consciousness, in political consciousness, say, in moral, artistic and other forms. Expressing the individual's attitude to various spheres of social life, value orientations are at the same time related to the general spirit determined by the individual's adherence to a certain social class. Although they may be contradictory, the basic contents of value orientations in a normal person usually coincide. The system of such orientations may be defined as the general orientation or ethos of the personality, the generalising principle that embraces all spheres of a person's mentality—from needs to ideals. The ethos is not the sum total of many orientations, it is a qualitatively different formation permeating all the various forms of value orientations. The ethos of the personality is expressed in the world outlook, in moral principles and political views. In generalised form ethos equals belief.

We thus obtain a system of need, interest, precept, orientation and ethos that allows us to describe the structure of the individual mentality. But this structure is predicated on the external world, whence it draws its knowledge and experience, notions of the rules of behaviour and appraisals of social phenomena, ideals and goals. Whereas in the first case we refer to the connection between the first and second signal systems, to the interaction between the subconscious and the conscious, in the second case we are noting the orientation of the individual consciousness towards social relations and social consciousness, including any given world view or system of moral values.

---

[1] V. V. Vodzinskaya, "The Concept of Precept, Attitude and Value Orientation in Sociological Research" in *Philosophical Sciences* No. 2, 1968, pp. 50-54 (in Russian).

The ethos is the leading element in the psychological structure of the individual personality. It exerts a decisive influence on the other elements, on the amount of knowledge and the way biologically conditioned qualities such as temperament and natural abilities are manifested. The analysis of the ethos is essential to the study of the social structure of the personality.

Sociological analysis of personality is unthinkable without a definition of its place in the social relations and roles, without some indication of how a person performs this or that role. "...Personality is characterised not only by *what* it does, but also by *how* it does it...."[1] The latter stems from the precepts, value orientations and ethos of the individual personality. Here, depending on the ethos of the personality, we have different attitudes to one's role and, consequently, different types of behaviour and essentially different social types of individual. Lenin pointed this out on several occasions.

The social structure of the individual personality is built up out of the individual's place in the system of social relations and social roles and his attitude towards them, which stems from the ethos of his personality. Only by analysing the various combinations of the objective position of man's roles and spiritual make-up can we begin to define social types, which is one of the key tasks of sociological analysis.

Ethos and Social Types of Personality

In its most general form the task of the classification of social types consists in singling out the essential characteristics of the basic forms of activity, attitude to work, social activity, conditioned by a person's place in society and his general orientation or ethos. Ethos and type are closely interconnected characteristics of personality, because the very concept of ethos implies its plurality, and plurality is realised and exists in the form of types. At the same time ethos and type are the most generalised indicators of the social content of personality.

Whereas characterisation of the social type requires us

---

[1] K. Marx and F. Engels, *Selected Correspondence,* p. 140.

to reveal the content of the basic features of the group, ethos is the generalised, integrative indicator that allows us to single out the typical features. Ethos is the main thing in the type. Having discovered the ethos of a particular type, the investigator can go on to elucidate (1) the general qualities that the individual personality shares in common with society, class, nation or other social group and which characterise it as the representative of a certain social type, and also the features of this type, (2) the effects of the ethos of the personality and its inner world on the fulfilment of the basic forms of activity (roles) of the social type, i.e., the individual existence of social relations, and (3) the general and concrete-historical laws of the development of the personality. In other words, it is through revealing the ethos that we are able to make a proper study of the personality as the individual existence of historically concrete social relations, or, as Marx described it, "the subjective existence of thought and experienced society present for itself".[1]

By type we usually understand a generalised image, the characteristic features of a certain group of people, or specimen models for groups of objects, phenomena and individuals. The social type of personality designates the means by which a person carries out various forms of activity, a certain combination of qualities expressing the adherence of an individual to a social group.

Through belonging to a certain social group, through the special circumstances of his path in life and his inner state of mind, the individual chooses one or several patterns of thought and behaviour which, while predominant in him, also bear a resemblance to other characters that are more or less widespread in society. The mode or pattern of thinking which a person chooses, or rather assimilates, under the influence of the social conditions, produces a definite type of personality. The various conditions in which people may find themselves give rise to a whole system of types of consciousness and behaviour and, hence, a system of types of personalities. "There are, of course, and always will be individual exceptions from group and class types," Lenin observes. "But social types remain."[2]

---

[1] K. Marx, *Economic and Philosophic Manuscripts of 1844,* p. 105.
[2] V. I. Lenin, *Collected Works,* Vol. 27, p. 276.

Whereas a type of psychological activity is formed as a result of the peculiarities of the activity of the nervous system, a certain relationship of the processes of excitement and inhibition, equilibrium and mobility, the social type is made up of a combination of social qualities.

The formation of the basic social types in the conditions of an antagonistic society is founded on the division of that society into classes, on people's different relationships to the means of production, their different roles in the social organisation of labour, and the different amounts of income they receive.

But the peculiarities of a certain type depend not only on the individual's predetermined position in society but also on the individual's attitude to his position.

If his objective position and spiritual and moral qualities coincide, we have classical social types—slave and slave-owner, serf and feudal lord, proletarian and capitalist. Lenin gives a clear definition of social types of personality, based on their orientation. "The slave who is aware of his slavish condition and fights it is a revolutionary. The slave who is not aware of his slavish condition and vegetates in silent, unenlightened and wordless slavery, is just a slave. The slave who drools when smugly describing the delights of slavish existence and who goes into ecstasies over his good and kind master is a grovelling boor."[1] Here we find three different social types in one and the same social position.

Thus, the interests of a large group by no means automatically determine the behaviour of each and every individual belonging to that group.

There are other social distinctions within classes and various social groups that have subtle effects on outlook and behaviour. Take contemporary bourgeois society: the ordinary worker and the skilled man belonging to the "workers' aristocracy", the farmer and his hired man, the conscious revolutionary and the religious preacher, the recidivist criminal and the social philistine, the prosperous broker and the prostitute, the civil servant and the person who has been seeking work for years. The contrasts are not the same as those between class types, but they are very considerable

[1] V. I. Lenin, *Collected Works*, Vol. 13, p. 53.

both in respect of material conditions, character of activity and individual psychology. Each individual's thoughts, feelings and notions of morality and the meaning of life differ vastly on account of the differences in level and source of income, occupation, education, etc. But even so, belonging to a certain class remains the chief foundation on which social types of individual are formed in class society.

No matter how the social types of individual are formed, we always observe that the distinctions between them are connected with their relationship to the product of their labour, to their own activity, to other people. The relationships in these spheres of being are the foundation on which the basic qualities of the social type evolve. We have taken these extremely broad parameters because in a certain sense they extend over the whole being of man and form its main element. Marx used them when he was considering the problem of alienation and the movement of society towards communism.[1]

The structure of the types of personality in a given society, its typological or personality structure[2] corresponds on the whole to its social class structure and in one way or another reflects the state of harmony or conflict between the productive forces and the production relations, between the basis and the superstructure, between the interests of classes. It, therefore, seems to us that the use of the concept "personality structure of society" when considering the Marxist methodology of the problems of the individual in society is fully justified.

We speak of the personality structure corresponding "on the whole" to the class structure deliberately because this personality structure is relatively independent of the social structure. The variety of social types, including the intermediate and temporary types, is sometimes so great that sociologists are often tempted to give a positivist description of

---

[1] K. Marx, *Economic and Philosophic Manuscripts of 1844*, pp. 98-112.

[2] The personality structure of society should not be confused with the structure of the personality. The latter is the combination of features possessed by a given type of personality. The personality structure of society is the combination of types of personality that corresponds to the social structure of that society.

existing social types, to substitute unscientific, subjectivist, ephemeral criteria for the scientific criteria of historical materialism. The observance of a strictly scientific, historical materialist approach to the analysis of the personality structure of society does not stand in the way of the description and analysis of the intermediate or temporary social types, which are not obviously and directly connected with the basic classes and strata of a given society, which have come about as the concentrated expression of certain more or less stable conditions of social psychology.

Thus, two factors are particularly important when we are dealing with the problem of typing as a method of sociological research. First, the personality is always a definite social type. As a bearer of the general and the particular, one person may possess typical qualities of various kinds and, consequently, be a mixed-type person, personifying various social phenomena. Whereas a certain type may be described without reference to the characteristics of any particular individual, in fact, always is so described, the personality cannot possibly be described without elucidating its typical features, because there is no personality that is completely removed from all types. Second, the personality as a reflection of society, as a definite type, expresses something essential from its social environment, from a definite system of social relations—a class, group, phenomenon, trend or conflict. But neither the single individual nor even a type of individual is capable of expressing the sum total of these relations. Only a system of types can adequately reflect the structure of society, and this system is of particular interest as the personified expression of the social structure of a given society, and any changes that may be observed in it are the personified movement of the social organism, its rise, its crisis, its decline. The characterisation of certain social relations or laws is bound to look incomplete until it is rounded off with an exposition of the types of individual that represent these relationships and laws in a definite personal structure of society.

Karl Marx's *The Eighteenth Brumaire of Louis Bonaparte* and many of Lenin's works provide splendid examples of this approach.

Foundations and Methods
of the Classification of Personality

Every given society gives us a great number of types of personality reflecting the mosaic of social conditions that is made up of class and intraclass structural formations, national peculiarities, professional occupations, ideological aspirations and political activity.

If we proceed further than the basic class types, we arrive at a vast range of types that are to be found within these large and extremely general social types.

And if we approach this great variety without considering its foundations we can easily get lost in it. But there is in this multiplicity and seeming chaos a quite definite pattern and hierarchy, various degrees of subordination, because each of these types has a definite basis.

The characterisation of social types always demands elucidation of the general features of the various social groups. In respect of the individual this means finding out his objective position in this group, his social role, the essence of which is always determined by his attitude to the interests of the classes, of the group, and the way he performs this role which will depend on his general orientation or ethos. Classification, therefore, lies in the definition of socio-economic features, ideological and moral values, goals, methods of activity of groups of people by way of singling out what is general, stable and essential for the group and, hence, for the type. This definition is made either by means of describing the dominant features or by extracting certain combinations of qualities that reflect the content of the type.

There are different approaches to the explanation of the class and intraclass type. The content of the class type is determined by the identity of its features with the features of the class—its socio-economic position, ideological and moral features, culture, everyday life (of proletarians, capitalists, etc.). When characterising other social types, we must find in addition to their class features certain features that are also common to this particular group, since there is no such thing as a singular type.

The basis for defining intraclass types may be schematically presented as follows: (1) attitude to the means of production, i.e., amount of property and level of income; say, the big, medium and small bourgeoisie; the industrial proletarian, the worker who owns a strip of land, etc.; (2) production activity; for the working class and the professional people, this is a matter of trade or profession—metallurgist, miner, weaver, teacher, doctor, etc.; in respect of the bourgeoisie, the commercial bourgeoisie, the industrial and the financial bourgeoisie; (3) attitude to ideological values and the political struggle of the classes; depth of understanding of the interests of the class and its politics, consistency in defending its interests, attitude to methods of activity (conservatives and liberals among the ruling classes, revolutionaries and reformists among the working class), degree of participation in the struggle, political role. If we bear in mind these comparatively few attributes as foundations for our classification into types, as we are bound to do, we shall find that their various combinations yield an enormous number of typological phenomena reflecting sociohistorical situations.

What is more, one must remember that there are always separate elements of one or another class that choose to be oriented by the ideological values and even the outward forms of behaviour of another class or group (reference group). These types, of course, represent or reflect social conflict. The typological structure of society is not confined to types that reflect its structural formations, just as life itself does not consist of the peaceful, stable coexistence of classes and other groups. Just as the development of antagonistic society finds its expression in the struggle of classes, of the old and new, the existence of fundamental and intermediate, wavering sections, the victory of some and the defeat of others, in transitional phenomena and slow changes, so does the typological structure reflect all this in the existence of broad, stable and definite types or unstable, wavering and intermediate types.

The relation of broader types to the narrower ones is that of a whole to its parts. A whole must always consist of parts that differ from one another. Moreover, "the part must conform to the whole, and not vice versa",[1] and consequently

---

[1] V. I. Lenin, *Collected Works,* Vol. 12, p. 486.

the broader type and its qualities are determinant in relation to the features of the types that form part of it. The
parts, however, play a definite role in characterising the
whole.

Belonging to a social type, apart from the fact that it is
governed by social laws, is also quite a strict and serious
matter. It places a definite stamp on a person's character
and through the inner logic of group interests and psychology
obliges or actually forces him to act in a certain way and
not otherwise. People belonging to a particular social group
may be kind or unkind, of cheerful or gloomy disposition,
but they carry out their decisive acts in approximately the
same way because of this inner logic and the demands of
the psychological stereotype. Referring to this situation,
Lenin wrote: "...There are many most sincere Cadets who
really believe that their party stands for 'people's freedom'.
But the dual and vacillating class basis of their party inevitably engenders their double-faced policy, their fallacies and
their hypocrisy."[1]

In contrast to the Marxist approach, which is based primarily on the individual's class adherence, bourgeois sociologists
usually avoid class characteristics and are guided either by
psychological features or character of occupation. Max
Weber's classification of individual social behaviour was
characteristic in this respect. He laid down four types of
behaviour. The first type was behaviour guided by reason
and the will; the second, by rational values; the third, by
affectively controllable moods, passions; and the fourth, by
tradition. This classification has certain clearly pronounced
social and psychological characteristics. It completely avoids
any reference to production relations or the class division of
society.

In a number of his works Robert Merton develops a
conception diametrically opposed to that of Freud, according
to whom man's rebellious instinct is rooted in human nature
(a variant of original sin). Merton, on the other hand,
assumes that the infringement of social codes is a "normal"
response to a given situation and calls this point of view
the doctrine of socially derived sin. Developing this idea,

---

[1] V. I. Lenin, *Collected Works*, Vol. 10, p. 215.

Merton uses as his criteria for typing individuals people's attitudes to the goals, intentions and interests accepted in bourgeois society and to the means for attaining these goals. People differ according to whether they accept or reject these goals.

Having obtained a positive or negative answer to the question of attitude to these "culture goals" and the means of attaining them, Merton stipulates five logically possible, alternative ways in which individuals may adapt to social conditions.

Adaptation I consists of people who accept both the goal and the means. Merton holds that this is the most widely diffused adaptation. People of Adaptation II accept the goal but reject the means (hence innovation). This may involve the use of means which, though generally regarded as prohibited, are extremely effective for obtaining wealth, power, and so on. This adaptation includes criminals. Adaptation III (ritualism) rejects the goal but adheres to the means approved by society, even though the goal may have lost their meaning. Adaptation IV rejects both goal and means. This category includes psychotics, vagrants, drug addicts, i.e., people who have put themselves outside society. And finally, Adaptation V is the type of rebellion, i.e., rejection of both goals and means and their replacement by new ones.

Merton makes a particularly close analysis of what he calls the "illegitimacy adjustment", i.e., the category of people who, while accepting a goal approved by society, while accepting the values approved by society, employ means which though technically expedient are not morally acceptable to society. His concrete example was the specialised areas of vice on the near north side of Chicago constituting a "normal" response to a situation where the cultural emphasis upon pecuniary success had been absorbed, but where there was little access to conventional and legitimate means for attaining such success.[1]

Merton's reasoning is not lacking in realism and his method of studying the attitude to goal and means has been

---

[1] Robert K. Merton, "Social Structure and Anomie" in the *American Sociological Review*, Vol. 3, 1938, pp. 676, 677, 678.

fairly widely used for a long time. It may also be applied to the study of types in socialist society. Nevertheless his classification still makes no reference to classes, though it is regarded as universal.

The tendency to avoid analysis of the relationship between class structure and types of personality is a general feature of bourgeois sociology, which Lenin noted and criticised in his day. Struve, following Zimmel, propounded the idea that there was a direct connection between the differentiation of the group and the development of the individual belonging to that group. "In order that the individual may be differentiated, he must live in a differentiated environment," Struve wrote. Lenin called this abstract proposition completely unscientific "because no correlation can be established that will suit every form of social structure. The very concepts 'differentiation', 'heterogeneity', and so on, acquire absolutely different meanings, depending on the particular social environment to which they are applied".[1]

The term "differentiation" was so indefinite that it could be (and was!) interpreted in completely different ways when concrete analysis was attempted. Mikhailovsky, for example, regarded the abolition of serfdom as a weakening of differentiation (abolition of the estates), while Struve saw this as a strengthening of differentiation, in view of the widening economic gap, and so on. Lenin gives an analysis of the development of social life in Russia and its significance for the individual and reaches the following conclusion: "The 'old-nobility' economy, by tying men to their localities and dividing the population into handfuls of subjects of individual lords, brought about the suppression of the individual. And then capitalism freed him of all feudal fetters, made him independent in respect of the market, made him a commodity owner (and as such the equal of all other commodity owners), and thus heightened his sense of individuality."[2] Capitalism created conditions that made it possible for the individual to protest against Russian capitalism. Thus, the class approach to the problem gives concrete substance to the type of personality.

---

[1] V. I. Lenin, *Collected Works,* Vol. 1, p. 412.
[2] Ibid., p. 415.

Unless we study the typical qualities of the individual there can be no science of personality. If we are guided only by a person's individual peculiarities we are left at the mercy of chance. Only investigation of what is typical in the individual takes us into the sphere of laws, and the inferring of laws is always the crown of scientific knowledge.

Marxism-Leninism regards the study of types of personality, their scientific and artistic characterisation as a way of demonstrating the basic, determining qualities of social groups and phenomena. By studying the peculiarities of any social type we come to grips with the essential aspects of social development and are able to predict the behaviour not only of an individual of that type but also the behaviour of social groups and hence the development of events, and thus to exert a certain influence on people's actions.

The significance of types in art deserves special mention. Engels wrote that "realism implies, besides truth of detail, the truth in reproduction of typical characters in typical circumstances".[1] The artist's perception of types of personality is a fertile source of knowledge and education.

The essence of the artist's approach is to reveal the universal through the individual. When this requirement is not fulfilled, authenticity is lacking and the artistic effect is lost. Similarly, if a theoretical analysis fails to consider the origin of socially significant features or to disclose individual qualities from the standpoint of their social content, it falls short of its criteria and cannot be considered adequate. On the other hand, if in a work of art a character displays only typical and general qualities and there is no individuality, the effect is unnatural and uninteresting.

Thus, we see that scientific and artistic perception of the human personality is achieved by different methods. Both, however, solve certain general problems. Both the scientific and artistic study of life is concerned with singling out the essential, the important things, the things that interest and stir humanity. They solve this problem by showing the individual in close connection with his surroundings, with other people, with society. Both science and art sum up their activity by producing certain general attributes and qualities

---

[1] K. Marx and F. Engels, *Selected Correspondence,* pp. 478-79.

that indicate the social significance of what has been investigated or portrayed.

                                    *   *   *

Such are some of the basic features of the Marxist-Leninist conception of personality.

Marxism-Leninism brings an entirely new approach to the problem of the relationship between society and the individual. The idea of the socialist transformation of society by revolutionary means is implicit in the demands of the natural-historical development of society itself. Its purpose is to free the working man from exploitation and oppression and to abolish parasitism as a way of life. It corresponds to the interests and aspirations of the proletariat and of all working people.

The appearance of Marxism proclaimed the historical fact that the cult of abstract man must surrender the stage to the science of real people, the science of their historical development.[1] Not only was the secret of capitalist exploitation laid bare. Not only was it proved that capitalism must inevitably perish and be replaced by communism. This, of course, is Marxism's main achievement. But at the same time a number of specific anthropological problems were thoroughly examined and put on a scientific basis. Marx, Engels and Lenin frequently considered the problems of personality and illuminated numerous personal aspects of the development and functioning of bourgeois and socialist society—the social nature of man's essential being, of the individual's creative activity, the correlation between essence and existence, between the material and the spiritual, the rise and evolution of alienated labour and the alienated individual. They showed that belonging to a certain group or class explained the basic qualities of the individual. They evolved scientific methods for classifying types of individual. New light was thrown on every aspect of the relationships between collectivity and individuality, freedom and necessity, freedom and individual responsibility, and the idea that the individual's all-round development depends on the character of his work and social conditions was substantiated.

Marxism-Leninism is deeply opposed to the normative

---

[1] K. Marx and F. Engels, *Selected Works,* Vol. 3, p. 360.

approach to the definition of the ideal individual and always infers the qualities of the personality from life, from objective conditions. Man develops as an individual through active social participation in the course of which he transforms the world around him and himself. Rejecting the absurd charge that Marxism sought to destroy the personality, Marx and Engels stressed that they were opposed to the kind of personality that identifies itself with owning a bank account, a private estate, riding stable, pleasure yacht, and so on. You must confess, they wrote, "that by 'individual' you mean no other person, . . . than the middle-class owner of property. This person must, indeed, be swept out of the way and made impossible."[1] This is why the imperialist bourgeoisie in the shape of its ideologists—Marxologists, Sovietologists, Kremlinologists, i.e., professional anti-Communists—does all it can, by every method and means, to overthrow the Marxist-Leninist ideas of humanism.

Marxist-Leninist humanism, however, has nothing to do with the anarchistic repudiation of morality in general or with the infantile idea of the moral sovereignty of the individual. More than any other ideological system, Marxism-Leninism elevates the idea of the individual's creative activity, the free and all-round development of his aspirations and abilities. At the same time Marx, Engels and Lenin pointed quite definitely to the class character of morality, to the fact that the individual is bound by moral ties to his class.

Marx, Engels and Lenin devoted much time and effort to studying the general laws of social development, the strategy and tactics of revolutionary struggle, and the practical political problems. But all this was done in the name of emancipation of the individual and mankind in general from all forms of enslavement. Marxism-Leninism thus provides the theoretical basis of successful practical efforts to refashion human society and produce a new kind of man. Discovery of the laws of motion of society, organisation of the proletariat's political forces leads to the realisation of the ideals of humanism. Communism, in the words of Marx, equals humanism, is practical, positive humanism.

---

[1] K. Marx and F. Engels, *Selected Works*, Vol. 1, p. 122.

CHAPTER TWO

THE HISTORICAL PRECONDITIONS AND FUNDAMENTAL STAGES OF THE FORMATION OF THE SOCIALIST PERSONALITY

History is present in some way or other in every individual.

This is because the world around us is the product of historical development and because any significant historical event continues to exert an effect on succeeding generations. Here we have a very obvious law: the more deeply any particular event transforms the foundations of social life, the stronger and longer its effect will be on subsequent history. So, if we wish to understand how and in what direction contemporary society is developing, we must first of all find out where that society came from.

The social types of personality that society creates in the preceding stages of its development and leaves to the new age as the *dramatis personae* of subsequent history play their part in historical continuity.

Thus, we must examine not only the general socio-economic, political and ideological preconditions but also the structure of social types that takes shape in the prerevolutionary period and reflects the social conflict in a society pregnant with revolution. Social types, their political and moral peculiarities give us a tangible conception of the ideological content of the class struggle and form an inseparable part of the general picture of this struggle, of the spread of socialist consciousness, and the ultimate emergence of socialist ideas and active revolutionaries. The types that were formed before the revolution continue to exist after the revolution, and their role, their evolution constitute essential elements in the general process of development of socialism.

The family tree of Soviet man has deep roots in the history of the revolution. Our contemporaries, their ideals and basic features cannot be understood unless we are aware of the continuity between them and the generations of Bolsheviks who prepared and carried out the socialist revolution—the continuity of the thought and morals that the older generations inherited from the middle-class revolutionaries of the 19th century and which they consolidated and developed in the struggle against tsarism and Russian capitalism.

1. HOW THE SOCIAL CONFLICT WAS EXPRESSED IN THE PERSONALITY STRUCTURE OF TSARIST SOCIETY

The personality structure of tsarist Russia reflected both the general features of the socio-economic development inherent in countries in the middle stages of capitalist development and also some special features that were purely her own. "Sharp contrasts were a characteristic feature of the Russian scene: an agrarian country with a predominantly rural population, it had at the same time a high degree of concentration of industrial production and of revolutionary organisation of the working class. A big world power, it was invariably involved in rival imperialist blocs, while remaining dependent on the more developed capitalist states. Russian culture gave the world classical works in literature, art and science. Yet three-quarters of the population were illiterate."[1]

Russia entered the socialist revolution before she had solved many of the problems posed by the bourgeois revolution. The relentless exploitation of the workers, the peasants' poverty and lack of land, the absence of all political rights for the people, the subjection of the national minorities, the survivals of serfdom and patriarchal life, and much else, all made Russia a nodal point of social and national oppressions and predetermined the tremendous intensity and acuteness of the political events at the beginning of the 20th century.

---

[1] *On the Centenary of the Birth of V. I. Lenin*, Moscow, 1970, p. 8.

The multistructural nature of the economy placed in the fore-
front of the political struggle, along with the basic classes,
a multitude of intermediate social groups (and social types)
displaying a vast variety of political beliefs and programmes.
Suffice it to say, that after the February revolution of
1917 there were more than fifty political parties reflecting
the conflict-torn economic and social diversity of the period.

Russian society was not only a class society; it also had
a hierarchy of social estates. The development of capitalism
set afoot violent processes destined to sweep away the hierarchical distinctions by the deepening division of labour, the
migration of wealth from the nobility to the bourgeoisie, the
spread of education, and so on. A certain differentiation also
occurred in the political views of the ruling class concerning
the methods of administration; even this class acquired its
"Left" wing and part of the bourgeoisie became actively
opposed to the government.

Confronted with this mêlée of political programmes and
phraseology, the revolutionary proletariat badly needed to
be able to make assessments based on clear criteria of class,
to recognise the social types that represented the interests
of one class or another. By studying the pattern of economic
development, of the class struggle, Lenin was able to present
a whole gallery of social types representing the personality
structure of society and reflecting the prerevolutionary social
conflict. In his works we find living portraits of types of
reactionary monarchists, public men from among the liberal
bourgeoisie, or the peasant bourgeoisie, the type of worker
who lived in a village and owned his own strip of land,
the rural proletarian type, the middle peasant, the proletarian revolutionary, the political opportunist, etc.

In a country like Russia with a predominantly rural
population the fate of the revolution depended in large
measure on the behaviour of the peasantry, on the development of its revolutionary consciousness. The peasantry's
evolution under the influence of economic processes, its
awareness that its own interests were close to the proletariat's, the emergence of peasant types with similar aspirations to those of the proletariat were salient features to
which Lenin paid the closest attention.

The key event is the abolition of serfdom in 1861. On

the one hand, because of the subsequent robbing of the peasants, this led to a growth of revolutionary feeling among the peasant masses, and on the other, it started a rapid and profound disintegration of village life, an exodus of peasants to the cities and, at the same time, a sudden proliferation of new social types.

The peasants reacted to robbery by means of reform with a fresh wave of unrest and rebellions. Peasant revolts occurred in nearly every decade of the 19th century. "The peasant needs land, and his revolutionary feeling, his instinctive, primitive sense of democracy *cannot* express itself otherwise than by laying hands on the landlords' land."[1] The reform swelled the numbers of rebellious peasants and widened the sphere of irritated consciousness. In the second half of the century the people's discontent gushed forth so violently that revolutionary situations followed one another in quick succession without, however, leading to revolution, to the radical solution of social problems.

The break-up, the differentiation of the peasantry was expressed in the collapse of the village communities with their rigid framework of life, and in profound changes in the character of the peasants, the producers themselves. In Lenin we find a thorough analysis of such changes as "depeasantisation", i.e., transformation of the peasant with property of his own into a propertyless proletarian. "Migration to the town" in search of work "elevated the peasant as a citizen".[2] But another line of development was also to be observed. The peasant broke his ties with serfdom in a different way— by becoming a property-owner, a kulak, and thus swelling the ranks of the exploiters. The squeezing out of the middle peasants created a layer of rural bourgeoisie, of kulaks, on top of the mass of proletarianised rural poor—agricultural workers with a strip of land.

Lenin regarded the Russian peasantry as a revolutionary force capable of forming an alliance with the proletariat. Referring to the results of the revolution of 1905, he noted with satisfaction: "A new type appeared in the Russian village—the class-conscious young peasant. He associated

---

[1] V. I. Lenin, *Collected Works*, Vol. 8, p. 247.
[2] Ibid., Vol. 3, p. 576.

with 'strikers', he read newspapers, he told the peasants about events in the cities, explained to his fellow-villagers the meaning of political demands and urged them to fight the landowning nobility, the priests and the government officials."[1] At the same time Lenin pointed out the dual nature of the peasant: on the one hand, a property-owner, on the other, a toiler. Hence his differing behaviour in a revolution. ". . .The small master (a social type existing on a very extensive and even mass scale in many European countries), who, under capitalism, always suffers oppression and, very frequently, a most acute and rapid deterioration in his conditions of life, and even ruin, easily goes to revolutionary extremes, but is incapable of perseverance, organisation, discipline and steadfastness. A petty bourgeois driven to frenzy by the horrors of capitalism is a social phenomenon which, like anarchism, is characteristic of all capitalist countries."[2] Lenin went on to show the instability of such revolutionariness, its futility, its tendency to collapse suddenly into submission, apathy, wild imaginings, even a "frenzied" enthusiasm for the latest "fashionable" bourgeois trend.

A new class, the proletariat, the antipode of the bourgeoisie, quickly took shape during the reform period. Its main source of growth was the bankrupt rural masses. In 1913, Russia had about 17.8 million people working for hire, including domestic servants. More than half of them, those employed in industry, transport and communications, were organised.

The exodus from the countryside was largely instrumental in moulding the class of proletarians and the personality of the proletarian in Russia. Every year from the mid-seventies onwards not less than three million people quitted the villages to take up work in industry or subindustries in the cities. The factories moved out into the country and many manufacturing villages developed into large industrial centres. Finally the subindustries were capitalised with a consequent increase of hired labour in the villages. All this, of course, held back the development of consciousness among the workers at the beginning of the first period of the work-

---

[1] V. I. Lenin, *Collected Works*, Vol. 23, p. 243.
[2] Ibid., Vol. 31, p. 32.

ing-class movement. On the other hand, it brought the workers' vanguard closer to the peasant masses.

Lenin examined the process of the formation of proletarian consciousness with great care. He noted to what extent a person's psychology was influenced by his objective status. If a person merely took up work at a factory without becoming aware of his own change of status, he was still not a full-fledged proletarian. "Our 'proletarian'," Marx maintained, "is economically none other than the wage-labourer who produces and increases capital, and is thrown out on the streets, as soon as he is superfluous for the needs of aggrandisement of 'Monsieur capital' ".[1]

Characteristically, in their first actions against the capitalists the workers were steadier and better organised than the peasants. This irreconcilable class feeling of the workers was immediately noted by the servants of the autocracy—the secret police. In his political review for 1883 the chief of the St. Petersburg secret police wrote: "Most prominent among the general species of workers is the type of the permanent factory worker.... This type produces the dangerous element on which the anarchists, with some justification, hope to graft dreams of socialist utopias."[2]

It is factory production that forms the typical features of the worker's personality. In his book *The Condition of the Working Class in England,* Engels describes the unselfishness and solidarity of the workers. "To them every person is a human being, while the worker is less than a human being for the bourgeois." For the workers money has not the "value of a god" that it has for the bourgeoisie. The worker is less greedy for money than the bourgeois, and he is "much less prejudiced, has a clearer eye for facts as they are than the bourgeois, and does not look at everything through the spectacles of personal selfishness."[3]

Karl Marx noted in the workers the intensity of their social interests. "When communist *workmen* associate with one another, theory, propaganda, etc., is their first end. But

---

[1] K. Marx, *Capital,* Vol. I, p. 614.

[2] *The Working-Class Movement in Russia in the 19th Century,* Vol. II, Part 2, Moscow, 1950, p. 634 (in Russian).

[3] K. Marx and F. Engels, *On Britain,* Moscow, 1962, p. 158.

at the same time, as a result of this association, they acquire a new need—the need for society—and what appears as a means becomes an end. You can observe this practical process in its most splendid results whenever you see French socialist workers together. Such things as smoking, drinking, eating, etc., are no longer the means of contact or the means that bring together. Company, association, and conversation, which again has society as its end, are enough for them; the brotherhood of man is no mere phrase with them, but a fact of life, and the nobility of man shines upon us from their work-hardened bodies."[1]

The approaching revolution demanded of the broad masses that they should be clearly aware of their class interests, and the complete opposition of those interests to the interests of the exploiters. Lenin propounded and persistently developed the idea of the hegemony, the leadership, of the proletariat in the imminent revolution and regarded workers as different social types according to their attitude to this idea. "The proletariat is revolutionary only insofar as it is conscious of and gives effect to this idea of the hegemony of the proletariat. The proletarian who is conscious of this task is a slave who has revolted against slavery. The proletarian who is not conscious of the idea that his class must be the leader, or who renounces this idea, is a slave who does not realise his position as a slave; at best he is a slave who fights to improve his condition as a slave, *but not* one who fights to overthrow slavery."[2]

The Russian working class had all the qualities that were needed to make it the progressive, revolutionary class of society. It was the most irreconcilably opposed to exploitation and political oppression, it showed a capacity for discipline and organisation, for steadfastness and helping each other in a tight corner. And because of these qualities it was most receptive to the socialist ideology and was able to conduct a conscious, organised struggle for the interests of all the working people. It was the way the working class conducted itself that decided the fate of the revolution. From the working-class environment came the steadfast and consistent fight-

---

[1] K. Marx, *Economic and Philosophic Manuscripts of 1844*, p. 124.
[2] V. I. Lenin, *Collected Works*, Vol. 17, p. 232.

ers for the cause of the revolution, the outstanding organisers of socialist construction.

The working class was faced with a strong political opponent. After the reform of 1861 a certain differentiation occurred among the landowners. Some of them used the redemption payments they had received for the land to set up businesses, thus producing a type of nobleman-bourgeois that advocated either restriction of the monarchy or the setting up of a bourgeois republic. It was they who later formed the core of the liberal opposition, the Zemstvo movement and the Octobrist party (Guchkov, Rodzyanko, Shidlovsky and others). Another part of the landowning class went bankrupt and joined the ranks of officialdom. Some were able, thanks to the size of their estates, to carry on as before, exploiting the labour of their former serfs.

Huge semi-feudal estates continued to exist. Their owners were the most reactionary force of all and the main bulwark of the autocracy. It was this class that supplied the provincial governors, the governors-general, the top military, the government ministers, and so on. The key positions in the government apparatus were still controlled by the nobility.

The transformation of the aristocratic landowner class went hand in hand with important changes in the bourgeoisie, which in Russia was represented mainly by merchants. The reform of 1861 introduced the figure of the modern, more or less educated capitalist running his business on upto-date lines. The former merchants, tax-farmers, grain dealers, the newly rich village kulaks and money-lenders became speculators into railway, industrial and banking capital. To defend their interests various groups of the bourgeoisie joined together in special organisations of a class-economic and, later, political nature. Their interests were represented by the Cadets (Constitutional Democrats, and from 1906, the People's Freedom Party), led by Milyukov, Nabokov, Muromtsev, Gessen and others.

Taken as a whole, the Russian bourgeoisie, as Lenin noted in his book *Two Tactics of Social-Democracy in the Democratic Revolution*, was not revolutionary.[1] The liberal

---

[1] V. I. Lenin, *Collected Works*, Vol. 9, p. 15.

camp constantly manoeuvred between Social-Democracy and reaction and at all critical points in the revolution supported tsarism. The Russian bourgeoisie gave history not a single revolutionary-bourgeois type of public figure.

Lenin frequently pointed out the dangers that liberal representatives of the ruling classes presented to the revolution and relentlessly exposed the counter-revolutionary exploitative essence of liberalism. In the article "In Memory of Count Heyden", replying to the "liberal and democratic droolers" who were making too much of the late count's educatedness and humanity, Lenin wrote sarcastically: "The educated counter-revolutionary landlord knew how to defend the interests of his class subtly and artfully; he skilfully covered up the selfish strivings and rapacious appetites of the semi-feudal landlords with a veil of noble words and outward gentlemanliness; he insisted (to Stolypin) on the protection of these interests by the most civilised forms of class domination."[1]

When classifying the types of the ruling class, Lenin takes into consideration various methods of achieving one and the same goal. If the tactics of the bourgeoisie were always the same or at least always of the same kind, he explained, the working class would rapidly learn to reply with similarly unchanging tactics. "But, as a matter of fact, in every country the bourgeoisie inevitably devises two systems of rule, two methods of fighting for its interests and of maintaining its domination. ... The first of these is the method of force, the method which rejects all concessions to the labour movement, the method of supporting all the old and obsolete institutions, the method of irreconcilably *rejecting* reforms. ... The second is the method of 'liberalism', of steps towards the development of political rights, towards reforms, concessions, and so forth."[2]

Lenin often reminded us that Russia was the most petty-bourgeois of all European countries, particularly in its cities. After the bourgeois reforms of the 1860s and 1870s the *meshchanstvo,* the urban petty bourgeoisie, acquired wide access to the civil service with the right of individual (i.e.,

---

[1] V. I. Lenin, *Collected Works,* Vol. 13, p. 55.
[2] Ibid., Vol. 16, p. 350.

not hereditary) elevation to the nobility. With the development of capitalism the upper crust of the *meshchanstvo* moved up into the ranks of the bourgeoisie, while the lower part became craftsmen and proletarians. Many entered the liberal professions (medicine, law, etc.).

The *meshchanstvo* combined the greed of the property-owner with the ignorance of the semi-educated and the pretentiousness of the urban leisured classes. They gravitated towards the ruling class in spirit and acted as a militantly reactionary force against the progressive trends. These peculiarities of the *meshchanstvo* made the word a synonym of vulgarity and ignorance. When Gorky said of one of Dostoyevsky's characters that "this is, undoubtedly, the Russian soul, amorphous and multicoloured, simultaneously cowardly and audacious, and above all pathologically vicious", Lenin firmly disagreed: "...You condescended to say very truly about the *soul:* only you should have said, not 'the Russian', but the *petty-bourgeois*, for the Jewish, the Italian, the English varieties are all *one and the same devil;* stinking philistinism everywhere is equally disgusting—but 'democratic philistinism', occupied in ideological necrophily, is particularly disgusting."[1]

The small property-owning strata are the bulwark of reformism. Lenin showed the objective conditions behind this type of behaviour. "This wavering flows in two 'streams': petty-bourgeois reformism, i.e., servility to the bourgeoisie covered by a cloak of sentimental democratic and 'Social'-Democratic phrases and fatuous wishes; and petty-bourgeois revolutionism—menacing, blustering and boastful in words, but a mere bubble of disunity, disruption and brainlessness in deeds. This wavering will inevitably occur until the taproot of capitalism is cut."[2]

Servility is a political feature of a certain social type. Lenin was particularly scornful of those who looked up in awe at Heyden's education without noticing the class essence of his activity. Though not members of the ruling class themselves, they served it diligently. And this feature—or what some sociologists would call "reference group orientation"—is a

1 V. I. Lenin, *Collected Works*, Vol. 35, p. 123.
2 Ibid., Vol. 33, p. 21.

characteristic of the "lackey", the prostituted type of individual. "You are mean-spirited boors, and your education, culture, and enlightenment are only a species of thoroughgoing
prostitution."[1]

And even clearer characterisation of the same social type
is to be found in the article "In the Servants' Quarters" which
deals with its psychological qualities as well. Speaking of the
lackey as a social type, Lenin wrote, "Here it is a case of a
social type and not of the qualities possessed by individuals.
A lackey may be the most honest of men, an exemplary
member of his family, an excellent citizen but he is fatally
doomed to hypocrisy because the main feature of his trade is
the combination of the interests of the master whom he is
'pledged to serve truly and faithfully' and those of the milieu
from which servants are recruited. If this problem, therefore,
is studied from the political point of view, i.e., from the
point of view of millions of people and the relations between
millions, one must come to the conclusion that the chief
features of the lackey as a social type are hypocrisy and cowardice. These qualities are inculcated by the lackey's trade,
and they are the most important from the point of view
of the wage-slaves and the mass of working people in any
capitalist society."[2] The qualities of hypocrisy and cowardice
would seem to be produced by the effort to combine extremely
contradictory interests, because the very fact of combining
them makes a person put on a false face and tremble with
fear for his own well-being.

The second half of the 19th century, particularly the reform period, produced immense cultural advances. Outstanding talents appeared in the most varied branches of science
and art. And yet the culture of the ruling classes was incapable of creating progressive spiritual values. It was designed
mainly to preserve the semi-feudal regime and was very
much inclined to kneel in awe before anything foreign. On
the other hand, the liberation movement of the 1860s to
1890s gave a powerful impetus to the development of democratic culture, which in its turn had a colossal influence in
developing the activity of the fighters for freedom and dem-

---

[1] V. I. Lenin, *Collected Works*, Vol. 13, p. 53.
[2] Ibid., Vol. 29, pp. 541-42.

ocracy, and is to this day tremendously effective in shaping the minds of the rising generations.

The deepest features of the progressive men of science, literature and art of those days were the ardent championing of education, their revolutionary spirit, the service in the interests of the people and the materialist tendency of their views. As Marx wrote: "The intellectual movement now taking place in Russia testifies to the fact that deep below the surface fermentation is going on. Minds are always connected by invisible threads with the body of the people...."[1] Russian progressive thought of the 19th century, Lenin wrote, reflected not an "intellectual" mood but the mood of the serfs rebelling against serfdom, the history of protest and struggle by the broadest masses of the population "against the survivals of feudalism throughout the whole system of Russian life...".[2]

The complex, dramatic history of the democratically-minded intelligentsia yielded a number of correspondingly contradictory types, which Lenin also analysed. One of them was Alexander Herzen. In an examination of Herzen's complex career as a revolutionary and assessment of his personality, Lenin wrote: "Herzen belonged to the generation of revolutionaries among the nobility and landlords of the first half of the last century.... The uprising of the Decembrists awakened and 'purified' him. In the feudal Russia of the forties of the 19th century, he rose to a height which placed him on a level with the greatest thinkers of his time. He assimilated Hegel's dialectics. He realised that it was 'the algebra of revolution'. He went further than Hegel, following Feuerbach to materialism....

"Herzen came right up to dialectical materialism, and halted—before historical materialism.

"It was this 'halt' that caused Herzen's spiritual shipwreck after the defeat of the revolution of 1848....

"Herzen's spiritual shipwreck, his deep scepticism and pessimism after 1848, was a shipwreck of the *bourgeois illusions* of socialism. Herzen's spiritual drama was a product and reflection of that epoch in world history when the revolutiona-

---

[1] K. Marx and F. Engels, *Selected Correspondence*, p. 311.
[2] V. I. Lenin, *Collected Works*, Vol. 16, p. 125.

ry character of the bourgeois democrats was *already* passing away (in Europe), while the revolutionary character of the socialist proletariat had *not yet* matured. . . .

"With Herzen, scepticism was a form of transition from the illusion of a bourgeois democracy that is 'above classes' to the grim, inexorable and invincible class struggle of the proletariat. . . . In breaking with Bakunin, Herzen turned his gaze, not to liberalism, but to the *International*—to the International led by Marx. . .".[1]

Lenin's analysis of such a complex personality as Herzen, his evolution from the positions of the nobleman revolutionary through the illusions of bourgeois socialism to proletarian socialism is a splendid example of how to take into consideration changing objective conditions, shifts in the relationship of class forces, and also the inner, intellectual hesitations of the individual.

Lenin also gave a subtle and profound analysis of the work and personality of Leo Tolstoy and characterised him as a social type. We are shown a landowner and man of letters, a thinker, but not the kind of thinker who expresses the interests of his own class. Tolstoy was a writer and thinker who had adopted the positions of the patriarchal peasantry and was expressing its condition and status. "The protest of millions of peasants and their desperation—these were combined in Tolstoy's doctrine."[2]

But it was not only a matter of defending the interests of the peasantry. Taken as a social type, Tolstoy is a focal point of conflicting prerevolutionary tendencies.

"The contradictions in Tolstoy's views are not contradictions inherent in his personal views alone, but are a reflection of the extremely complex, contradictory conditions, social influences and historical traditions which determined the psychology of various classes and various sections of Russian society in the *post*-Reform, but *pre*revolutionary era."[3] The great artist and the landlord obsessed with Christ; the powerful protest against falsehood and hypocrisy and the appeal for moral self-perfection; the merciless criticism of the

---

[1] V. I. Lenin, *Collected Works*, Vol. 18, pp. 25-27.

[2] Ibid., Vol. 16, p. 332.

[3] Ibid., p. 325.

system and the teaching that evil should not be resisted by force; the most sober realism and the preaching of religion—"one of the most odious things on earth".[1] In the divided inner world of the artist we see the contradictory conditions of the social environment, the objective position and subjective aspirations of the various sections of society. Not for nothing did Lenin call this contradictoriness in Tolstoy's views, in his writings "a mirror of the Russian revolution". The metaphor symbolises Tolstoy's work and also characterises a definite social type peculiarly subject to inner contradiction.

The *raznochintsi*—people of various rank and title who had acquired an education and broken away from their former social environment, people who came from various estates, the merchants, the *meshchanstvo,* the clergy, the peasantry, and also the minor officials and nobles—played a special part in the development of a critical and, later, revolutionary consciousness. Lenin characterised the *raznochintsi* as educated representatives of the liberal and democratic bourgeoisie.

Politically speaking, the *raznochintsi* were represented by whole generations of fighters against the autocracy and serfdom. The best part of intellectual Russia, people dedicated to thought and honour, feverishly sought a way out of the impasse to which the autocratic-landowner system had reduced the country. Despairing of finding truth on the "legal" path, the young people took up arms and began shooting at the tsars and their satraps, turned to books and studied the intricacies of socio-economic science and looked to the working class that was just beginning to take shape.

Such are some of the peculiarities of the personality structure of tsarist Russia, which reflected the main social conflict of the prerevolutionary epoch. In 1913, the socio-class structure of Russian society presented the following picture: 17 per cent workers and employees, 66.7 per cent peasants and small craftsmen, 16.3 per cent bourgeois, landowners, traders and kulaks.

The basic questions that stirred society were the questions of the land, of the equality of nations, of democratic free-

---

[1] Ibid., Vol. 15, p. 205.

doms and later—during the war—of peace. People's attitude to these questions determined the positions of the social groups and, consequently, the formation of the social types of individual, and their polarity—revolutionary or reactionary types. The actions and aspirations of these types reflected the social conflict that led to the revolutionary explosion of 1905, and then to the victorious socialist revolution of 1917. The people who actually personified these typical features became the main participants in the historical events of that time.

Thus, we find that the system of types of personality, or the personality structure of society, is a special personified expression of the socio-class structure of the given society, while any change in this structure represents the personified motion of the social organism, its rise, crisis or decline. At the turn of the 19th century the popular consciousness was still dominated by submission to the tsarist autocracy. This state of consciousness corresponded, as Lenin put it, to the type of "a God-fearing and police-fearing person".[1] After the revolution of 1905 Lenin observed with enthusiasm: "The Russian proletariat can be proud of the fact that in 1905, under its leadership, a nation of slaves for the first time became a million-strong host, an army of the revolution, striking at tsarism. And now the same proletariat will know how to do persistently, staunchly and patiently the work of educating and training the new cadres of a still mightier revolutionary force."[2]

Other laws are to be observed in the movement of the personality structure of prerevolutionary Russia apart from the general law of its being dependent on the socio-class structure. One of these laws is that intensification of the social conflict and the build-up of the revolutionary situation generates an ever greater variety of class types with a definite social significance and makes the class features and qualities of individuals even more striking. As the struggle grows more intense, the intermediate strata also throw up growing numbers of eclectic, opportunist types expressing the changing fortunes of the struggle at every given stage.

---

[1] V. I. Lenin, *Collected Works*, Vol. 19, p. 144.
[2] Ibid., Vol. 15, pp. 351-52.

Yet another law is to be observed in the fact that the transition from the old society to the new, from capitalism to socialism is accompanied by the mass degradation of the individuals of the reactionary, declining class and, on the contrary, the promotion by the ascending revolutionary class of outstanding individuals displaying energy and ability in all spheres of social life. Moreover, the "process of dissolution going on within the ruling class, in fact within the whole range of the old society, assumes such a violent, glaring character, that a small section of the ruling class cuts itself adrift and joins the revolutionary class, the class that holds the future in its hands. Just as, therefore, at an earlier period, a section of the nobility went over to the bourgeoisie, so now a portion of the bourgeoisie goes over to the proletariat, and in particular, a portion of the bourgeois ideologists, who have raised themselves to the level of comprehending theoretically the historical movement as a whole."[1]

The contradictory character of the working man's personality becomes more and more apparent as the social conflict develops into a revolutionary situation. There are exploitation, political and spiritual oppression on the part of the landowner-bourgeois system and at the same time a "mounting feeling of individuality", the growth of revolutionary self-awareness of the proletarian and peasant masses. This, too, is a law of the development of the working man's personality in conditions of capitalism, which is also clearly defined by Lenin in a number of his works.

2. FORMATION OF THE PERSONALITY OF THE PROLETARIAN REVOLUTIONARY

A particularly interesting feature of the development of the personality structure of Russian society is the formation of the personality of the proletarian revolutionary, which embodied the finest qualities of the working class, the revolutionary vanguard of the whole people.

---

[1] K. Marx and F. Engels, *Selected Works,* Vol. 1, p. 117.

Scientific Socialism Combined with Revolutionary Struggle as a Condition of the Formation of the Proletarian Revolutionary

The formation of the personality of the proletarian revolutionary was connected with the spread of Marxism in Russia. "The ground for the assimilation and application of Marxism in Russia was prepared by her socio-economic development, the sharpness of class contradictions and revolutionry traditions originating in peasant revolts, in the activities of A. N. Radishchev and the Decembrists, A. I. Herzen, N. G. Chernyshevsky and other democrats of the 60s and the revolutionary Narodniks (Populists) of the 70s of last century."[1]

Bolshevism, Lenin wrote, grew up on the firmest of all foundations, on the theory of Marxism, which had been proved correct not only by the world experience of the 19th century but also and in particular by the experience of the straying and vacillation, the mistakes and disillusionment of revolutionary thought in Russia.[2] In 1912, reviewing the path of the revolutionary struggle, Lenin noted three stages in history and three types of revolutionary representing three classes: ". . . we clearly see the three generations, the three classes, that were active in the Russian revolution. At first it was nobles and landlords, the Decembrists and Herzen. These revolutionaries formed but a narrow group. They were very far removed from the people. But their effort was not in vain. The Decembrists awakened Herzen. Herzen began the work of revolutionary agitation.

"This work was taken up, extended, strengthened and tempered by the revolutionary *raznochintsi*—from Chernyshevsky to the heroes of Narodnaya Volya. The range of fighters widened; their contact with the people became closer. The young helmsmen of the gathering storm is what Herzen called them. But it was not yet the storm itself.

"The storm is the movement of the masses themselves. The proletariat, the only class that is thoroughly revolutionary, rose at the head of the masses and for the first time aroused millions of peasants to open revolutionary struggle. The first

---

[1] *On the Centenary of the Birth of V. I. Lenin,* p. 8.
[2] V. I. Lenin, *Collected Works,* Vol. 31, p. 25.

onslaught in this storm took place in 1905. The next is beginning to develop under our very eyes."[1]

The great service that the forerunners of Marxism performed for Russia was their creation of brilliant, deep-going and influential traditions of democratic struggle against the tsarist autocracy. Lenin called Herzen, Belinsky, Chernyshevsky and the revolutionaries of the seventies (P. Alekseyev, A. Zhelyabov, N. Morozov, V. Figner, S. Khalturin and others) the forerunners of Russian Social-Democracy.[2] In the revolutionary movement of the seventies he saw the great inspirational power of the ideas of the peasant socialist revolution. The moral qualities of the great thinkers of the seventies, so he believed, must be inherent in the masses of the proletariat.

Needless to say socialist ideas could only be spread by overcoming difficulties, in the course of a desperate struggle. Scientific socialism in Russia was confronted by three basic adversaries: the hidebound, reactionary ideology of the ruling class, essentially expressed in the famous formula, "autocracy, orthodoxy and nationalism"; then the liberal intelligentsia, which was wavering between revolution and reaction and which hated socialism more than tsarism, and, as a rule, at the critical moments in history decamped to the

---

[1] V. I. Lenin, *Collected Works*, Vol. 18, p. 31.

[2] V. I. Lenin, *Collected Works*, Vol. 5, p. 370. Chernyshevsky's ethical views had much to offer the working class. They demanded that a fighter for the people's cause should serve the people devotedly, subordinate his personal interests to these of society, to the task of emancipation of the people.

Noting the beneficial influence of *What Is To Be Done?*, Lenin pointed out the moral effect of the novel: "Before I got acquainted with works by Marx, Engels and Plekhanov the chief, overriding influence was exerted on me by Chernyshevsky alone, by his *What Is To Be Done?* The greatest service performed by Chernyshevsky was his proof that every thinking and truly honest man must be a revolutionary. Besides he showed, which is more important, what kind of a revolutionary he must be, what rules must govern his activity and how he must approach his aim and by what ways and means he must achieve it." (V. I. Lenin, *On Literature and Art*, Moscow, 1967, p. 655, in Russian.) N. K. Krupskaya writes that as a personality Chernyshevsky impressed Lenin with his irreconcilability, his staunchness and the dignity and pride with which the great revolutionary democrat endured the unbelievable hardships allotted him by fate (V. I. Lenin, *On Literature and Art*, Moscow, 1970, p. 239).

monarchists; and finally, the imitators of utopian socialism—the liberal Narodniks, whose views dominated the
consciousness of the revolutionary intelligentsia until the
appearance of Marxism in Russia.

In the period from 1883 to 1904, from the beginning of
the activity of the Emancipation of Labour group to the appearance of Bolshevism, Marxism won the day over the petty-
bourgeois, utopian theories of socialism and became the dominant ideology in the Russian working-class movement. In
the controversy with the Narodniks the truth was established that Russia had long since entered upon the capitalist
path of development, that its proletariat was growing rapidly,
and that the worker was becoming the "man of the future".
The inadequacy both of adventurist terrorist tactics and of
the reformism of the liberal Narodniks was laid bare.

It was the Bolshevik Party led by Lenin that performed
the historical service of uniting scientific socialism with the
working-class movement. Lenin regarded it as one of the
most essential conditions of success to bring socialist consciousness into the movement. He attached the greatest
importance to Social-Democratic propaganda in the performance of revolutionary tasks. In this he saw one of the main
differences between the revolutionary and the philistine. "The
philistine," he wrote, "is satisfied with the undoubted, holy
and *empty* truth that it is impossible to say in advance whether there will be a revolution or not. A Marxist is not satisfied with that; he says: our propaganda and the propaganda
of all worker Social-Democrats is *one of the factors determining* whether there will be a revolution or not."[1]

The Marxist-Leninist approach to the political education
of the masses, the propaganda is fundamentally different
from the bourgeois approach. From the bourgeois theoreticians' standpoint, propaganda is a deliberate spreading of
illusions with the aim of stimulating people to act in accordance with the predetermined goals of certain interested social
groups. Michael Choukas, an American student of propaganda, for instance, writes that the function of science is
cognition and education, while the function of propaganda is
manipulative influence. Since the interests of the ruling class

---

[1] V. I. Lenin, *Collected Works*, Vol. 18, p. 383.

are alien to the people, the common bourgeois attitude is cynical admission of the deceptive nature of propaganda. Falsehood is in the interests of the bourgeoisie and is, in fact, one of its class characteristics.

The essence of the Marxist-Leninist conception of propaganda is determined by the fact that socialism expresses the interests of the working people, the majority of society, and embodies its progressive development. Socialist propaganda aims at developing in the consciousness of the workers, of all working people, scientific knowledge of the world, of the present-day socio-economic system, of the various classes of society, of the struggle between these classes, and of the role of the working class in this struggle.[1]

Despite mass illiteracy there were nevertheless among the proletariat of Russia many people with enough education to be able to consciously absorb the ideas of socialism and bring them to the masses. The anti-Communists, who spread the false idea that Russia was not ready for the October Revolution, talk of the "immaturity" and "backwardness" of the Russian working class as downtrodden illiterate "semi-peasants" rather that the "type of industrial worker". The West German publicist H. Falk maintains that the proletariat, the masses in Russia, adopted Marxism and socialism merely as a new religion since they were allegedly at a low level of development and had no revolutionary or cultural traditions. According to Falk, "with regard to ideas Lenin found an almost complete vacuum, which he was able to fill with the Marxist ideology."[2]

Bourgeois Sovietologists distort and speculate on some of the facts and play down the others. By the beginning of the 1860s, according to Chernyshevsky, six per cent of the population were literate. By the time of the revolution the figure had risen to 30 per cent. The democratic critic Shelgunov recalled: "In the sixties, as if by a miracle... there was suddenly created a quite new, unusual reader with social feelings, social thoughts and interests, who wanted to think about social matters, who wanted to study to acquire the

---

[1] V. I. Lenin, *Collected Works*, Vol. 2, p. 329.
[2] Heinrich Falk, *Die ideologischen Grundlagen des Kommunismus*, München, 1961, S. 12.

knowledge he desired." Characteristically, there were quite
a few workers among such readers. In some public libraries
nearly half the readership consisted of workers.

Thus, it was not a vacuum but a mass of proletarians that
eagerly accepted the scientific truths of socialism. A large
number of proletarians thirsted for knowledge, read and
studied, were informed about the struggle of the West European proletariat and the history of the liberation movement
in their own country, were proud of their revolutionary
traditions and observed them.

What is more, one must bear in mind that the proletariat
in general, thanks to its position, absorbs Marxism more
quickly than the *"learned* scribes".[1] The bourgeois lie about
a "vacuum" is countered by the Marxist-Leninist teaching on
the class character of culture and morality. Engels showed
in *Anti-Dühring* that in bourgeois society a proletarian
morality exists side by side with the bourgeois morality.[2]
This idea is developed by Lenin's proposition on different
cultures within each national culture under capitalism. Lenin
wrote that alongside the bourgeois culture "the *elements* of
democratic and socialist culture are present, if only in rudi-
mentary form, in *every* national culture, since in *every*
nation there are toiling and exploited masses, whose conditions of life inevitably give rise to the ideology of democracy
and socialism."[3]

Relying on the proletariat's spontaneous leanings toward
socialism, the Bolshevik Party launched a campaign of mass
propaganda and agitation for socialist and democratic ideas
through the system of study circles, and the medium of the
Russian Social-Democratic press. The success of this ideological and political work was based on the elaboration by
Lenin and his associates of the theoretical problems of the
class struggle. They examined and explained basic directions
of the country's economic and political development, the
distribution of the class forces, the ways, means and forms
of class struggle, the content and basic stages of the forthcom-
ing revolution, the question of the hegemony of the working

[1] K. Marx and F. Engels, *Selected Correspondence,* p. 253.
[2] F. Engels, *Anti-Dühring,* Moscow, 1969, pp. 113-15.
[3] V. I. Lenin, *Collected Works.* Vol. 20, p. 24.

class in the revolution, the problems of building the future socialist state, and so on. This meant that the political precepts, tasks and slogans of the Party were based on a sound theoretical foundation, and the consciousness of the active fighters from the working class was formed on the basis and in the process of assimilating the scientific and revolutionary theory of the working class.

Political Struggle as a Means of Shaping the Personality of the Revolutionary

Unlike the reformist working-class parties, the Bolshevik Party was created by Lenin as a party of revolution, as a party of a new type. Lenin and his associates proceeded from the fact that only under the leadership of the proletariat can the working people achieve victory in the socialist revolution and build socialism. Nothing can be achieved without political struggle, this being the main factor in the victory of the working class. It is also the chief means of moulding the personality of the revolutionary fighter. The revolutionary, socialist consciousness of the workers, the proletarian vanguard, can take shape only in persistent class, political struggle. "Only struggle educates the exploited class," Lenin said. "Only struggle discloses to it the magnitude of its own power, widens its horizon, enhances its abilities, clarifies its mind, forges its will."[1] The Party Programme, passed by the 2nd Party Congress, stipulated the ways and means of attaining the final goal of the revolutionary proletariat. It inspired the proletarians of Russia with faith in victory and became an inexhaustible well of optimism and fighting spirit.

When all other circumstances are equal, the working class and its ideologists are best able to absorb and master socialist teaching in conditions of highly developed heavy industry, whereas backward economic relations breed supporters of the working-class movement who comprehend only some aspects of Marxism, only parts of its world view or isolated slogans and demands, and are incapable of breaking with the traditions of the bourgeois outlook in general and the bourgeois-democratic outlook in particular. This generates different

[1] V. I. Lenin, *Collected Works*, Vol. 23, p. 241.

attitudes to the aims of revolutionary struggle and, consequently, different personal qualities, different types of personality taking part in the movement.

The amateurish activities of the Economists, the local
miscellaneous experience gained within the narrow confines
of the economic struggle, breeds an opportunist type of
politician, brilliantly described by Lenin. "A person who is
flabby and shaky on questions of theory, who has a narrow
outlook, who pleads the spontaneity of the masses as an
excuse for his own sluggishness, who resembles a trade union
secretary more than a spokesman of the people, who is
unable to conceive of a broad and bold plan that would
command the respect even of opponents, and who is inexperi-
enced and clumsy in his own professional art—the art of
combating the political police—such a man is not a revolutionary, but a wretched amateur!"[1]

The dispute over Article I of the Party Rules at the 2nd
Party Congress played an important part in shaping the
personality of the revolutionary. The question at issue was
what kind of person the professional revolutionary, the
champion of the working-class cause, should be. Lenin proposed writing into the Party Rules: "Anyone may be considered a member of the Party who acknowledges its Programme and supports the Party both materially and by personal
participation in one of the Party organisations."[2] In contrast,
Martov proposed that anyone could be considered a Party
member who accepted its programme, supported the Party
materially and rendered it regular personal assistance under
the leadership of one of its organisations.

The hotly debated alternative was whether a Party member should be a disciplined, active fighter for the cause of the
working class or whether he could allow himself a "free"
programme of life.

Criticising Martov's formulation, Lenin stressed the
practical needs of the political struggle: "This formulation
necessarily tends to make Party members of *all and sund-*

---

[1] V. I. Lenin, *Collected Works*, Vol. 5, p. 466.
[2] *The CPSU in the Resolutions and Decisions of Congresses,
Conferences and Plenums of the Central Committee*, Vol. I,
Moscow, 1970, p. 66 (in Russian).

ry.... But that is precisely what we do not like! And that is precisely why we are so adamant in our opposition to Martov's formulation. It would be better if ten who do work should not call themselves Party members (real workers don't hunt for titles!) than that one who only talks should have the right and opportunity to be a Party member."[1]

Supporting Lenin at the Congress, Plekhanov contrasted proletarian collectivism with bourgeois individualism. He emphasised that "workers wishing to join the Party will not be afraid of entering an organisation. They are not afraid of discipline. Many intellectuals saturated in bourgeois individualism will be afraid to enter it. But this is all to the good. These bourgeois individuals are usually also representatives of all kinds of opportunism. We must keep them at a distance. Lenin's draft may serve as a barrier to their invasion of the Party, and for this reason alone all opponents of opportunism should vote in favour of it."[2]

Yet another very important, educative aspect of Lenin's proposal should also be noted. Lenin believed it to be an important duty of the Social-Democrat to put every worker with any ability into conditions in which he could fully develop and apply his abilities.

Thus, from the outset the Bolshevik Party imposed on its members political and moral demands that had deep foundations in life. These moral principles were worked out by the working class in the struggle for its fundamental interests, for its communist ideals. The moral norms of the revolutionary proletariat became in their highest development the norms of Party life. They played a decisive role in training steadfast, disciplined and convinced fighters for the revolution. The whole experience of the Party in the course of three revolutions and the period of socialist construction bears this out.

The principles evolved by our Party are still relevant today and have acquired international significance.

Lenin's position defined a principled approach to the solution of certain important problems of the relationship

---

[1] V. I. Lenin, *Collected Works*, Vol. 6, p. 503.
[2] *Second Congress of the RSDLP,* Minutes, Moscow, 1959, p. 272 (in Russian).

between the individual and a society organised on socialist lines.

Naturally they have nothing in common with Nechayev-ism. It is hard to find a book by any of the ideologists of imperialism about Bolshevism which does not come up in some form or another with the idea that Lenin and the Bolsheviks borrowed a great deal from Nechayev's doctrine. What has prompted the anti-communists to revive the forgotten name of Nechayev? Their motives are the same as those that led the Russian and international reactionaries to make a sensation out of the Nechayev trial in St. Petersburg in 1871. Nechayev himself, although he pretended to be an emissary of the International Working Men's Association (the International), never was anything of the kind, as Karl Marx pointed out. A combination of *agent provocateur* and adventurer, Nechayev preached as methods of "revolutionary work" deception, slander, intimidation, the stab in the back and systematic assassinations. He condemned science and idealised ignorance and violence. In his practical activity, using the name of the International as a cover, Nechayev committed various crimes ranging from fraud to murder.

The bourgeois press even in those days sought to place the blame for Nechayev's immoral ideas and crimes on the International, and on revolutionaries in general. This is why Nechayevism is today still so dear to the hearts of the anti-communists. They are not in the least concerned with the fact that Marx and Engels waged an irreconcilable struggle against the ideas and practice of Nechayev's spiritual mentor and leader, the apostle of Russian anarchism, Mikhail Bakunin, that they exposed before the whole world the essentially treacherous role of Nechayevism. Nor are they bothered by the fact that Lenin himself waged a determined, consistent struggle against the principles of Blanquism and anarchism. The Marxists-Leninists always stressed the absolute incompatibility between the proletarian ideology, the theory of scientific communism, and the ignorant notions of historical development, class struggle and the future society. The Bolshevik Party was guided in its work by the truth that the socialist consciousness of the proletariat's vanguard, the features of the proletarian revolutionary's personality should be moulded and tempered in wide-ranging revolutionary struggle.

Analysing the development of working-class consciousness Lenin takes into consideration above all (a) the adherence of any participant in the struggle to a particular inner class group, (b) the scope and intensity of the struggle. In his "Lecture on the 1905 Revolution", which he delivered in Switzerland in 1917 to an audience of young people, he said: "Let us examine more closely the relation, in the 1905 strike struggles, between the metalworkers and the textile workers. The metalworkers are the best paid, the most class-conscious and best educated proletarians. The textile workers, who in 1905 were two and a half times more numerous than the metalworkers, are the most backward and the worst-paid body of workers in Russia, and in very many cases have not yet definitely severed connections with their peasant kinsmen in the village. . . .

"Throughout the whole of 1905, the metalworkers' strikes show a preponderance of political over economic strikes, though this preponderance was far greater toward the end of the year than at the beginning. Among the textile workers, on the other hand, we observe an overwhelming preponderance of economic strikes at the beginning of 1905, and it is only at the end of the year that we get a preponderance of political strikes."[1]

As for the scope of the revolutionary struggle and its influence on the further development of the consciousness of the various strata, Lenin observed: "Only the waves of mass strikes that swept over the whole country, strikes connected with the severe lessons of the imperialist Russo-Japanese War, roused the broad masses of the peasantry from their lethargy. The word 'striker' acquired an entirely new meaning among the peasants: it signified a rebel, a revolutionary. . . ."[2]

Here we have a clear example of how Lenin takes his analysis of working-class development to the point of concrete socio-psychological characterisations of types of personality, which personify the disposition of class forces.

---

[1] V. I. Lenin, *Collected Works*, Vol. 23, pp. 241-42.
[2] Ibid., p. 243.

The proletarian revolutionary personality began to take shape particularly rapidly in Russia in the period of the 1905 revolution and the years that followed.

During the revolution of 1905, in the process of sharp political struggle for democracy and freedom, for the setting up of the Soviets, which achieved its culmination in an armed uprising, the Russian proletariat showed its implacability towards the autocracy, its initiative, discipline, understanding of the need for it to have its own political organisation operating on a broad scale.

The revolution signified a steep decline in the prestige of the tsar and the tsarist autocracy, of the whole establishment. The active support for tsarism on the part of the liberal bourgeoisie not only exposed its counter-revolutionary essence, but at the same time compromised it in the eyes of considerable sections of advanced, politically conscious workers. Noting this circumstance, Lenin wrote that the proletariat had "won the *emancipation* of the working masses *from the influence* of treacherous and contemptibly impotent *liberalism*. It won *for itself the hegemony* in the struggle for freedom and democracy as a precondition of the struggle for socialism."[1]

After the 1905 revolution reaction made extremely active efforts to corrupt the working class; the church became militant. Very serious confusion arose in the ranks of the radical intelligentsia. This was to be seen particularly in "god-seeking" and "god-building", and in repudiation of the revolutionary ideals. Vorovsky described the situation as follows: "The necessary altruism of previous generations was countered by 'natural' egoism; their socialism, by individualism, their concept of duty, by freedom of individual; their idea of social good, by personal happiness."[2] In preaching individualism the former "legal Marxist" Nikolai Berdyaev sank to the very depths of obscurantism and counter-revolution.[3]

---

[1] V. I. Lenin, *Collected Works*, Vol. 16, p. 387.

[2] V. V. Vorovsky, *Works*, Vol. II, Moscow, 1931, pp. 96-97 (in Russian).

[3] N. Berdyaev preached the idea that social changes cannot change the personality because even "the most radical social upheavals do not touch the roots of human existence, do not destroy evil...." (N. Ber-

Reaction, however, was unable to check the course of history, to prevent a new upsurge of revolutionary struggle. In the moral sense the postrevolutionary period was fruitful in giving the working class a deeper understanding of its own class interests, its role of hegemony in the revolution. In this situation Lenin frequently returned to the question of how the personality of the worker-revolutionary is formed. He wrote that it is not enough for a revolutionary merely to belong to the revolutionary class. Each representative of this class must be aware of his position, goals and interests.

Social-Democracy worked steadily and persistently to bring representatives of the so-called ignorant masses of the workers and peasants into the revolution and the revolutionary struggle. For instance, in 1906, N. Vasilyev published his booklet *The Ten Commandments of the Social-Democrat,* which gives an interesting description of how the advanced workers, the Social-Democrats pictured the tasks of the proletarian. The introduction states that it is intended for workers who are as yet outside the organisation. Having sketched the glaring injustices of the existing regime, the booklet formulates ten principles of morality by which the proletarian should be guided in his conduct.

I. Remember that you are a poor man (proletarian) and that all poor men are your brothers.

II. Do not sell your soul to the capitalists, who buy your body and the bodies of your brothers.

III. Do not forget that the poor are as an ocean, while the rich are only few; believe that victory is not difficult if a ray of light enters the ignorant heads of your brothers and sisters.

dyaev, *The Philosophy of Freedom,* Moscow, 1911, p. 194, in Russian.) The Bolsheviks, Berdyaev maintained, fail to understand that the ideal values of the personality cannot be explained by the influence of the "external" social environment, because man's essence is not social in origin, and just because people are liberated from poverty and starvation, oppression and humiliation they will not become happier, calmer and more contented. "People," he wrote, "anticipating" the existentialists of today, "will be a thousand times more unhappy when their consciousness is not diverted by external oppression and disorder from the most appalling questions of existence. Then their life will become unbearably tragic...." (N. Berdyaev, *Sub specie aeternitatis. Philosophical, Social and Literary Essays (1900-06),* St. Petersburg, 1907, p. 369 (in Russian).

IV. Educate yourself and educate your sisters and brothers.

V. Lay down your life for them, if necessary.

VI. Unite your sisters and brothers in unions: the peasants according to villages, volosts, uyezds and gubernias; the workers according to factories, trades and cities... all poor people in one mighty union.

VII. Serve not dissent, but serve conciliation between the unions. Teach by example. Forget your own *Self* and remember the sacred cause.

VIII. Aim at one goal—socialism, that is, a free society, where everyone works and the fruits of your labour are not eaten by the drones.

IX. Remember that the first steps toward this goal are: organisation, education and self-education, daily united struggle for existence and for the conquest of state power.

X. Remember well that the cause of the people's emancipation can be only the cause of the people united in a single great army and striving consciously for this goal.

This booklet clearly indicates the frame of mind of the Party propagandists who were working among the masses and who strove to counter the corrupt influence of reaction with the clear class-consciousness of the revolutionary proletarian. Despite all the efforts of the servants of the autocracy, the growth of the people's awareness could not be reversed. Lenin summed up the results of 1905 in a brief, expressive phrase: "After December they were no longer the same people. They had been reborn."[1]

The outbreak of the imperialist war and the consequent redoubling of the people's troubles and sufferings gave a powerful boost to the revolutionary processes and helped to make the broad masses of the proletariat and the peasantry aware of the exploitative, anti-popular essence of the rule of the tsar and the landowners. It made them understand that it had to be overthrown and replaced by a just social system. Analysing the situation that developed during the war years, Lenin gives a socio-psychological characterisation of the condition of the masses. "The war cannot but evoke among the masses the most turbulent sentiments, which upset the

---

[1] V. I. Lenin, *Collected Works,* Vol. 28, p. 373.

usual sluggish state of mass mentality. . . . What are the main currents of these turbulent sentiments? They are: (1) Horror and despair. Hence, a growth of religious feeling. Again the churches are crowded, the reactionaries joyfully declare. . . . (2) Hatred of the 'enemy', a sentiment that is carefully fostered by the bourgeoisie (not so much by the priests), and is of economic and political value *only to the bourgeoisie*. (3) Hatred of one's *own* government and one's *own* bourgeoisie—the sentiment of all class-conscious workers. . . ."[1] Heterogeneous, contradictory, violently intense, these moods and aspirations indicated the approach of revolution, an imminent explosion.

The socialist consciousness of the advanced section of the working class comprises not only hatred of the exploiting classes but also a conscious desire for a just social system. In the theory of scientific communism the proletariat's aspirations acquire a precise theoretical elaboration and are formulated in a system of ideas, arguments and programme precepts. The process of prerevolutionary political development brought into being a militant proletarian vanguard, armed with a clear understanding of the socialist aims of the revolution. The broad masses of the people acquired a firm belief in the injustice of the bourgeois-landowner system and the inability of the autocracy to satisfy the interests of the country and people. Socialist aspirations and democratic demands were closely interwoven.

Revolutionary traditions, general political tension throughout the country, the working class's growing awareness of its own interests, its joining first in the economic and then the political struggle, the spread of socialist ideas and intensive propaganda of Marxism, the appearance of a political party of the working class, steering a definite course towards the revolutionary overthrow of the landowner-bourgeois system, the stormy events of the 1905-07 revolution (the dress rehearsal for 1917), the imperialist war and the upsurge of popular discontent—such was the general context in which the revolutionary consciousness of the masses matured and which moulded and developed the personality of the Bolshevik, the socialist type of revolutionary.

---

[1] Ibid., Vol. 21, pp. 279-80.

Features of the Bolshevik Type of Revolutionary

Generations of splendid revolutionaries were forged and grew up during the years of arduous struggle against the autocracy and capitalism, in conditions of undercover and open political struggle, in prison and exile. The Communist Party "absorbed everything honest, thinking, courageous and self-sacrificing that had been accumulated by generations of revolutionaries".[1] These were the people who led the social-ist revolution to victory in 1917, who rallied the masses at all stages of socialist construction, whose courage and self-lessness were an example to all.

The Bolshevik as a type of personality does not accept the existing capitalist system and seeks to overthrow it by revolutionary means.

The characteristic element in the Bolsheviks' ideological make-up is the organic combination of a profound dedication to the interests of the working class and the working people, with a scientific, realistic conception of the aims and ways of remaking society on communist principles, an understanding of the international as well as the national tasks of the work-ing class. All the Party Programmes, all the ideological and political precepts passed at its congresses and conferen-ces, bear this out. The Bolsheviks became the personification of the strictest devotion to the ideas of communism, no matter what changes occurred in the means and forms of struggle.[2] "It would not be worth living," Felix Dzerzhinsky wrote from a tsarist prison, "if mankind was not illuminated by the star of socialism, the star of the future."

The Bolshevik is the revolutionary of the masses. He is a revolutionary not only because he represents the people's interests but because he cannot conceive of revolutionary struggle without the participation of the working masses. Lenin devoted his whole life to the development of the mass revolutionary movement, its strategy and tactics, to elabo-ration of its organisational principles and combining the various forms of this movement. He trained the Party cadres

---

[1] *Fiftieth Anniversary of the Great October Socialist Revolution*, Moscow, p. 6.

[2] V. I. Lenin, *Collected Works*, Vol. 31, p. 95.

in this spirit. No matter what work the Bolshevik did (as organiser, propagandist, agitator, etc.) he always remembered that success ultimately depends on the level of consciousness, on the actions of the masses. This special feature of the Bolshevik springs from and is fostered by his ties with the masses.

The Bolshevik orientation on the mass movement was brilliantly vindicated by the victory of the revolution as an armed uprising of workers and peasants, soldiers and sailors. The source of the victories of the October Revolution, as Lenin said, lay in organisation of millions of working people. "And it is this feature of the proletarian revolution which, in the course of the struggle, brought to the fore those leaders who best expressed that specific feature of our revolution that was never seen in revolutions before, namely, the organisation of the masses."[1]

Another essential feature of the Bolshevik is his irreconcilability towards the enemy, which stems from the revolutionary character of the Party. At the critical moments in history the Bolsheviks displayed maximum flexibility in their tactics and used extremely varied forms of struggle, but they also won a reputation for irreconcilability. There is no contradiction in this because both features were conditioned by the high sense of the responsibility which they had undertaken for the fate of their class and the revolution. "...Supreme clarity of the aims and objectives of struggle," Frantz Mehring wrote, "fosters the moral energy, the high degree of persistence, honesty, courage, readiness for self-sacrifice by which the party struggle of the workers is so profoundly distinguished from the party struggle of other classes."[2]

Thus, the Bolsheviks as revolutionaries are people who have absorbed the wisdom of scientific knowledge, who express the interests of the working class, of all the working people, who are close to the broadest masses and inspired by a spirit of irreconcilability in the cause of emancipation of the working people.

These features show the aspirations of the revolutionary proletariat in high relief against the background of Menshe-

---

[1] V. I. Lenin, *Collected Works*, Vol. 29, p. 90.
[2] F. Mehring, "Ethik und Klassenkampf", *Die Neue Zeit*, No. 20, XI. Jahrgang, I. Band, 1892-93, Stuttgart, S. 701.

vik opportunism. Lenin's works give a full description of the opportunist type of personality. Its characteristic features, Lenin pointed out, are a tendency to lag behind and compromise in forming a world view, to seek autonomy, a lordly anarchism in matters of organisation, indefiniteness, vagueness, elusiveness in conduct. These features, in their turn, reflected the positions of the section of society that the Mensheviks represented, namely, that part of the working class that cherished bourgeois illusions.

The qualities of the proletarian revolutionary mentioned earlier characterise fully enough the social type of personality because they express quite definitely its connection with its social group, its attitude to the interests and aims of that group and to the methods of realising these interests and aims. These revolutionary characteristics form the source of the Bolsheviks' tremendous prestige and influence among the masses.

" ...The foremost sections of the proletariat have by their example shown the mass of the working people... a *model* of such devotion to the interests of the working people, such vigour in the struggle against the enemies of the working people, such firmness in difficult moments, such self-sacrificing resistance to the bandits of world imperialism, that the strength of the workers' and peasants' *sympathy* for their vanguard has proved *by itself* capable of *performing miracles.*"[1]

Maxim Gorky, who was deeply interested in the character of the Leninists, wrote of them: "...The *Russian* revolutionary—with all his shortcomings—is in spiritual beauty, in love for the world a phenomenon of which I know no equal."[2]

The statistics of the 6th Party Congress, which assembled on the eve of the October Revolution of 1917, give a highly representative picture of the character of the Bolsheviks. Delegates of 12 nationalities attended the Congress. Out of 171 interviewed delegates, 79 were under 29 years of age, 79 between 30 and 39, and the average age was 29. Educationally, the figures were: 55 (including students) with a higher education, 39 secondary, and 60 primary, etc. Oc-

---

[1] V. I. Lenin, *Collected Works,* Vol. 30, p. 72.
[2] Maxim Gorky, *Collected Works,* Vol. 29, p. 74 (in Russian).

cupations: 70 workers, 22 in white-collar occupations, 20 writers, 12 teachers, 7 medical workers, 6 lawyers, 2 soldiers, and 23 without any definite occupation. Work for the Party: 114 agitators, 103 organisers, 85 propagandists, 57 writers, 37 secretaries, 30 chairmen and committee members, 18 lecturers, 3 treasurers, 1 publishing house manager. Taken together, the delegates had worked 1,721 years in the Social-Democratic movement, and 1,400 years in Bolshevik organisations. Participants in the Congress had spent 245 years in prison (110 people), 127 years and 5 months in exile (55 people), 73 years in restricted residence (24 people), 41 years in penal servitude (10 people). 150 Congress delegates had been arrested 549 times. When the February revolution of 1917 occurred, only 79 of the delegates were at liberty. The rest were in prison, in exile, doing penal servitude, and so on.[1]

This cross-section of the Congress, which to a certain extent reflects the composition of the Party, or at least its directing force, indicates that the Bolshevik hard-core activists were international, had a fairly high level of education, represented the most active, proletarian section of the population, had taken part in the struggle since the first years of the Social-Democratic movement and had often been persecuted by the tsarist autocracy.

Lenin was the ideal embodiment of the personality of the proletarian revolutionary. On the eve of the centenary of Lenin's birth the Central Committee of the CPSU stated:

"Lenin was a political leader of a new type, a scholar, tribune and propagandist, an organiser of the masses. He was distinguished for his profound scientific approach in the analysis of events, sober assessment of the correlation and alignment of class forces, consistency and firmness in upholding Marxist principles, purposefulness in action, flexibility of tactics in the struggle, and selfless service to the interests and aims of the proletarian movement. . . .

"Lenin's whole life was an exploit. It was a life spent in creative thought and unflagging revolutionary action, in ideological and political battle. Lenin combined the most distinc-

---

[1] *6th Congress of the RSDLP (Bolsheviks)*, Minutes, Moscow, 1958, pp. 294-300 (in Russian).

tive qualities of the proletarian revolutionary: a powerful intellect, an indomitable will, passionate hatred of slavery and oppression, revolutionary fervour, consistent internationalism, boundless faith in the creative powers of the masses and immense organisational talent. His life and work were one with the struggle of the working class and the Communist Party."[1]

From the ranks of the proletariat came such splendid revolutionary leaders as I. Babushkin, K. E. Voroshilov, G. I. Petrovsky, V. P. Nogin, V. A. Shelgunov, F. A. Sergeyev (Artyom), P. I. Voyevodin and others. A galaxy of outstanding Party workers from the intelligentsia won their spurs in the struggle. These included V. V. Vorovsky, P. A. Japaridze, R. S. Zemlyachka, P. A. Krasikov, L. B. Krasin, N. K. Krupskaya, M. M. Litvinov, A. V. Lunacharsky, F. N. Petrov, I. V. Stalin, M. G. Tskhakaya and others.

Ivan Babushkin provides a concrete example of the worker-revolutionary. A fitter at the Semyannikov Works in St. Petersburg, Babushkin became a revolutionary at an early age and worked actively under Lenin's leadership. In 1905, he was executed in Siberia. Lenin regarded him as one of the advanced workers who ten years before the revolution had set about building up a working-class Social-Democratic Party. "Had it not been for the tireless, heroically persistent work of *such* militants among the proletarian masses the RSDLP could not have existed ten months let alone ten years,"[2] Lenin wrote. People like Babushkin "did not dissipate their energies on the futile terrorist acts of individuals, but... worked persistently and unswervingly among the proletarian masses, helping to develop *their* consciousness, *their* organisation and *their* revolutionary initiative. They are people who stood at the head of the armed mass struggle against the tsarist autocracy when the crisis began, when the revolution broke out and when millions and millions were stirred into action. Everything won from the tsarist autocracy was won *exclusively* by the struggle of the masses led by such people as Babushkin.

"Without such men the Russian people would remain for-

---

[1] *On the Centenary of the Birth of V. I. Lenin,* Moscow, pp. 4-5.
[2] V. I. Lenin, *Collected Works,* Vol. 16, p. 363.

ever a people of slaves and serfs. With such men the Russian people will win complete emancipation from all exploitation."[1]

Yakov Sverdlov was another striking representative of the Bolsheviks. According to Lenin, he most fully and organically expressed the main and essential features of the proletarian revolution. And Sverdlov's personality certainly did embody ideological conviction, orientation on the movement of the masses, and implacability towards the enemy. In his "Speech in Memory of Y. M. Sverdlov at the Extraordinary Session of the All-Russia Central Executive Committee, March 18, 1919", Lenin pointed to the fact that "the history of the Russian revolutionary movement over a period of many decades contains a list of martyrs who were devoted to the revolutionary cause, but who had no opportunity to put their revolutionary ideals into practice. In this respect, the proletarian revolution, for the first time, provided these formerly isolated heroes of the revolutionary struggle with real ground, a real basis, a real environment, a real audience and a real proletarian army in which they could display their talents. . . .

". . .The long period of illegal activity most of all characterises the man who was constantly in the fight, who never lost contact with the masses, who never left Russia, who always worked in conjunction with the best of the workers, and who, in spite of the isolation from general life to which persecution condemned the revolutionary, succeeded in becoming not only a beloved leader of the workers, not only a leader who was most familiar with practical work, but also an organiser of the advanced proletarians."[2]

There were not so many people in the Party with talent and ability equal to Sverdlov's; leaders are naturally few in number. But there was a host of people of Sverdlov's type, i.e., similar to him, with the same orientation, the same views. The Communists absorbed the best features of Lenin, Sverdlov, Dzerzhinsky, Kalinin, Orjonikidze, Kirov, Frunze, Kuibyshev and other outstanding Bolsheviks. The Communists are the part of the people comprising the most active and

---

[1] Ibid., p. 364.
[2] Ibid., Vol. 29, pp. 90-91.

thinking force of our society. They form the model from which are fashioned new generations of Communists, new generations of builders of communism.

3. BASIC FACTORS AND STAGES IN THE FORMATION OF THE SOCIALIST PERSONALITY SINCE THE OCTOBER REVOLUTION

Immediately after the October Revolution, along with many urgent tasks of building the new state and resisting the enemy, the Communist Party was faced with the problem of spreading socialist ideology among the broad masses, of educating the new man, of drawing the working people into vigorous social activity.

Political Division and Development of the Socialist Activity of the Masses

The law discovered by Marx, which states that "with the thoroughness of the historical action the size of the mass whose action it is will... increase",[1] affects the development of socialist consciousness and, consequently, the formation of the new socialist personality. Lenin concretised, developed and added to this proposition, which is one of the most important in Marxism. He wrote: "The greater the scope and extent of historical events, the greater is the number of people participating in them, and, contrariwise, the more profound the change we wish to bring about, the more must we rouse an interest and an intelligent attitude towards it, and convince more millions and tens of millions of people that it is necessary."[2]

The October Revolution of 1917 and the changes that followed it, altered the whole life of the country. The national wealth, political power and the ideological media were now in the hands of the workers and peasants. The might of the exploiting classes had been decisively reduced, although they were still strong. This led to a sharp division within the broad masses between those who supported the new power and those who opposed it. Millions of workers and peasants

---

[1] K. Marx and F. Engels, *The Holy Family*, p. 110.
[2] V. I. Lenin, *Collected Works*, Vol. 31, p. 498.

supported the new power and acted to uphold the ideas of socialism. The interests of the workers and peasants were affected too deeply by such vital questions as the question of peace, of land, of rights and freedoms, for them to stand aside from the struggle.

Lenin wrote: "...A majority of the workers (or, at least, a majority of the class-conscious, thinking and politically active workers) should fully realise that revolution is necessary, and that they should be prepared to die for it."[1]

The political division ran right through the country during the Civil War and brought out people's attitude to Soviet power, and hence their attitude to the ideological positions of the Communists and their opponents. After the Soviets had proved victorious in the Civil War the defeated enemy could muster no ideological support among the majority of the population.

As for the ruling classes, they had been politically and ideologically defeated during the intense class struggle evoked by the terrorism of the counter-revolution and the huge scale of the Civil War. The influence of their ideology on the development of social consciousness subsequently shrank to a minimum. Needless to say, bourgeois psychology and ideology continued to exist and had its carriers among the peasantry, the urban petty bourgeoisie and sections of the intelligentsia.

The ideological and subsequent political breakaway from the petty-bourgeois political parties was dominated by the questions as to whether the proletariat should take power into its own hands and whether it was possible to build socialism in Russia. The Mensheviks believed that even if the workers did take over the government of the country they would not be able to carry out a socialist programme because of Russia's economic and cultural backwardness and would not be able to retain state power.

With splendid insight Lenin foresaw long before October that the question of power would be the key question of the socialist revolution. History decided the argument in favour of the Bolsheviks. Relying on working-class rule, the working people of our country have built a socialist society and

---

[1] Ibid., p. 85.

defended the achievements of socialism from its enemies. Experience has shown that the stability and effectiveness of the people's power is the first essential condition for consolidating and developing socialist social relations and for their growing into communist relations.

In the course of the Civil War the petty-bourgeois parties were driven by the logic of the class struggle into the camp of the whiteguard counter-revolution. In this situation only the Bolshevik Party, revolutionaries of the Bolshevik type expressed the interests of the revolutionary proletariat and all working people. They were able to understand the working people's real needs, the changes in their psychology at various turning points in history, and to take this into consideration in their political tactics.

The heroism, the inspiration of establishing the new, the traditions that acquired full scope for the first time in the period of the Civil War exerted and still exert a tremendous influence on the formation of the new personality of the working man. New, socialist forms of administration, forms of relations between people and forms of everyday life were evolved during the Civil War. Although they still retained much that had been left over from the old society, this was a period of mass creativity both in civil and military life and in the sphere of social and state administration.

A rapid process of character forming was afoot, a process that was giving the young state the new type of personnel it needed—the commanders, commissars, managers, Soviet administrators, cultural workers, people from the working class and the peasantry and those of the intellectuals who were willing to co-operate with Soviet government. Soviet policy and the communist ideology became the main orientation for the new personality that was beginning to emerge. This meant a great deal, but at the same time it was only the beginning of the enormous task of education and re-education of the broad masses of the working people.

Basic Factors of the Development
of the Socialist Personality

The young Soviet state and the Bolshevik Party was confronted with the tremendously complex task of raising to active, socialist life the largely peasant population of a vast country, three-quarters of whom were illiterate, a country devastated by two wars that had lasted a total of seven years.

When they undertook the revolution Russia's Communists were theoretically prepared for socialist changes. They had creatively assimilated and developed the teaching of Marx and Engels. The service performed by Lenin and the Party is that the most general theoretical propositions, the highest ideals were elaborated as programme precepts, political slogans and specific practical tasks. All the Party's policy statements are permeated with the idea of creating the requisite material and spiritual conditions for the development of the working man's personality, for establishing a correct relationship between society and the individual.

The RSDLP Programme, passed at the 2nd Party Congress, points out, for instance, that the substitution of social ownership for private ownership of the means of production and exchange and the planning of social production were to be carried out "to ensure the well-being and all-round development of all members of society", and that the "proletariat's social revolution will destroy the division of society into classes and thus emancipate all oppressed humanity, since it will put an end to all forms of exploitation of one part of society by another".

The Second Party Programme, passed in 1919, contains an even more profound and detailed elaboration of the problems of the interrelationship between society and the individual. It states that the socialist type of democracy, as the highest type of democracy, demands for its correct functioning a constant raising of the culture, organisation and initiative of the masses. "...Proletarian democracy," the Programme stresses, "replaces the formal proclamation of rights and freedoms by making them actually available above all and most of all to the classes of the population that were oppressed by capitalism, i.e., to the proletariat and the peasantry....

"The task of the RCP is to induce increasingly broader masses of the working population to make use of their democratic rights and freedoms, and to widen the material possibilities for this."

The development of the personality is what the Party seeks to achieve by making cultural progress one of its main tasks. Lenin said that the old educational system worked to produce humble and efficient servants of the bourgeoisie, slaves of capital, and never bothered to make the schools an instrument for the moulding of the human *personality*. "And now it is clear to all that this (educaiton of the personality— G. S.) can be done only by socialist schools, which have inseparable bonds with all the working and exploited people and wholeheartedly support Soviet policy."[1] Lenin regarded every factory and every village from which the exploiters, the capitalists and landlords, had been expelled as "a field in which the working man can reveal his talents, unbend his back a little, rise to his full height and feel that he is a human being."[2]

The question, however, was what kind of personality was to be produced, with what qualities, aspirations and ideals. Lenin always had in view a definite ideal in which he saw the demand of the proletariat. The general problem on whose solution the education of the specific qualities of the new personality depends Lenin formulated in the briefest possible terms: "Learn communism". This task signifies above all struggle for the consolidation and completion of communism, and is the basis of communist training, education and teaching.[3]

All Lenin's works and speeches are infused with the idea of the formation of certain general, essential features of personality that would belong specifically to the builders of socialist society:

devotion to the ideas of communism and deep understanding of them;

mastering of knowledge and professional skill;

socio-political activity and discipline.

The basic task of upbringing, education and training of the young, Lenin proposed, should be the fostering of *communist morality*.

The ideological opponents of communism constantly re-

---

[1] V. I. Lenin, *Collected Works*, Vol. 28, p. 408.
[2] Ibid., Vol. 26, p. 407.
[3] Ibid., Vol. 31, p. 295.

peat the legend they have created that Lenin ignores morality. But they conceal or distort the fact that it was Lenin who went to the trouble of specifying the basic content of communist morality, of defining what communist morality actually is.

The profoundly humane significance of communist morality lies in the fact that it is inferred from the interests of the class struggle of the proletariat—the most revolutionary, the most advanced class of modern society.[1] "When people tell us about morality, we say: to a Communist all morality lies in this united discipline and conscious mass struggle against the exploiters. We do not believe in an eternal morality, and

---

[1] An interesting document recording an attempt to create something in the nature of a communist moral code has come down to us in the present day. The draft on Party Ethics, proposed by the Presidium of the Central Control Commission of the RCP(B) to a plenary meeting in 1924, states that in the current circumstances the part played by Communists in the moral education of the masses should be enhanced. The difficulties of the country's internal life and the international situation, the draft states, compel us "to work out norms of comradeship among its (Party) members, relationships between ourselves, norms of conduct towards the non-Party worker and peasant masses that will attract to communism the maximum number of new forces from the worker and peasant masses, ensure maximum confidence in us as the progressive revolutionary vanguard of the working class, and facilitate the transition to the new system."

Below we cite some of the points in this document:

"(1) He is not a Communist for whom the Party is not an *aim* but a *means*, who enters the Party in order to use his Party membership to obtain all kinds of privileges and advantages.

(2) He is not a Communist who does something against which the Party is fighting.

(3) He is not a Communist for whom the Party does not come first, but who gives first place to something else—his own household, family, and so on.

(4) *Therefore, the Communist must think not only of his work but also of how to give others the opportunity of carrying on this work as well; hence the duty to show concern for one's comrades at work.*

(5) The same attitude must be extended to the field of family relations. In present circumstances the communist family should be a group which, relying on natural feelings of attachment, seeks to create favourable conditions for the communist work of all members of the family, making it into a working comradely commune."

This document testifies to the character of the demands presented to Communists. It sets out the essentials of a number of norms that later became part of the moral code of the builder of communism.

we expose the falseness of all the fables about morality. Morality serves the purpose of helping human society rise to a higher level and rid itself of the exploitation of labour."[1] Communism, Lenin emphasised, begins when the rank-and-file workers show concern for the general good.[2] "We shall work to inculcate in people's minds, turn into a habit, and bring into the day-by-day life of the masses, the rule: 'All for each and each for all'. . . ."[3]

In this treatment of the question there is no counterposing of the moral principles of communism to the universal human norms of morality. On the contrary, Lenin drove home the significance of the latter for the new society. In April 1918, when formulating the general slogan of the moment in his work *The Immediate Tasks of the Soviet Government,* he pointed out the necessity in the critical situation resulting from the war and general dislocation for prolonged, persistent effort on the part of "the best and most class-conscious workers and peasants in order to bring about a complete change in the mood of the people and to bring them on to the proper path of steady and disciplined labour."[4] He described as absolutely elementary such demands as "keep regular and honest accounts of money, manage economically, do not be lazy, do not steal, observe the strictest labour discipline", and said that the practical implementation of these slogans by the mass of the working people was "the *sole* condition for the salvation of a country. . . ."[5]

The appeal to observe elementary norms was dictated by the special demands of the moment. This will always remain one of the tasks of education, but Lenin regarded learning communism as the young people's main and most worthy task.

As a great realist, Lenin was profoundly opposed to the various high-flown notions of building socialism out of some new "material". He mercilessly ridiculed such intentions. "We want to build socialism with the aid of those men and

---

[1] V. I. Lenin, *Collected Works,* Vol. 31, p. 294.

[2] Ibid., Vol. 29, p. 427.

[3] Ibid., Vol. 31, p. 124.

[4] Ibid., Vol. 27, p. 244.

[5] Ibid., pp. 243-44.

women who grew up under capitalism, were depraved and corrupted by capitalism, but steeled for the struggle by cap- italism."[1] And he shows the structure of social types pre- sent in Russia at that time. "There are proletarians who have been so hardened that they can stand a thousand times more hardship than any army. There are tens of millions of op- pressed peasants, ignorant and scattered, but capable of unit- ing around the proletariat in the struggle, if the proletariat adopts skilful tactics. And there are scientific and technical experts all thoroughly imbued with the bourgeois world out- look, there are military experts who were trained under bour- geois conditions—if they were only bourgeois it would not be so bad, but there were also conditions of landed proprietor- ship, serfdom and the big stick. . . . We must build socialism out of this culture, we have no other material. We want to start building socialism at once out of the material that cap- italism left us yesterday to be used today, at this very moment, and not with people reared in hothouses, assuming that we were to take this fairy-tale seriously."[2]

But the task was not confined to the peasantry and the old intelligentsia. It was necessary to "remake" and "re-educate" the proletarians themselves, who would not shed their petty- bourgeois illusions at once but only in the course of pro- longed and difficult mass struggle against petty-bourgeois influence.

It was essential to combat the opposition of the capital- ists, not only the political and military, but also the ideolog- ical opposition, which is the deepest and most powerful. "The force of habit in millions and tens of millions is a most formidable force. . . . It is a thousand times easier to van- quish the centralised big bourgeoisie than to 'vanquish' the millions upon millions of petty proprietors; however, through their ordinary, everyday, imperceptible, elusive and demoral- ising activities, they produce the *very* results which the bour- geoisie need and which tend to *restore* the bourgeoisie."[3]

Lenin was deeply convinced that changing the social re- lations would correspondingly change man. In Lenin's solu-

---

[1] V. I. Lenin, *Collected Works*, Vol. 29, p. 69.
[2] Ibid., pp. 69-70.
[3] Ibid., Vol. 31, pp. 44-45. See also pp. 363-73.

tion of the tasks of educating the new man we find the same consistent materialist monism that was organically inherent in Lenin himself: in order to educate a new man one must build new forms of social intercourse between people, new forms and methods of inducing people to work, of bringing the millions into this work, that is to say, one must create a new social environment.

In this gigantic task Lenin placed exclusive importance on the role of the working class. Without the dictatorship of the proletariat, without the party of the proletariat enjoying the trust of all that is honest in this class, and capable of sensing the mood of the masses, it would be quite impossible to carry on such a struggle successfully.

Another task of great importance was to master the whole wealth of knowledge accumulated by mankind. "We can build communism only on the basis of the totality of knowledge, organisations and institutions, only by using the stock of human forces and means that have been left to us by the old society. Only by radically remoulding the teaching, organisation and training of the youth shall we be able to ensure that the efforts of the younger generation will result in the creation of a society that will be unlike the old society, i.e., in the creation of a communist society."[1]

These ideas have been widely introduced in practice. Only a few days after the people's seizure of power A. V. Lunacharsky, People's Commissar for Education, issued a proclamation "To the Workers, Peasants, Soldiers and Sailors, to All Citizens of Russia". It ran as follows: "Besides natural wealth the working people have inherited an enormous wealth of culture: buildings of wondrous beauty, museums full of rare and beautiful objects that can teach and elevate the soul, libraries preserving immense values of the spirit, and so on. All this does indeed now belong to the people. All this will help the poor man and his children rapidly to outgrow the previous ruling classes in education, will help to become a new man, master of the old culture, creator of a culture such as has never been known before.

---

[1] V. I. Lenin, *Collected Works*, Vol. 31, p. 284.

"Comrades! This property of the people must be carefully and vigilantly safeguarded!"[1]

Lenin paid close attention to the development of the working people's interest in knowledge and observed with satisfaction in March 1919, at the 8th Congress of the RCP(B) "a tremendous thirst for knowledge" and "tremendous progress in education"[2]. "The working people are thirsting for knowledge because they need it to win."[3] He had in mind political as well as general education.

Lenin saw knowledge as an instrument for building communism and constantly stressed the need to integrate study, work and struggle. "Without work and without struggle, book knowledge of communism obtained from communist pamphlets and works is absolutely worthless."[4] This idea of the merging of study and practice is the underlying theme in all Lenin's speeches and writings on matters of education.

The desire to single out what is essential and important for building new social relationships, for moulding the new man from life itself, from the practical experience of the workers and peasants themselves is extremely characteristic of Lenin. The launching of the movement for a communist attitude to work, which he rightly described as "a great beginning", may be numbered among his immortal services to history. Noting the tremendous importance of the workers' labour enthusiasm, Lenin simultaneously emphasised the importance of personal material incentives for the building of the new society and educating the new man. He was interested in the various forms of free distribution and called them "*the shoots* of communism".[5] But in a context of general desire to make everything "free of charge" and to set up forms of distribution claiming to be communist, Lenin was the first to declare that the new society could and should be built with the aid of personal material incentives as well as enthusiasm.

Lenin attached no less importance to the problem of com-

---

[1] *Izvestia,* CEC and the Petrograd Soviet of Workers' and Soldiers' Deputies, November 4, 1917 (in Russian).
[2] V. I. Lenin, *Collected Works,* Vol. 29, p. 183.
[3] Ibid., Vol. 28, p. 88.
[4] Ibid., Vol. 31, p. 285.
[5] Ibid., Vol. 29, p. 429.

bining personal and social interest in drawing up the plan for the co-operation of peasant farms. In co-operation, he wrote, "we have now found that degree of combination of private interest, of private commercial interest, with state supervision and control of this interest, that degree of its subordination to the common interests which was formerly the stumbling block for very many socialists.... It is still not the building of socialist society, but it is all that is necessary and sufficient for it."[1]

The general rise in the consciousness of the working people after the revolution was not confined to labour heroism. Socialism is first and foremost political activity of the masses. To this aspect of the building of the new society Lenin devoted great attention. He saw two sides of the question: the need for sharing the burden of administering society among all members of society and the inculcation of a sense of responsibility for the common weal. "We must go on extending the participation of the working people in economic administration and in building a new economy. We shall never bring the work of communist construction to its completion unless we cope with this task, unless we convert the trade unions into organs for training ten times as many people as at present for direct participation in state administration."[2]

Lenin always stressed the need for variety and initiative in work. Characteristically, one of his first articles of this period dealt with how to organise competition. "...Centralism, understood in a truly democratic sense, presupposes the possibility, created for the first time in history, of a full and unhampered development not only of specific local features, but also of local inventiveness, local initiative, of diverse ways, methods and means of progress to the common goal."[3]

Tens and hundreds of thousands of the common people became active in economic management and were able to display their splendid talents and abilities.

Finally, we must recall yet another form of social activity of which Lenin wrote as an indispensable condition of the

[1] V. I. Lenin, *Collected Works,* Vol. 33, p. 468.
[2] Ibid., Vol. 28, p. 426.
[3] Ibid., Vol. 27, p. 208.

success of the communist education of the working people. He had in mind social control over the activities of members of society. In his work *The Immediate Tasks of the Soviet Government* he wrote that "without comprehensive state accounting and control of the production and distribution of goods, the power of the working people, the freedom of the working people *cannot* be maintained, and... a return to the yoke of capitalism is *inevitable*."[1] Lenin was particularly emphatic about the various anti-social elements. "No mercy for these enemies of the people, the enemies of socialism, the enemies of the working people! War to the death against the rich and their hangers-on, the bourgeois intellectuals; war on the rogues, the idlers and the rowdies!"[2] Lenin demanded that idlers, rogues and rowdies "must be placed under the special surveillance of the entire people; they must be ruthlessly punished for the slightest violation of the laws and regulations of socialist society. Any display of weakness, hesitation or sentimentality in this respect would be an immense crime against socialism."[3]

But Lenin considered accounting and control to be not merely a measure for the transitional period, designed to restrain the anti-social elements. This measure would be a condition for the functioning of a more mature society. "Accounting and control—that is mainly what is needed for the proper functioning of communist society."[4]

Thus, we have a consistent system of factors constituting the basic elements of the new social environment, which was to mould the individual's new socialist orientation and, naturally, his new behaviour.

Lenin's ideas and instructions have been widely practised in socialist construction, in communist education and have produced their splendid fruit. The lofty ideological and moral qualities that were characteristic of the advanced proletarians are now shared by millions of working people. This is the highest achievement of socialism.

---

[1] Ibid., pp. 253-54.
[2] Ibid., Vol. 26, p. 411.
[3] Ibid.
[4] Ibid., Vol. 27, p. 304.

Stages of the Development
of the Socialist Personality

Owing to the inherited varying level of economic, political and cultural development, the changes in the condition of the mass of the people belonging to different classes, groups and strata, the formation of their socialist consciousness came about unevenly.

The various classes, groups and strata entered socialism from the capitalist mould with their own specific notions of values, their own habits and moral standards, their old way of life. The socialist consciousness and the socialist personality came about through the gradual erasure of a whole series of substantial differences between various groups of working people and through the growth of increasingly significant common features. Moreover, the various classes had their own peculiarities of development.

Both the working class and the peasantry shook off exploitation and poverty and set out on the path of socialist development, culture and technical progress. But the working class, in getting rid of its former trade narrowness waxed even stronger during the years of Soviet power and grew up to be a bearer of the socialist mode of production and socialist ideology. In other words, its most essential features gained new strength. The development of the peasantry took a different course. In the same period the peasantry lost one of its important peculiarities. It ceased to be a class of small property-owners. In embarking on the socialist path of production (collective and state farms) the peasants moved forward a long way towards mastering the socialist ideology. Their cultural level also rose, and this helped to bring them into closer contact with the working class and the intellectuals.

Whereas the psychology of the working class, its social attitudes, sympathies and antipathies had been to a certain extent the source of socialist consciousness, the psychology of the petty-bourgeois strata was of a dual nature—worker, on the one hand, and property-owner, on the other. Whereas the working class in absorbing the socialist consciousness and shaking off traces of bourgeois consciousness could rely on its own class proletarian psychology, the petty-bourgeois

strata, in assimilating the socialist consciousness, had to overcome the psychology of the small property-owner.

The peculiarities of development of the socio-class structure in the USSR gave rise to certain distinction of a political and legal nature. In the early years of Soviet power democracy was proclaimed for the overwhelming majority of
the population—for the working people, but at the same time
there was a restriction of the rights of the exploiter minority. The state proceeded from the fact that at a time of decisive struggle with the exploiters there could be no place
for them in any of the organs of power. Accordingly, the
former landowners, capitalists, kulaks, private traders, police-
men, secret police, etc., were deprived of the franchise.
The first Soviet constitutions (RSFSR Constitution of 1918
and the USSR Constitution of 1924) also established a certain advantage in electoral rights for the workers compared
with the peasants.

Later on, when the peasantry adopted collective farming,
the alliance between the workers and peasants grew even
stronger and the need for unequal franchise disappeared. Nor
was there any further need to isolate from political life the
people of the former exploiting classes, since the majority
of them had begun to co-operate honestly with the workers
and peasants and had ceased to present any serious threat
to Soviet power. The Constitution of 1936 introduced equal
electoral rights for all citizens. All this widened the social
base of the dictatorship of the working class.

During the Great Patriotic War against Hitler Germany,
and in the postwar period, all Soviet people became still more
united around the Communist Party on the basis of the Marxist-Leninist ideology. In these circumstances the need for
any franchise restrictions on political grounds has completely disappeared. The situation was reflected in the 1958 decision of the USSR Supreme Soviet, which ruled out of the
Constitution of the USSR the point on disfranchisement by
court decision.

When considering the unevenness of the development of
socialist consciousness in the USSR one must not forget the
economic backwardness of tsarist Russia and the need to make
up for the lag rapidly. In the period of the first five-year
plans the people's efforts were concentrated mainly on build-

ing up heavy industry. Naturally, although rural life also developed quickly in those years, the urban population was in the lead. Moreover, the country could not fully satisfy the needs of the population for certain important consumer goods. Such shortages were exploited by irresponsible elements for purposes of profiteering. Unsatisfactory living conditions also created difficulties in educating the working people. The war caused still more difficulties, which took many years to overcome.

The unevenness of the development of socialist consciousness is also linked with the specific character of certain forms of social consciousness. Always and under any circumstances political consciousness changes first, because it directly expresses economic interests. As socialist society developed and grew stronger, the existence of common economic interests promoted the political consolidation of Soviet society and unanimous active support of the policy of the Communist Party. These changes in political views provided a great stimulus to the assimilation of other forms of socialist consciousness: communist morality, the materialist philosophy, scientific knowledge and art. The acquisition of these forms of consciousness is a more complicated process, which involves raising the general educational level of the population, persistent educational work and considerable time.

Thus, while expressing the dialectical interaction of social being and social consciousness, the uneven development of various forms of mass consciousness is a factor that determines the level of consciousness of various types of personality. On the other hand, the people's newly acquired sociopolitical and ideological unity provided a firm foundation for rallying people with different levels of education and culture to achieve further progress in moral, legal and artistic consciousness, scientific world outlook and general cultural level.

All stages of the history of socialist construction have seen a steady development of all forms of socialist consciousness and ousting of the survivals of the past, the traces of bourgeois, self-seeking consciousness.

Let us take the period of socialist reform of the intellectual life of society during the proletarian revolution and the transition from capitalism to socialism, a period that lasted approximately to the mid-thirties, when socialism had in the main been built in the USSR. Nationalisation of the land and capitalist property, the restriction and ousting of capitalist elements destroyed the economic and political domination of the exploiting classes. In the course of a fierce class struggle the landowners and capitalists were abolished as a class, and the proletariat became the ruling class. In the villages the number of middle peasants increased and poor peasants became less numerous, but there were still poor people in the rural areas.

An important achievement of this stage was that a significant majority of the population, with the exception of the kulaks, nepmen, clergy and part of the old, bourgeois intelligentsia, had, as a result of the alliance of the working class mainly with the poor and middle peasants, in the course of socialist construction, become imbued with the ideology of the Communist Party.

At the same time a great change came about in people's attitude to the law. The development of socialist consciousness ran into considerable complications in the sphere of economics, although from the very first years the practices of giving free labour to society and of joining in socialist competition were widely adopted among the workers. The process of instilling scientific knowledge, the scientific world view, the new morality and release from religious beliefs took longer than the establishment of the new political and legal ideology.

The socialist consciousness of the working class, the peasantry and the Soviet intelligentsia grew and asserted itself in this period in sharp ideological class struggle against the anti-socialist, bourgeois and petty-bourgeois ideology, psychology and morality, in the course of criticism of incorrect political, legal, philosophical, aesthetic and other conceptions alien to Marxism-Leninism. This struggle, the tremendous struggle of the Party and state to refashion the whole pattern of social life and educate the working people was crowned by a radical change in the consciousness of the broad masses and a rapid and all-round rise in socialist culture.

Industrialisation and collectivisation, the victory of socialism on all fronts transformed the class structure. The personality structure of society also began to change rapidly.

Small industrialists and traders were the only exploiters left in the cities, as were the kulaks in the villages. But the businessman that emerged in the period of the New Economic Policy was opposed by the Soviet industrial manager, while in the villages the communard and then the collective farmer made their appearance. The intelligentsia in this period presented a somewhat motley picture of former government officials, people of the "liberal professions", people from the former nobility and the big, medium and small bourgeoisie. At the same time a worker-peasant intelligentsia was beginning to emerge. Young workers and young people from the villages went to study. New types of people the country had never seen before came into being: shock-workers, Stakhanovites, collective farmers, girl tractor-drivers, airwomen, explorers of the Soviet Arctic. "Red" specialists—engineers, planners, teachers—appeared on a big scale.

In the second stage (from the mid-thirties to the mid-fifties), on the basis of the policy of industrialisation and collectivisation and a cultural revolution, socialism won decisive victories, resulting in a new class structure. Whereas in 1913, the landowners, the big and petty urban bourgeoisie, the traders and kulaks accounted for 16.3 per cent of the whole population, by 1937, these social groups no longer existed as such. In 1913, peasants working their own farms (not counting kulaks) and workers outside the co-operatives—tinkers and craftsmen—accounted for 66.7 per cent of the population, in 1928, for 74.9 per cent, and in 1939, for 2.6 per cent. On the other hand, by 1939, 47.2 per cent of the population were collective farmers and small craftsmen working in co-operatives, and the share of the working class had grown to 32.5 per cent. Intellectuals, office and professional workers accounted for 17.7 per cent of the population. With the abolition of private ownership of the means of production and elimination of the exploiting classes there took shape in the Soviet Union for the first time in human history a society of working people consisting of workers, collective farmers and working intellectuals.

Further progress was made in consolidating and developing the socialist consciousness among the masses of the workers of socialist society, fighting the survivals of capitalism in the sphere of ideology, psychology and morality, and in developing the people's culture. This stage was marked by the consolidation of the socio-political and ideological unity of Soviet society and an upsurge of Soviet patriotism and friendship of the peoples of the USSR. The victory of the socialist ideology in the consciousness of the mass of members of Soviet society was manifested in the Great Patriotic War of 1941-45.

The war confirmed the great significance of what had been achieved by socialism. The Soviet people displayed such spirit, such outstanding ideological and moral character that the whole world bowed their heads in acknowledgement of the Soviet people's great achievement. The exploits of soldiers, officers, political workers, partisans, scouts, workers and collective farmers, women, youth and even children amounted to mass heroism. Patriotism and the communist ideology merged into one.

The postwar restoration of the economy was a feat of the Soviet people that comes second only to the exploit of their victory in the war. These were grim years full of inconsolable grief for the losses of family and near ones that could never be made good, of a devastated economy, of drought, lack of trained personnel, lagging agriculture and food shortages. The war wounded had to be nursed back to health, many people's lives had gone awry. But the joy of victory and the optimistic prospects generated determination and mass labour heroism. The devastated cities, factories and collective farms were restored. New projects got under way. The soldier was able to return to the bench and the tractor, to take up studies.

The present stage of development of Soviet society dates from the mid-fifties. It is connected with the decisions taken at the Party congresses.

The Report of the Central Committee to the 24th Party Congress states: "The experience of past years has convincingly shown that the surmounting of the consequences of the personality cult and also of subjectivistic errors has favourably affected the general political and, above all, the ideological situation in the country."[1]

---

[1] *The 24th Congress of the CPSU*, Moscow, 1971, p. 123.

The Party did tremendous work in overcoming the violations and developing the Leninist norms of Party life, the Leninist principles of administration in all spheres of Party, state, ideological and economic activity. Important measures to raise production and the people's material standard of life have been carried out. New successes have been achieved in science and technology. The world has seen new Soviet exploits in space, in the cultivation of vast tracts of virgin land, in industry and construction. In passing through this period Soviet people have become more experienced and mature both politically and ideologically.

The present period is characterised by the further development of socialist consciousness, by its beginning to grow into communist consciousness, by the all-round development of the spiritual life of society, by the creation of the essential ideological and spiritual prerequisites for the victory of communism.

All these years there has been a steadily growing tendency towards extension and deepening of the mass socialist consciousness, towards a socialist orientation of the personality. This has been expressed in the ideological and political unity of Soviet society, in the perfecting of the forms of socialist labour and distribution, in the further elimination of class distinctions and making society more homogeneous, in raising the general cultural level of the whole population. Millions of people have acquired a profound understanding of the common cause and learned to treat it as their own.

The efforts by the Party and by the people have brought about the social relations of developed socialism: socialist production relations, a socialist class structure and socialist political organisation. A cultural revolution has been carried out. This means that a qualitatively new social environment has been created for the development of the personality. The individual has been placed in a different position from what he was in under capitalism, in a different position with regard to the system of social interconnections, in a new relationship to society, to his own activity, to other people. All the material and spiritual wealth of society has been made available to the man of toil. The obligation to work has been established as one of the basic principles. The great goal of remaking society on just communist principles, and the great things achieved on the path of socialism have inspired masses of people to devote themselves to serving the interests of society.

Thus, socialist society has been not only the soil from which new people have sprung. It is itself a product of the creative work of these people. History has confirmed one of the fundamental propositions of Marxism-Leninism, which demands a combination of "complete scientific sobriety in the analysis of the objective state of affairs and the objective course of evolution with the most emphatic recognition of the importance of the revolutionary energy, revolutionary creative genius, and revolutionary initiative of the masses—and also, of course, of individuals, groups, organisations and parties that are able to discover and achieve contact with one or another class."[1]

It must be borne in mind, of course, that the tremendous positive advances under socialism by no means dispose of all problems. The development of the personality proceeds on the basis of forms of life and traditions, habits and customs that have taken shape in the course of centuries. These old ways, which often contradict the new, are as yet inevitable, while the material resources, the knowledge or the skill to create new ones are still lacking. But the problems that still remain in the sphere of education in no way belittle what has been achieved.

[1] V. I. Lenin, *Collected Works,* Vol. 13, p. 36.

CHAPTER THREE

SOCIALIST SOCIETY AS THE ENVIRONMENT OF THE PERSONALITY

The building of socialist society has provided a new social environment for the development of the personality. The new system of social relations has a decisive effect in forming the needs, interests, ideals, value orientation and ethos of the personality and, therefore, creates general and specific human characteristics, and, consequently, a system of social types of personality, a personality structure of society.

Before the revolution the proletariat's class-consciousness and revolutionary moods were generated mainly by its oppressed condition, by hatred of the squalor of the exploitative system, but in conditions of socialism all the basic social forms of the new society contribute to the socialist consciousness of the working masses. Moreover, it is not only the content of the social experience assimilated that changes; the character of its interaction with society as a whole and with the social groups is also transformed.

In order to understand how the content of the new environment affects people's position in society, their attitude to society, to themselves and their own activity, and to other people, one must examine the character of the work of the members of society, the sources that satisfy their material needs, the size and nature of their income; the way belonging to a certain class or group within that class influences the formation of special class or group features of the personality along with common features; the available means of drawing people into activity connected with the management of social affairs and realising their civil rights and obligations, and the ways of protecting the interests of society and the individual; and finally the principles of the educational system, thanks to which the knowledge and spiritual values of socialism become available to the individual and mould his personality.

Socialism is a fundamentally new system of social relations. To properly understand its new features one should remember that it is a product of the old society. Karl Marx, in his *Critique of the Gotha Programme,* and Lenin, in his *The State and Revolution,* both stressed that socialism is a society that in every respect—economic, moral, and intellectual—is still stamped with the birthmarks of the old society from whose womb it emerges.[1]

1. MAN IN THE SYSTEM OF ECONOMIC RELATIONS OF SOCIALISM

Socialism was inferred by Marx from the economic law of the motion of capitalist society. Emphasising this fact, Lenin wrote: "There is no trace of utopianism in Marx, in the sense that he made up or invented a 'new' society. No, he studied the *birth* of the new society *out of* the old, and the forms of transition from the latter to the former, as a natural historical process."[2] This is the key to the Marxist-Leninist, scientific, realist understanding both of the inevitability of socialism and its historical advantages, and the not as yet complete maturity that is characteristic of socialism as the first phase of communist society.

Socialist Property as the Basis of the New Position of the Worker in the System of Economic Relations

When considering the problems of the formation of the individual's socialist consciousness one must take into consideration a whole set of factors, economic and otherwise: public ownership, work at a socialist enterprise, distribution according to work, political life, legal system, ideological and educational work, and so on.

At the same time one must bear in mind the special, de-

---

[1] K. Marx and F. Engels, *Selected Works,* Vol. 3, p. 17.
[2] V. I. Lenin, *Collected Works,* Vol. 25, p. 425.

termining role of the ownership of the means of production. It is on the basis of these property relations that the whole system of economic, political and other relations is built. Ownership of the means of production plays a decisive part in determining the destination of the product of labour and, accordingly, people's attitude to labour, their place and role in the social organisation of labour, membership of a group or class, the character of their consciousness and behaviour.

In his *Economic and Philosophic Manuscripts* Marx analyses the position of the worker under capitalism, his social essence and traces three elements in social relations that indicate the basic characteristics of a person's position in society and that may be regarded as the foundations for the formation of the social qualities of the personality: (1) the character of property, i.e., the form of appropriation of material and spiritual wealth, its purpose and application and, hence, the worker's attitude to the product of his activity; (2) the character of a person's labour, i.e., the purpose of human activity, and the workman's attitude to his own labour; (3) the attitude of one man to another, to other people.[1]

Under the conditions of capitalist private property, "the object which labour produces—labour's product—confronts it as *something alien*, as a *power independent* of the producer"[2]. In other words, the realisation of labour, its objectification, acts as the loss of the object and enslavement by the object. The wealth created and accumulated by the workers' labour, since it is in the hands of the capitalists, becomes an instrument of exploitation, the material force that brings down on the worker all the means of political coercion, economic compulsion and spiritual deception. Naturally, "the worker is related to the *product of his labour* as to an *alien object*",[3] "as an alien world antagonistically opposed to him."[4]

Insofar as the product of labour is self-alienation, so production itself is active self-alienation. "...Labour is *external* to the worker, i.e., it does not belong to his essential being;

---

[1] K. Marx, *Economic and Philosophic Manuscripts of 1844*, pp. 67-83.
[2] Ibid., p. 69.
[3] Ibid., p. 73.
[4] Ibid., p. 73.

that in his work, therefore, he does not affirm himself but denies himself, does not feel content but unhappy, does not develop freely his physical and mental energy but mortifies his body and ruins his mind. The worker, therefore, only feels himself outside his work, and in his work feels outside himself. He is at home when he is not working, and when he is working he is not at home."[1] Thus production activity— the species life of man, i.e., that which distinguishes him from the animals and constitutes his essential attribute— turns out to be merely a means of supporting life. "Life itself appears only as a *means to life*."[2] Or to put it in yet another way, man's species essence becomes a means for his individual existence. The activity of the worker is not self-activity, it belongs to another; it is the worker's loss of his own self. Hence the worker's relation to his own activity appears as a relation to something alien, which does not belong to him.

The alienation of the product of labour itself leads us to examine the alienation of man from man. Since man is alienated from the product of his own labour, from his life activity, from his species essence and, consequently, is opposed to himself, this is also expressed in the opposition of one man to another. One man is estranged from another, as each of them is from man's essential nature. In real life this is represented by the fact that labour and the product of the worker belongs not to the worker but to the capitalist.[3] Therefore, the relations that develop between them are relations of domination and subordination. Enmity is the natural condition of this relationship.

A little later, in *The German Ideology*, Marx and Engels, developing the theme of man's estrangement from man, the theme of the antagonism of classes, point to alienation in the form of the state and religion. In the division of society into classes with their mutually opposed interests, in the separation of the general interest from the particular, when the general interest of the ruling class in the form of the state assumes an independent form, divorced from the real—both

---

[1] K. Marx, *Economic and Philosophic Manuscripts of 1844*, p. 72.
[2] Ibid., p. 75.
[3] Ibid., pp. 76-79.

separate and common—interest and at the same time the form of illusory generality, Marx and Engels see the highest stage of the development of the alienation of individuals.[1] The social and political forms of alienation are compounded by forms of spiritual alienation in the form of the subordination of man's thought, his will to illusory "symbols", to the "fantasies" of thought and sensation (idealism and religion), aspirations and incitements (egoism, individualism, etc.). The conception of alienation is further developed and concretised as the exploitation of man by man, as coercion and domination by the bourgeois state.

Thus, a relationship to the product of one's labour as to an alien and hostile world, and to labour as merely a means of subsistence, and the inimical, antagonistic character of relations between people belonging to the exploited and exploiting classes—such, according to Marx, are the fundamental characteristics that sum up the position of the working man under capitalism. Such are the relations that undergo radical change with the victory of socialism and the establishing of public ownership of the means of production.

Since the *product of labour* now belongs to all society and the socialist state has become the subject of the property relations and represents all members of society, it is natural that the purpose of production should be the satisfaction of the needs of members of society. For the first time in history the material and spiritual wealth is used in the interests of all members of society, of the working man. Society takes responsibility for the development of education, protection of health and social insurance. These branches of state activity are oriented on development of such needs and abilities of man as are important for his life and happiness.

The product created by the workers under socialism does not become the property of other people who can rule over them and become their masters. The fruit of everyone's work is everyone's property: no member of society can give society anything but his labour, and no one can receive from society anything but objects of use, consumer goods. Here the ruling principle is "From each according to his abilities, to each according to his work". The product of labour thus becomes

---

[1] K. Marx and F. Engels, *The German Ideology*, pp. 26-96.

not an instrument of exploitation, not an alien and hostile force, but a means of satisfying the demands of the members of society, of developing their abilities. The relationship between producer and owner, in which Marx saw "the most profound mystery, the hidden basis of the whole social system", has lost not only its opposedness but even its distinction; a member of socialist society combines in one person both the master of the conditions of production and the immediate producer. Hence the general, social interest objectively becomes the interest of all members of society, and this is the most essential, most important characteristic of the objective position of the worker in socialist production. Naturally, the elimination of the objective opposition between the product of labour and the worker's interest generates mass perception of the social wealth as belonging to the workers, as their own.

Work under socialism is work at a public enterprise and for the whole people. Society, emancipated from the parasitism of the exploiting classes, is an association of working people. Work is the source of the wealth of society as a whole and the well-being of all. Consequently, the worker's labour has not yet ceased to be a means of his subsistence. The strict dependence between each person's contribution to the common cause and the amount of goods he receives from society disappears only with the achievement of communist abundance and a high level of consciousness of all members of society. But already under socialism work at a public enterprise becomes the civic obligation and duty of everyone. The economic basis of this legal norm is the economic fact that work is the sole source of the well-being of all members of society and the basic criterion of a person's position in society. It is quite natural then that the individual should assert his human dignity primarily in work.

Between serving one's employer under capitalism and working in the interests of the people under socialism there is a tremendous difference reflecting the transition from one historical epoch to another. Work under socialism is thus a means for supporting life, a means for the development of one's abilities and social activity for the common good.

New relationship of man to man is expressed mainly in the elimination of the antagonisms between classes and the establishment of the community of the fundamental interests of the working people. Since public ownership of the means of production rules out exploitation of man by man, it unites the fundamental interests of all social groups, all nationalities and members of society. And although by no means all their interests coincide, although the contradictory character of social development remains (but these contradictions are no longer antagonistic) nevertheless a radical advance has been made in integrating people's interests and society has acquired ideological and political unity. These relations between people find their expression in socialist democracy, in the policies of the socialist state, whose activities are all aimed at serving the interests of the whole people.

Thus, the socialising of production fundamentally changes the content of the production, economic relations and the position of the worker in production. In the position of all working people, regardless of what class they belong to, important common features are shaped that provide the basis for the formation of certain general interests, for qualities of the personality that characterise its socialist ethos.

Socialist Relations in the Immediate Process of Production

Socialism inherits the division of labour and organisation of production that have taken shape under capitalism, and only gradually transforms them. But public ownership immediately has a marked effect on the position and behaviour of the worker in production. This is expressed in his relation to the general problems of the development of social production and his own work, in the development of mass production activity on the part of the working people. In other words, socialist relations assert themselves in the immediate process of production.

Many bourgeois work-study experts are worried by the grim picture of human relations at capitalist enterprises today. The mortally dangerous disease which, they believe, has struck the "world of labour" is due to the elimination from the labour process of all emotional and mental activity on the part of the worker, to his complete lack of any interest in his work.[1] The bourgeois authors cannot but point to the degradation of the worker's personality under capitalism.

But the very same authors, adhering to the positions of defence of capitalism, make every effort to disprove Marxist views on this question and, hence, the practice of socialism. The main target of attack is Marx's proposition that the emancipation of labour can be brought about only on condition of the abolition of capitalist ownership of the means of production. It is asserted that the depressing picture presented by work, its joyless character are not the result of capitalist exploitation but something quite different, something puzzling and mysterious—the fate, the destiny, the tragedy of mankind. The blame for the working people's unhappy plight is placed on the technological process, on machines, which are alleged to be responsible for the unnatural separation of intellectual from physical work and to destroy the worker's interest in his work[2]. The remedies proclaimed by these bourgeois writers are highly reminiscent of the Narodnic palliatives that Lenin subjected to such devastating criticism[3]. We are told of the need for partnership between owners and workers, particularly in the sphere of "joint consideration" of production targets and "redistribution of operations and giving the worker a part in the organisation of labour".

In short, this is a case of all critical themes being blotted out by apologetic arguments and proposals aimed against the revolutionary character of the Marxist solution to the problem of personality, and also against the practice of socialism. The development of socialist production relations, however, confirms Marx's prevision and confounds his critics.

---

[1] See, for example, H. Weinstock, *Arbeit und Bildung*, Heidelberg, 1956. Weinstock supports his case with references to the book of the Swedish worker Friedel. Friedel's book is indeed a grim indictment of capitalist production. He writes, for instance: "Machine operators have no right to be people.... We, ordinary workers, seem to be running alongside life. For democracy and freedom we mean just about as much as manure means for the growth of a plant.... Not for a single hour in the course of the whole twenty-eight years I have worked in the textile industry have I felt the slightest joy in my work" (p. 46).

[2] H. Weinstock, *Arbeit und Bildung*, S. 52-57.

[3] V. I. Lenin, *Collected Works*, Vol. 1, pp. 409-10.

Marx was the first thinker to give a profound scientific elaboration of the role of technology in the development of the forms of organisation of labour.[1] But nowhere, even in the early economic and philosophic manuscripts, which bourgeois ideologists so often counterpoise to *Capital,* did Marx examine the dialectic of the interaction between technology and man outside the definite economic relations between people. According to Marx, the machine eliminates the need to attach the worker forever to one and the same functions. At a mechanised enterprise it becomes possible to relieve personnel without interrupting the work process. Moreover, the speed at which a young man can master mechanised work in its turn eliminates the need to attach the worker to one particular operation for life. But the interests of the capitalist owner, the fierce competition and the race for profit necessitate systematic reduction of the workers' wages and introduction of narrow specialisation, and, consequently, make the worker a slave for life to one particular operation. This, on the one hand, cheapens labour power and, on the other, increases the workers' dependence on the capitalist and weakens their resistance to capitalist oppression. Marx and Engels wrote that the bourgeois "finds in this self-alienation its confirmation and its good," while the proletarian "sees in it its own powerlessness and the reality of an inhuman existence".[2]

Socialism has introduced in the division of labour a number of essential changes of a general, social character, which are of great importance to the development of a new attitude to work. It has liquidated the opposition between the town and country, between mental and manual labour, and has destroyed the ruling classes' monopoly of mental work. The peoples of the former colonial borderlands of tsarist Russia are now equal members of the Union of Soviet Socialist Republics. Thanks to this a community of interests has been established between the workers, collective farmers and intellectuals of all nationalities.

Public ownership of the means of production demands a planned economy. The practice of the USSR and other so-

---

[1] K. Marx, *Capital,* Vol. I, pp. 371-507.
[2] K. Marx and F. Engels, *The Holy Family,* p. 61.

cialist countries has clearly confirmed the advantages of centralised planning and direction of the national economy. This is shown by the rapid development rates in socialist production and the solution of fundamental problems of economic and cultural progress in a historically short period of time. Economic planning in the USSR has solved the crucial social problem of employment and has given direction and purpose to the implementation of measures for raising the people's living standards and culture.

The social significance of economic planning lies in the fact that the process of formation of national economic proportions, which under capitalism happens spontaneously, now comes within the scope of human control. People's activity thus produces the desired results and, as socialism develops, will continue to do so on an ever increasing scale. The goals and tasks set by the plans are comprehensible to the working people and this generates in the mass consciousness a confidence in the future and allows the working man to take an active part in their realisation.

Needless to say, the advantages of socialist planning do not materialise automatically. The 24th Congress of the CPSU emphasised that, although the USSR justifiably takes pride in its planning achievements, there is an urgent need to improve the planning methods, planning must rest on a more precise study of social requirements, on scientific forecasts of economic possibilities, on all-round analysis and evaluation of different variants of decisions and of their immediate and long-term consequences.[1]

To elucidate the new position of the working man we must consider for a moment the character of the exchange of activity under socialism. Commodity-exchange relations continue to exist, but commodity exchange under socialism differs from commodity exchange under capitalism just as social exchange differs from private exchange. Under socialism it is not private owners who enter into exchange but the workers, collective farmers and working intellectuals united in socialist enterprises. Commodity exchange ceases to provide individuals with a source of profit, a means of exploiting others.

The planned socialist economy gets rid of the fetishist

---

[1] *24th Congress of the Communist Party of the Soviet Union*, p. 80.

character of the commodity form. Although individual work under socialism manifests itself even before exchange as social labour, its social character also manifests itself in commodity exchange because certain social connections are realised in it and various forms of labour acquire their full social significance through the medium of commodity exchange.

The processes of exchange no longer occur behind the backs of the producers, separate from their will and consciousness, like a blind and alien force. The planned character of the development of exchange rules out any antagonistic contradiction between consumer value and the cost of the commodity. This means that under socialism there is no insoluble conflict between production and demand, and no crises of overproduction. Any overstocking of certain goods or shortages of others are overcome by improving organisation, without social conflicts. The socialist state, taking into consideration production and individual needs, organises planned distribution and exchange between the various branches of production for the satisfaction of the needs of the members of society, and the workers themselves take an active, conscious part in organising production.

Socialism has brought radical changes in the conditions and stimuli of economic activity. It has abolished private initiative as the driving force of economic activity. But despite the prophecies of the apostles of the "golden calf", this has not led to the collapse of society. On the contrary, socialism has proved its historical superiority over capitalism by creating on the basis of public property its special, fundamentally new system of stimulating the working people's activity. Public ownership of the means of production, the general obligation to work, the distribution of material goods in accordance with the quantity and quality of work done, and socialist democracy instil in the working people a high consciousness of their social duty, open up possibilities for releasing and applying tremendous social energy.

The specific forms of organisation and encouragement of economic activity may be varied in socialist conditions. This depends on the socio-economic and national peculiarities of the country in question, on the level of development of the productive forces. On the basis of these objective conditions the management bodies have full scope for creative activity on which the more or less effective use of the advantages of socialism depends.

In abolishing private property socialism at the same time puts an end to capitalist competition. But the disappearance of capitalist competition signifies the disappearance of the *bourgeois form of competition,* and not competition in general. Competition may arise wherever work is done by a number of people working together. "The socialists' attacks," Lenin wrote, "have never been directed against competition as such, but only against market competition. Market competition, however, is a special form of competition characteristic of capitalist society and consisting in a struggle of individual producers for a livelihood and for influence, for a place in the market. The abolition of competition as a struggle of producers that is connected only with the market does not at all mean the abolition of competition—on the contrary, the abolition of commodity production and capitalism makes it possible to organise competition in its human instead of its bestial forms."[1] Socialism, Lenin wrote, makes it possible for the first time to apply competition broadly, on a mass scale, to draw into it the millions of the working people.

Socialist competition is a law of social production under socialism. Its essence lies in bringing up low indices to the average level and average indices to the advanced level. Since in socialist society commodities are also exchanged according to their cost, here too the problem of the correlation of the socially necessary time with the individual working time, of social and individual cost, is solved by perfecting the methods of production, by reducing per-unit production costs. But in conditions of private property this leads to the ruin of some and enrichment of others, whereas under socialism the predominant role is played by relations of comradely mutual assistance.

The main stimulator of the working people's activity is their interest in the development of social production, which they regard as the universal source of public well-being. The history of the development of competition in the USSR is a splendid epopee of popular heroism and the formation of mass communist consciousness. Socialism, as Lenin foresaw,

---

[1] V. I. Lenin, *Collected Works,* Vol. 27, pp. 206-07.

took competition beyond the confines of the market and transformed it into a mass method of communist education and communist construction.

Thus, public ownership turns wealth to the service of the working man, transforms labour into public service and establishes a community of fundamental interests between social groups. Socialism puts an end to the alienation of the product of labour, of labour itself and of man from man. From being the self-alienation of the human personality work becomes the self-assertion of the dignity of the working man's personality.

Economic Differences in the Position of Members of Society

Certain essential differences in economic position of the working people are inherited from the prerevolutionary past and are the "birthmarks" of the old society of which both Marx and Lenin wrote. These differences are of definite significance in shaping some of the special qualities that go into the making of certain subtypes of personality within the general framework of the socialist type of personality.

People who formerly belonged to various patterns of social life have been drawn into socialism. Characterising the multistructural economy in the transitional period, Lenin indicated the following elements:

(1) patriarchal, i.e., to a considerable extent natural, peasant farming;

(2) small commodity production (this includes the majority of those peasants who sell their grain);

(3) private capitalism;

(4) state capitalism;

(5) socialism.[1]

The first four structures and consequently the corresponding groups of people disappeared entirely with the development of the socialist economy, not counting a small number of individual peasant farms.[2] The rise and development of

---

[1] V. I. Lenin, *Collected Works*, Vol. 27, pp. 335-36.

[2] Remaining individual peasant farmers and small craftsmen outside the co-operatives comprise 0.03 per cent of the population. *Narodnoye Khozyaistvo v 1969 godu*, p. 35.

socialist agriculture has eliminated the former antithesis between town and country, which was inherent in capitalism.
But even now, as a result of its past, the countryside lags
behind the town in the industrialisation of labour, the level
of culture and living standards. The social economies of the
collective and state farms cannot as yet fully satisfy all the
requirements of the population for food, so the personal
subsidiary holdings continue to exist.

The collective farmers' personal subsidiary holdings and
also those of the workers at state farms, and of some town
dwellers and people who live in workers' settlements have
a commodity character in cases when the produce is sold on
the market and a corresponding income received. It is possible to speak of a certain similarity with ordinary commodity production inasmuch as here the producer makes a product for exchange and is its owner. But the likeness ends
there, because the owner of the subsidiary holding is farming on socialised land, the size of his holding is limited and
there is no possibility of exploiting hired labour. The income from the subsidiary holding is not the sole or by any
means the main source of subsistence of the family, because
both the head of the family and its members are usually
employed at some socialist enterprise. In many cases the
produce is realised not on the market but through a co-
operative.

Economists consider trade at a collective farm market,
where the products of the personal subsidiary holding are
sold side by side with the products of the collective farms'
social economy, as socialist relations in the sphere of exchange. But one must note certain difference in the position
of the working man who has no subsidiary holding and the
one who has. In the former case, the family works at various
socialist enterprises, lives in a state-provided flat and the
only source of income is the wages it receives. In the second
case, the members of the family, while working at a socialist
enterprise, have their own house, orchard, vegetable garden,
water supply system, etc. In short, the two families are in
distinctly different positions. In the latter case, there are
more opportunities for the development of individualistic,
selfish aspirations, the property-owner's mentality. If control
and educational work are relaxed the personal holdings may

grow out of proportion and be used by certain elements for purposes contrary to the interests of society.

The new society inherits from the past the antagonistic opposition between intellectual and physical work. Social reforms and the cultural revolution have done away with this opposition, and the essential difference between the two forms of work are gradually being eliminated. The country has made a tremendous leap forward in the field of education and culture. Nevertheless, the legacy of the past still makes itself felt in a lower educational level of the main mass of people engaged in physical labour compared with intellectual workers, particularly in rural areas. The low level of education and general culture sometimes provides a favourable soil for preserving various superstitions, religious notions, and so on.

Among the birthmarks of the old society Marx and Lenin numbered also the economic inequality that remains under socialism. The principle of distribution according to work presupposes social ownership of the means of production, absence of any exploitation of man by man and a planned economy. The socialist nature of the principle "From each according to his abilities, to each according to his work" lies in the fact that, as Marx put it, no one can give anything but his work, and nothing can become the property of individuals except objects of personal use. This is the essential difference between such relations and bourgeois relations. Bourgeois relations are formed in a context of private ownership of the instruments of production and exploitation of hired labour, when distribution takes the form of income or payment for the labour sold by the workers.

The introduction of distribution according to work denotes a fundamental step towards the abolition of economic inequality. But this principle of distribution does not ensure complete equality. In other words, the introduction of the socialist principle of distribution according to work is still not enough to overcome inequality completely because society has not matured sufficiently for that: the level of development of the productive forces is not high enough, there are still distinctions between skilled and unskilled labour. Noting the fact of incomplete equality under socialism, Lenin wrote: "The first phase of communism, therefore, cannot yet provide justice and equality: differences, and unjust differences, in wealth will still persist, but the *exploitation* of man by man will have become impossible because it will be impossible to seize the *means of production*—the factories, machines, land, etc.—and make them private property."[1]

2. SOCIO-CLASS STRUCTURE AND INTEGRATION OF INTERESTS

Economic relations are directly reflected in the corresponding socio-class structure of society, in differences between the large social groups, in their having special common interests, and in the character of the interrelationships between general and individual interests.

To understand how the position of the individual in the system of social relations has changed one must consider two aspects of the socio-class structure: the common features that classes have acquired through socialist transformations, and the differences that characterise the working class, the collective farm peasantry and the intelligentsia. In doing so we must bear in mind the basic attributes of the classes indicated by Lenin: the relation of large groups to the means of production, their role in the social organisation of labour, the dimensions of the share of social wealth of which they dispose and the mode of acquiring it.[1]

If we take these indicators and attempt to apply them in characterising the class differences in the USSR, we obtain the following picture:

1. State property in the means of production is the possession of the whole people—workers, peasants and intellectuals. This means that the Soviet working class is the first working class in history to have ceased being proletarians in the actual sense of the term, since proletariat means a class deprived of property in the means of production.

Under socialism the peasantry has also undergone deep changes. Liberated from the landowner and kulak exploitation, it works a large-scale socialist economy based on modern technology and science. Collective farm and co-operat-

---

1 V. I. Lenin, *Collected Works*, Vol. 25, p. 466.
2 Ibid., Vol. 29, p. 421.

ive property belongs to certain collectives of working people and as such acts as an indicator of class differences between the workers and the collective farmers. But in its essence collective farm and co-operative property is a socialist form of property, because it excludes exploitation of man by man, serves the interests of the working people and is integrated in the general state system of national economic and socio-cultural planning.

There is yet another difference between workers and collective farmers in the sphere of property: the property owned by the whole people is not as yet equally used by workers and collective farmers. All the workers' labour is based on state property, whereas the collective farmers use mainly the land. There are also other differences—in capital investment, development of social funds, etc. As for the intellectuals, most of them are connected with the state property, fewer with the co-operative property, and in this sense these groups are no different from workers in the first case and collective farmers in the second.

2. In the sphere of social organisation of labour socialism is a society of working people, of toilers. In antagonistic formations the ruling classes control the function of management of production, and the exploited classes are engaged in the immediate process of production.

Under socialism there are no such class differences because with the overthrow of the ruling classes the monopoly of the function of management has disappeared. Both the working class and the peasantry themselves manage social production.

People engaged in intellectual work are not a special social group like a class. The differences between the working class and the peasantry, on the one hand, and the intelligentsia, on the other, are conditioned by the still surviving differences between manual and mental labour. The intelligentsia differs from the workers and peasants in respect of the content of its activity and cultural and technical level.

In conditions of socialism the intelligentsia is closely connected with the working class (engineers, technicians, etc.) or the collective farmers (agronomists, stock-breeders, etc.) by birth and social position. These groups of intellectuals are directly involved in the process of industrial and agricultural production. Teachers, doctors, scientists, artists, managers and professional military personnel constitute special groups of the intelligentsia. A large portion of the intelligentsia in socialist society comes under the heading of service personnel. But part of the artistic intelligentsia (writers, composers and others who do not work for hire in a state institution), and also the members of collective farms engaged in intellectual work, are not counted as service personnel. On the other hand, there are many service personnel performing unskilled or less skilled work who cannot be included among the intelligentsia.

Consequently, the various groups of intellectuals in socialist society, performing an important role in the organisation of production, management and the satisfaction of sociocultural requirements, do not on account of their social position and functions constitute a special class. Each of the above-mentioned social functions has meaning and significance only to the extent that it is connected with the interests of the main classes and the people as a whole.

3. With the socialisation of the means of production the dimensions of the share of social wealth received by the working people have increased and the mode of acquiring it has changed. The working people acquire their share of social wealth not by selling their labour, as under capitalism, but by distribution of part of the national income according to the quantity and quality of the work done by each worker; while the main source of the collective farm peasantry's income is work in a social enterprise, although the subsidiary personal holding at present plays a fairly considerable role in agricultural production. Consequently, the differences in payment for work, connected with the quantity and quality of the work of members of society, cannot be regarded as indicators, attributes of class membership. These differences depend on the level of skill of individual workers and the professional peculiarities of the groups within classes.

Thus, the indicators that signified division of people into classes in former times—relationship to the means of production, role in the social organisation of labour, mode of acquiring and size of income—now in all basic respects unite the working people of the USSR. As for the survivals of

class distinction, they, undoubtedly, still play an important
role in the life and development of the workers, collective
farmers and Soviet intelligentsia.

The leading role of the working class in Soviet society is
related to the nature of class differences. It is based not only
on the moral prestige derived from the revolutionary services performed by the working class in the past but also on
its present position in society, particularly in the system of
socialist production.

Connected with large-scale machine production and advanced technology, educated in the spirit of fine revolutionary traditions and loyalty to the ideas of Marxism-Leninism,
the working class is to play a particularly important part in
creating the material and technical base of communism. It
is the most consistent carrier of the socialist ideology, of
comradeship and collectivism, discipline and organisation.

The historical task now confronting Soviet society is to
make agricultural work into a form of industrial work, to
achieve a unified nationwide form of property and on this
basis raise the collective farm peasantry's consciousness, discipline and organisation to the working class level. While
class differences remain, the leading position in society belongs to the working class.

Hence the need to take into consideration the general and
particular in the development of the classes of socialist society. "... The Party's policy yields the required results only
when it fully takes into account both the interests of the
entire people and the interests of various classes and social
groups, and directs them into a single common channel."[1]

The change of the socio-class structure and the new status
of workers, peasants and intellectuals under socialism acquire their logical culmination in a fact of immense historical significance—the *integration of interests*[2]. The level of

---

[1] *24th Congress of the Communist Party of the Soviet Union*, p. 87.
[2] "Interest" is used here in the sense of a means of satisfaction of
need and the aim and motivation of separate individuals and groups.
This interpretation of interest presupposes that interest exists as an
objective category and does not coincide with need; its realisation is
to be regarded as an objectively essential condition for the development of the given individual or community and, therefore, may not
coincide with the subjective, erroneous notion of interests held by peo-

social homogeneity achieved is summed up in the appearance of fundamental interests that are common to different social groups, in a new relationship of social groups and separate individuals to the interests of society.

The establishment of social ownership of the instruments of production introduces a definite common element into the position of the workers, peasants and intellectuals in the system of social production, and on this basis, common economic, social, political and other requirements, common means of satisfying them and, consequently, unity of their fundamental interests. Such common interests of all social groups are the interest in the building of communist society, in multiplying social property and developing socialist production, in strengthening the socialist state and legal institutions, in growth of the people's well-being and culture, in defence of the socialist Motherland and development of international solidarity among the working people and in consolidating world peace.

It should be borne in mind, however, that the general exists only in the particular, while the particular is a part of the general and cannot exist outside it. Various groups and individuals take part in realising the general interests, carrying out certain functions and performing the tasks confronting them. Social interests are, therefore, expressed in the concrete interests that people acquire in the process of their work together, in the process of intercommunication, and are determined by the peculiarities of the position of various groups, collectives and individuals. Interests may be connected with production—interest in reaching certain production targets, in material and technical supplies, in finance, in training personnel. They may be connected with an interest in receiving one's share of the returns. They may be interests of a scientific or artistic nature, or interests in social work, and so on. Such concrete interests are a part of the social interest, the mode of existence of the social interest, the forms of its realisation. Social interests, being general interests, are impossible without realisation of con-

---

ple themselves; there are economic, political and spiritual interests, and also social, group (class) and personal interests; long-term and temporary interests and fundamental and secondary interests.

crete interests, and these last cannot be realised in isolation from general problems.

In stressing the tremendous significance of common fundamental interests, we presume the existence of other interests that are not fundamental interests, but are highly significant for social groups, collectives and individuals. These special interests reflect the specific position of those who have them. The great importance of the universality of the fundamental interests lies in the very fact that it makes it possible to satisfy the whole totality of interests to an optimal degree. But the fact that Soviet people's fundamental interests coincide does not mean that all interests—general interests, the interests of separate collectives, and personal interests—always and under all circumstances coincide.

The realisation of the special interests of the collective farm peasantry is connected with the technical equipment of production, with material and technical supplies, with the level of prices on deliveries of farm produce to the state, with the forms and level of capital investment and granting of credits to collective farms. Economic interest is also expressed in the level and forms of payment for work, in efforts to raise the income from the collective farm. All this underlines the need for attentive study and attention to the specific interests of the collective farm peasantry in political measures taken by the Party and state.

For example, the development of agricultural production answers the general interests of society as a whole, but it is the activity and stimulation of the economic activity of the collective farmers with which the growth of farm production is directly connected. Such Party and state measures as the fixing of firm plans for the delivery of farm produce over a long period, raising of state wholesale prices, increase of allocations for the production of agricultural machinery and mineral fertilisers, for the development of stock-breeding on an industrial basis, are all permeated with the urge to take into consideration the specific nature of the collective farmers' position, stimulate their activity, and steadily raise the cultural level of the villages.

A highly characteristic feature of the socio-class structure under socialism is that all members of society are interested in eliminating the vestiges of class distinctions or, to put it differently, they have no interest whatever in preserving class distinction. A humanist idea can become a reality, however, only if it flows from the objective processes of economic development. The elimination of class distinctions is an objective process developing under the influence of the growth of the productive forces. As the production processes are mechanised and automated and material and spiritual goods become more abundant, society will not only acquire the material capacity to eliminate the remaining social distinctions, it will have to do so out of necessity, because highly developed production demands a generally high level of education and culture and, therefore, complete equality of all members of society in work, distribution and everyday life.

At present the problem of raising the productive forces in the rural areas, the mechanisation of farm labour and its conversion into a form of industrial work is of primary significance in getting rid of class distinctions. It is on this basis that, as the technical equipment of all branches of agriculture approaches that of industry and the cultural and technical level of all rural workers rises, collective farm and co-operative property will become more socialised and more like state property and a unified nationwide communist form of property will emerge.

As for the distinctions between factory and office workers, the CPSU Programme sets the task of combining manual and mental work in production activity. It is assumed that in the course of time the intellectuals will cease to be a special social stratum and the workers will rise to the level of people engaged in mental work through improvement of their cultural and technical standards[1].

The unification of mental and manual work has to be tackled from two angles: by creating the material and technical base of communism and by developing public education in every possible way. The creation of the material and technical base of communism will sweep away the vestiges of

---

[1] In 1939, 82 workers out of 1,000 of the population had a higher, secondary or incomplete secondary education, in 1959, the figure had risen to 386, and in 1967, to 500. The equivalent figures for collective farmers were 18, 226 and 330 respectively (*Land of Soviets, 50 Years,* Moscow, 1967, p. 277, in Russian).

the old division of labour, abolish heavy physical toil and make work in general easier and more attractive.

Thus, the process of erasing class distinctions embraces all spheres of social life, economic, socio-political, and spiritual, and takes place in the sphere of real, objective relationships between people and is definitely reflected in the social and individual consciousness.

The integration of the interests of social groups has had the effect of creating new conditions in which social interests are becoming the interests of every member of society. In conditions when the fundamental interests of social groups are common and coincide with the interests of society, the individual finds that the general interests have become part of his own interests.

The common fundamental economic and political interests and goals of social groups make for fraternal mutual assistance and friendship between all nations and nationalities and bring them together ideologically, politically and culturally. The development of industry and agriculture has stimulated intensive economic intercourse between the Soviet constituent republics, the strengthening of ties and interdependency between them. The general connections a republic has with the Union as a whole are often more important nowadays for that republic than its own internal connections. Construction, the exploitation of mineral resources, the development of transport make for greater mobility of population between the republics. The economy today is an organic whole to which each republic makes its contribution. At the same time every nation, its economy and culture, enjoys all-round development in the conditions of socialism. Soviet people of different nations, besides making great strides in education and culture, which is national in form and socialist in content, have many common psychological and spiritual characteristics, generated by the new type of social relations and embodying the best traditions of the USSR—patriotism and internationalism, labour and political activity, collectivism and comradeship, and so on. For all nationalities of the USSR the Russian language has become a means of communication giving every nation, large or small, the opportunity of enjoying the cultural achievements of all the nations of the USSR and of world culture.

Thus, as a result of the transformation of the socio-class structure and the development of national relations in the USSR a new historical community has taken shape—the Soviet people.

The socio-political and ideological unity of society under socialism gives rise to an important circumstance affecting the formation of personality: here there is conformity between the goals proclaimed by society and the norms of behaviour sanctioned by society. While in the conditions of bourgeois society, between the goals officially approved by the bourgeois ideology and the actual norms of behaviour there is a sharp conflict which leads to the destruction of the personality.

3. MAN IN THE SYSTEM OF SOCIALIST DEMOCRACY

Socialism, having fundamentally changed the system of state power, has placed the individual in a completely new position in the system of political organisation of society; the content of the institutions of democracy and their impact on the individual have changed, and members of society now take a different attitude to state power.

The basic question on which social relations in the political sphere turn is the question of power, of to whom or to what class state power belongs, in whose interests the state laws are created and carried out.

"*L'état—c'est moi!*"—"I am the state!" was the dictum of Louis XIV.

"The executive of the modern state is but a committee for managing the common affairs of the whole bourgeoisie,"[1] is how Marx and Engels define the essence of the bourgeois state in *The Communist Manifesto*.

"We are the state!" say Soviet people today.

These aphoristic definitions vividly reflect the tremendous path of political development that society has travelled in 500 years, from the power of the feudal aristocracy to the socialist state of the whole people. In the first years of Soviet power Lenin noted that social property and the power of the people have provided the working people with "great-

---

[1] K. Marx and F. Engels, *Selected Works*, Vol. 1, pp. 110-11.

er practical opportunities for enjoying democratic rights and liberties than ever existed before, even approximately, in the best and most democratic bourgeois republics".[1]

The aim of the activity of state power under socialism is to serve the interests of the working people, because the existing class structure rules out protection of the advantages of any one class or group.

In accordance with the changes that have taken place in the class structure of society, and reflecting these changes, the dictatorship of the proletariat in the USSR has become a political organisation of the whole people. The essence of these changes lies in the extension of the social base of the socialist state, in the extension of socialist democracy: democracy for the majority, for the working people has become democracy for the whole people, for all working people. The Soviet state of the whole people is a socialist state of the working class, collective farm peasantry and working intelligentsia, where the leading role belongs to the working class.

The centre of gravity in state activity now falls on the organisation of production, distribution of the social income, implementation of the tasks of cultural and educational work, maintenance of public order and defence of the country from external dangers. All this is carried out on the basis of science, of studying and taking into consideration the whole diversity of interests of the classes, nationalities, working collectives and individual members of society.

It is an undeniable advantage of socialist democracy that the organs of power play such a role.

The 24th Congress of the CPSU, while noting the greater all-round activity of the Soviets of Working People's Deputies, set these Soviets the task of realising their functions more fully, exerting effective influence on the development of the economy and culture, in raising living standards, and of taking up matters concerning the provision of public facilities and maintenance of public order.

The existence of real—economic and political—guarantees of citizens' rights and freedoms is a vital distinctive feature of socialist democracy.

---

[1] V. I. Lenin, *Collected Works*, Vol. 28, p. 465.

The socialist planned economy and the people's government guarantee for all members of society the right to work and leisure, education, medical care and social security. Needless to say, the satisfaction of material requirements depends on the level of the productive forces, the amount of wealth at the disposal of society, but the socialist method of satisfying these requirements has a deeply democratic character. Full employment, education for all, the health service and social insurance create conditions for a profoundly humane solution to the vital problems of human life. Equality of all races and nationalities, equal rights for men and women in all spheres of state, economic and cultural life are also guaranteed in practice. This system creates the essential conditions for developing the abilities and talents of the broad masses of the working people, for promoting in the interests of society people with the most outstanding abilities and, on the other hand, it helps to endow the personality with such qualities as dignity, independence, assurance and optimism.

This foundation of socio-economic rights provides the basis for the system of political rights and freedoms of the individual—freedom of speech, the press, meetings and assemblies, the right to elect and be elected to the bodies of state power. Moreover, it must be particularly stressed that it is this unity of fundamental interests and aims, of common moral principles that is the main and essential guarantee of personal rights and freedoms. Only when people are equal in the main things, when they are united by common aims, are they able to express their will freely and realise their right to participate in the running of public affairs. Man is really free if he knows nothing of the humiliating dependence on a "boss" who dominates him by the right of private property. What matters under socialism is not property, class, religious or national differences, but the talents and abilities, the diverse activities of individuals and collectives, work for the common good.

In these conditions all the activity of the individual, aimed at the good of society, at strengthening and developing socialism, at protecting civic rights, is supported by the Party and the state and proceeds in conditions of complete freedom. During sessions of the Soviets of all levels, at meet-

ings and conferences and in the press the working people
widely discuss questions of economic, cultural and political
life and fight various departures from the norms of Soviet
morality and legality. Broad discussion of various points of
view and opinions, criticism and self-criticism, election of
government bodies and their accountability, conscious discipline and a high sense of social responsibility on the part
of every worker—all these are essential attributes of socialist democracy.

The political rights and freedoms of citizens not only
present opportunities for practical participation in public
affairs. They also develop specific administrative skills: understanding of the complexity of the tasks confronting us,
the ways of solving them effectively, a critical approach to
the results achieved, and so on. In this context rights acquire
the qualities of social duty: the right to take part in the
management of public affairs, for instance, is regarded as a
definite obligation.

*An important specific feature of socialist democracy is that
personal rights and freedoms may not be used against the
interests of the people.*

The Constitution of the USSR (Article 125) states that
freedom of speech, the press, assembly and meeting, street
processions and demonstrations of citizens of the USSR is
guaranteed by law in accordance with the interests of the
working people and with the aim of strengthening the socialist system. This principle of freedom is aimed not only
against any attempts to violate the public interests by individual citizens but also ensures protection of the rights and
freedoms of members of socialist society from the hostile, subversive activities of the imperialist camp.

The Communist Party and the Soviet state have set themselves the complex and responsible task of educating in Soviet people high ideological qualities, noble moral principles
and the thirst for varied knowledge. Hence the desire to
protect the rising generations from the corrupting influence
of bourgeois ideas is entirely natural.

The key to understanding the ideological, theoretical and
political struggle around the problems of democracy is Lenin's proposition on the opposition between socialist and
bourgeois democracy: "The Soviet system provides the max-

imum of democracy for the workers and peasants; at the same time, it marks a break with *bourgeois* democracy and the rise of a *new*, epoch-making *type* of democracy, namely, proletarian democracy, or the dictatorship of the proletariat."[1]

As early as 1918, Lenin foresaw that capitalism "will raise the standard of liberty against us".[2] And this is what has actually happened. The workers and peasants of Soviet Russia have abolished the freedom of private property and do not allow freedom to defend it. The Communists' position is that the working people have no desire whatever for the propagation in our country of bourgeois ideology expressing the interests of the deposed classes, that they do not want any return of private property (with the unemployment and rule of private bosses that it entails), any freedom to exploit, to carry on war propaganda, and so on. Guided by high ideals, Soviet society prohibits the "freedom" to spread antisocialist ideas, the propaganda of war and race hatred, because this is one of the essential conditions of protection of the freedom of socialist activity and socialist society.

At this point it is worth recalling Lenin's letter to G. Myasnikov of August 5, 1921 (after the victorious end of the Civil War, which is an important point to bear in mind). Myasnikov had proposed introducing "freedom of the press, from the monarchists to the anarchists, inclusively". Lenin put the question as follows: *What sort* of freedom of the press? What *for*? For *which class*? "We do not believe in 'absolutes'. We laugh at 'pure democracy'," Lenin wrote. "No country in the world has done as much to liberate the masses from the influence of the *priests* and *landowners* as the RSFSR has done and is doing."[3] Going on to analyse what freedom of the bourgeois press would mean, he points out that it means freedom of political organisation for the bourgeoisie and its most loyal servants, the Mensheviks and Socialist-Revolutionaries, and would help the force of the world bourgeoisie.

This is now an episode from history. But Lenin's approach to the question holds good even today.

---

[1] V. I. Lenin, *Collected Works*, Vol. 33, p. 54.

[2] Ibid., Vol. 29, p. 352.

[3] Ibid., Vol. 32, pp. 504-06.

*Another fundamental specific feature of socialist demo-
cracy is that state and public affairs are administered by the
working people themselves.*
The experience of the Soviet and other socialist states has
forever shattered the bourgeois propaganda myth that the
masses of the people are incapable of making a constructive
contribution to administration. From the Supreme Soviet to
the village Soviets the people are represented by those who
make steel and build machines, weave cloth and grow grain,
make scientific discoveries and bring up children, the people
by whose work material wealth and spiritual values are
created. In the present Supreme Soviet of the USSR out of
1,517 deputies 481 are workers and 282 are collective farmers, which accounts for more than 50 per cent of the whole
Soviet.

Participation of the working people in the management of
production is an inseparable part of socialist democracy.
Here the main role is played by the trade unions. The "Resolution on Socialist State Production Enterprises" states that
the management of an enterprise together with the factory
or local trade union committee shall draw up rules for internal working of the enterprise in accordance with model
rules for the industry or organisation as a whole; shall pass
the estimate for the use of enterprise funds, award bonuses
and subsidise out of these funds, and shall distribute apart-
ments in houses belonging to or provided for the enterprise.

The management of the enterprise is bound to report at
meetings of the factory or local trade union committee on
draft plans, on the results of production and economic activity, on the fulfilment of plans and obligations undertaken in
the collective contract between management and staff, on
measures to improve organisation and working conditions
and the material, general and cultural amenities enjoyed by
all members of the staff, and on elimination of defects in
the work of the enterprise.

Conferences of the enterprise staff discuss the management's reports on draft production plans, plan fulfilment reports, drafts of the collective agreements and their fulfilment, questions concerning production, living and cultural
services for the staff and the use of the enterprise funds. The

management also reports back on the fulfilment of decisions taken at previous meetings.

The trade unions take part in drawing up production plans, plans for the construction and repair of housing, cultural and other facilities, and also plans for the social development of collectives. The material-incentives fund and the fund for social and cultural measures and housing construction are distributed in close co-operation with the trade union committees. Trade union committees arrange production meetings and in co-operation with the management organise socialist competition and the movement for a communist attitude to work; they check up to make sure that inventions and rationalisation proposals that have been accepted are actually put into practice in good time; take part in fixing wage rates, work quotas and organisation of wage payment; decide whether overtime may be worked; organise state insurance of all members of the staff; and together with the management distribute housing accommodation, and so on.

The trade unions file proposals with superior economic and Soviet organisations on matters concerning the improvement of the work of the enterprise, institution or organisation that they represent. If necessary, the trade union organisations can appeal to the appropriate organisations for the dismissal and punishment of managers or other administrative personnel who do not carry out their obligations under the collective agreement, who act bureaucratically, violate labour legislation, and so on. The management must take into consideration the opinion of the trade union organisation when making appointments and promotions.

Both administrators and trade union officials are guided by the public interest—to raise the labour productivity and improve the material and cultural level of the working people. But in seeking to achieve this common aim, the manager and the trade union official may disagree as to the best way of dealing with a current problem or as to what tasks should be given priority, which department or workshop, which workers deserve encouragement or incentives and in what form. The main thing, however, is and always has been protection of the interests of the working people in production. Lenin said that "the trade unions no longer have to face the *class* economic struggle but the non-class 'economic

struggle', which means combating bureaucratic distortions of
the Soviet apparatus, safeguarding the working people's material and spiritual interests in ways and means inaccessible
to this apparatus, etc."[1]

*The organisational principle of socialist democracy is de-
mocratic centralism.*

As a principle of the structure of the organs of state administration democratic centralism could emerge only under
socialism, because a democratic, centralised, planned government presupposes public ownership of the means of production. On the other hand, socialism and communism can
be built only if millions of the people are taking part in it.
Democratic centralism is in line with the collectivism, the
democratic, humanistic nature of the socialist social system
as it draws the great mass of rank-and-file workers into
conscious social activity concerned with the management of
production and culture.

Consistent realisation of the demands of democratic centralism—subordination and accountability of lower bodies
to higher bodies, subordination of the minority to the majority, election of government bodies from top to bottom, collective leadership, strict discipline, etc.—offers broad opportunities for initiative to all administrative bodies and individual workers and at the same time makes it possible to
educate the individual in a spirit of strict discipline and responsibility.

*The Communist Party's leadership of society is an essen-
tial feature of socialist democracy.*

Government by the people cannot be a spontaneous expression of the will of various groups or separate individuals; all that comes of such a system is anarchy and arbitrariness, and this inevitably leads to restriction and destruction of the rights and freedoms of the members of society.
Only the Communist Party, armed with advanced social
theory, can perform the task of scientifically determining the
essential interests of society as a whole and its separate
social groups.

By its determined struggle for the interests of the working
people, its successful leadership of the work of building so-

---

[1] V. I. Lenin, *Collected Works,* Vol. 32, p. 100.

cialism, by the personal courage and heroism of its members the CPSU has deserved and won the people's acknowledgement, the respect and admiration of its friends, and the fear and hatred of its enemies. But it is not only a matter of the Party's historic services.

What really matters is the fact that the Party, by uniting in its ranks the best representatives of the working class, the peasantry and the intelligentsia, is the political guiding force that works out the scientifically based political line. By making a profound study of the vital processes the Party maps out the home and foreign policy of the Soviet state, elaborates the main directions of the development of the economy, science and culture, of ideology, and all forms of education, issues directives to the organs of state, which then turn these directives into detailed plans covering the activity of all state and economic organisations. The Party guides the trade unions, the Komsomol (Young Communist League) and other public organisations.

The Party sends its best people to decisive sectors of state and public activity and thus ensures that its policy is carried out unswervingly. It demands moreover that its members should be present on the toughest sectors of the struggle for communism—in factory workshops, in the mines, on the construction sites, in the sheds and fields of the collective and state farms. Since the Great October Socialist Revolution tens and hundreds of thousands of workers and peasants have come forward to take an active part in state and social activity. Outstanding statesmen, Party leaders, organisers of socialist production, scientists, engineers, technicians, cultural workers have emerged from the ranks of the working class, the peasantry and the working intelligentsia. The Party exercises constant control over the fulfilment of its instructions and takes stern measures in cases of inattention to the needs of the working people and any violation of Party discipline.

The 24th Party Congress has stressed that the strength of the CPSU lies in its keen sense of ideology, in the activeness and devotion of its members, that the Party will not tolerate passivity, indifference and apathy towards politics. Uniting Soviet society ideologically, organising the people for the successful performance of the tasks of communist construction, the Party acts as the people's political leader, as the ideological and moral model for the formation of the personality of the working man. Successful advance of socialist society along the road to communism is inconceivable without such a political force.

4. CHARACTER OF EDUCATIONAL INFLUENCE

The new economic, social and political relationships objectively determine the formation of a socialist tendency in the individual, his active participation in social production and public and political life. But a socialist personality cannot be moulded without educational work, without the purposeful influence of the Communist Party, the Soviet state and the public organisations, the family, the school and the work collective.

Basic Directions of Education and Methodological Principles of the Educational Process

The general and the particular in people's economic, social and political position finds its expression in the social consciousness under socialism, and this, in its turn, conditions the character of society's educational efforts. The characteristic feature of the social consciousness under socialism is that the majority of the people accept the ideas of the communist theory as their own—inevitability of the social transition from capitalism to socialism, and then to communism, the need for public ownership of the means of production, the obligation to work, distribution in accordance with the quantity and quality of work done, planned development of the economy, social and state structure, collectivism, patriotism and internationalism, and so on. Science, planning, basically similar principles and norms for all groups and strata of the population, class irreconcilability towards bourgeois ideology are the characteristic requirements for the development of the socialist consciousness.

Socialist consciousness is also communist consciousness in the sense that socialism is the first phase of communism. Socialist consciousness reflects the content of socialist life and registers the principle inherent in socialism: distribution according to work done, personal material interest, absence of full economic equality, and so on.

Just as socialist social relations cannot be identified entirely with all the relations existing in socialist society, so one cannot identify the socialist consciousness entirely with all the social consciousness existing under socialism. Under socialism there may be facts of anti-social, anti-socialist conduct testifying to the existence of non-socialist motives in people's minds, that is to say, survivals of the past. These include the urge to make money through embezzlement, profiteering, bribery, and so on, or blatant infringement of the rules and norms of socialist community life—hooliganism, indifference to another person's troubles, avoidance of socially useful work, and the like. It also includes opinions and beliefs incompatible with the principles of socialism, with the Marxist-Leninist ideology. Naturally, when we try to appraise these phenomena we must take an ideological-political, class approach to them. There still exists the religious consciousness, which is in conflict with the scientific view of the world.

The reasons why such phenomena persist in people's consciousness are that consciousness lags behind actual existence, that the economy and everyday life themselves still retain vestiges of the past, and also the influence of the capitalist world, and drawbacks in applying socialist principles. But education can play a great part in overcoming them. The point is that quite often under generally similar economic and living conditions different individuals behave differently. It is here that the orientation, the general precepts implanted in a person in the process of his education and upbringing make themselves felt. Thanks to effectively organised educational work the Party and the state have succeeded in elevating to an active conscious life millions of people whose conditions of life were extremely different and in many cases did not have the benefit of socialist reform in the early stages.

Leonid Brezhnev's report to the 24th Congress of the CPSU stressed the particular significance of educational work. "The moral and political make-up of Soviet people is moulded by the entire socialist way of our life, by the entire course of affairs in society and, above all, by purposeful, persevering ideological and educational work by the Party, by all its organisations."[1]

The Soviet Union has a system of education and upbringing and is constantly improving that system. School and out-of-school education are permeated with common aims and tasks and based on scientific methods of educational work. The system is on the whole effective in coping with the tasks of general, polytechnical and professional education and giving the rising generations a scientific world outlook, communist moral principles, a communist attitude to work and public property, and their aesthetic and physical education.

The Soviet experience and the experience of other socialist countries, having shown the possibility of producing on a mass scale individuals with a keen desire and ability to take part in social life, have at the same time revealed the full complexity of the problems confronting socialism in this sphere, the persistence of anti-socialist behaviour of various kinds. This has given the Marxists-Leninists a more sober, more realistic view of the difficulties connected with the achievement of ideals. What is more important, however, is that this experience has yielded a great variety of methods that may be adopted in the educational process and has brought to light some important methodological principles for organising it that are of general significance. These principles have been worked out by Marxist-Leninist science and are being practically applied in socialist societies.

The aim of the Communist Party and the Soviet state in their work of educating the working people is *to combine a high ideological level with professional skill and high moral qualities*. This is the first basic principle of education.

The education of a comprehensively developed personality is the communist ideal. This ideal can be achieved only gradually, as the necessary conditions, most of them material, are created. But ever since the early years of Soviet power large funds have been allotted to political education, to general and professional education, to inculcating a high sense of responsibility and organisation among all builders of the new life.

---

[1] *24th Congress of the Communist Party of the Soviet Union*, p. 100.

The same aim is pursued by the development of social autonomy, beginning with self-government in the schools. It is
here that we have found solutions to the problems of improving the management of society and also developing the
abilities of the working people.

The next principle is *the necessity for the whole population, all social groups, every member of society to come under
a unified educational influence.*

The realisation of this educational principle has been promoted on a broad scale by the general alignment of people's
fundamental interests. This is what has made possible the
general unanimity of mood and emotional response that we
observe in connection with events of state importance. Such
major historic achievements as the defence of revolutionary
gains in the Civil War, the overcoming of the dislocation
caused by that war, successful industrialisation and collectivisation, defeat of Hitler Germany in the Great Patriotic
War, the cultivation of the virgin lands, welded the people
together in a single whole and made the general goals those
of the individual as well. This was also true of less significant events—the Curzon ultimatum, the conflicts on the
Chinese Eastern Railway, the defeat of the Japanese militar-
ists on Lake Hasan, the saving of the Chelyuskin polar explorers, the flights to the North Pole, the space flights, etc.,
have always been treated as events of nation-wide importance.

The activity of the masses is directly dependent on the
scale and significance of the aims or, as Marx put it, great
energy is generated only for a great aim. This general law
comes out even more clearly in the period of the building
of the new society. Lenin said that "only the millions can
build this society. In the era of serfdom these builders numbered hundreds; in the capitalist era the builders of the state
numbered thousands and tens of thousands. The socialist revolution can be made only with the active and direct practical participation of tens of millions in state administration".[1]

The building of communism involves a great number of
highly complex socio-economic, organisational and technical problems. This requires tremendous social energy. Such

[1] V. I. Lenin, *Collected Works*, Vol. 28, p. 426.

energy can be generated only by uniting the efforts of the whole population. Another side of the same question lies in the fact that to make the principles and norms of the new society work there will have to be a high level of education, culture and morality.

Yet another methodological principle of socialist education lies in *the planned organisation of the whole educational process*. This stems from the planned character of social life under socialism and corresponds to the scientific approach to the question of the tasks and aims of communist education.

The Soviet sociologist Z. I. Fainburg has expressed the view that in antagonistic socio-economic formations and under socialism there can be only directed socialisation of the personality, while planned socialisation of the personality will be possible only in communist society. This view probably does not go to the heart of the matter. And not only because it unites socialism with antagonistic formations, which in itself evokes surprise, but also because, and mainly because, under socialism there is in fact considerable planning of the educational process. It consists in projecting the basic qualities of the personality, which emerge as the aim of educational work; then in the planned realisation of a whole complex of educational measures in educational establishments, work collectives, in villages, towns, districts, regions and country as a whole. And although there are many problems and shortcomings of all kinds, the fact remains that the educational process takes place according to plan. One could speak of a significant difference in the level of planning under socialism and what we may expect to achieve under communism, but to place socialism on the same footing in this respect as the antagonistic formations is to argue against the facts.

The system of perspective goals evolved by the Soviet educationalist A. S. Makarenko is of particular interest in this connection. It may be briefly summed up as follows: educating a person means educating his perspective. "A person who is guided in his actions by the nearest perspective is the weakest person. If he is satisfied only by his own perspective, even a long-term one, he may appear strong but he evokes no sense of a noble personality and its real value. The wider the collective whose perspectives are a person's personal perspectives, the more noble and elevated is that person."[1]

It is by combining the short-term, medium and long-term perspective in the life of the collective, by relating people's everyday activity to the significant events of the collective and the country as a whole that one reaches the "interesting line, from the simplest, primitive satisfaction to the most profound sense of duty".[2]

The essence of such relating is to unite people's practical everyday activity with an understanding of its place and significance in the life of the collective, the city, the country, to unite essential interests with ideals. It may be asserted that this idea is widely applied in the practice of educational work, although not everywhere with sufficient skill and consistency.

An important step forward in this respect is the practice of drawing up plans of social development of production collectives, which was approved by the 24th Party Congress. Social development plans are an attempt to combine the general aims of our movement towards communism with current practical tasks that face collectives in their daily life.

Besides trying to provide all people with certain general qualities, educational efforts are aimed at *developing a person's individuality*. This principle is based on the general sociological law of the formation of personality, which consists in the unity of the intercourse and isolation of the human individual. While seeing the key to the moulding of the personality in the solution of the general problems of transforming the social environment, Marxists-Leninists at the same time view the development of collectivity and individuality in their dialectical unity: the more original and individual the personality the more profoundly does it express the social nature of society, the dialectic of social relations, because this uniqueness expresses, on the one hand, the depth of the individual's abilities and, on the other, his assimilation of the features of society.

The educational process can be successful only if it is

---

[1] A. S. Makarenko, *Works*, Vol. V, Moscow, 1957, p. 74 (in Russian).
[2] Ibid.

guided by respect for the autonomy of the individual, for a man's personal life. This is not a matter of the bourgeois cult of individualism, of counterposing the individual to the social, but of wisely restricting outside interference in the delicate sides of personal life. The readiness of a person to engage in active social life depends also on the observation of a certain boundary between the personal and social spheres.

Another principle of education that needs to be pointed out is the necessity for *constant occupation of a person's attention, his involvement in changing emotions.*

Keeping a person occupied is often understood merely as providing him with work. In reality the problem is much wider. It is both a psychological and social problem. Man is by nature an active being. Consequently, idleness, lack of occupation, of stuff for the mind to chew on, not only leads to the destruction of the personality, but also harms society. Just as there is no such thing as an ideological or moral vacuum, there is also no such thing as an emotional vacuum. The absence of emotional experience inflicts irreparable damage on the personality. Hence the need to bring a person into the system of social activity.

What is more, in order to function normally the mind demands changes of condition, changes of occupation. The planning of social undertakings and regulation of information, the alternation of negative and positive emotions are essential conditions for effective educational work. The success of the educator, particularly in difficult cases, is more likely to be assured when he is able to work indirectly towards his aim, not by means of didactic methods, but by creating a general atmosphere of enthusiasm, interest and active participation, which later become effective allies of the educator.

Formation of the Personality at Home and at School

In early life family and school play a decisive role in forming the personality. It is here that a person experiences the first effects of education, first enters the sphere of realisation of the essential potentialities of his personality.

The family is a social unit embracing man and wife and

their progeny. As such it has been and remains the source from which a person receives his first elementary knowledge about the surrounding world, habits and notions of behaviour.

Relationships within the family always bear the stamp of the socio-economic and political conditions in which the family exists. Where private property rules, the family is dominated by the despotic power of the husband and father and there is inequality between man and woman. In some capitalist countries women to this day are discriminated against, restricted in their political rights, receive less pay than a man for doing the same work as he does, and so on.

Naturally, the abolition of bourgeois property and the other changes brought about by socialism have had a corresponding effect on the family as a community, and on the relationships between man and wife, and between parents and children. The paramount feature of the Soviet family is equality of the sexes. Socialism has given women wide access to professional and social activity on equal terms with men. This has made them economically and legally independent of their husbands, with the result that mutual love, respect and help are becoming the decisive family ties.

The characteristic features of the Soviet family is devotion to the interests of society, and this creates the moral atmosphere that correspondingly moulds the character of the children. Since the family is a union of equals, the relationships between parents and children are based on comradeship and friendship of young and old, and this is helped along by the fact that the question of education, the question of providing work and qualifications for work is largely taken care of by society.

There is, undoubtedly, an art in family upbringing. Not everyone has equal mastery of this art. But although the way a child's character is formed in the family does depend on parental tact, it is, nevertheless, decisively influenced by the whole family structure, the example of the parents' work and behaviour. In other words, upbringing is the result of a whole set of circumstances and not merely of teaching or even mainly of teaching. If words and actions are at odds in the family there is bound to be a conflict either between the children and parents (when the children protest against

the parents' hypocrisy), or between children and society (when the children grow up in the image of their
parents).

The formation of the new family is a complex process.
The family absorbs not only progressive but also obsolete
traditions, and although a family based on love and mutual
respect is incomparably higher than one that is based on an
economic bargain, the creation of this new family makes far
greater demands on people in terms of kindness, respect,
responsibility and patience. As a cell of the social organism,
the family reflects all aspects of society, including "vestigial"
phenomena. It is the family of a certain kind that is to
blame for the fact that new bearers of a selfish morality
enter society and, vice versa, a family reflecting the new
social and moral structure as a rule succeeds in bringing up
good citizens of socialist society.

The further development of the Soviet family will give
women complete equality of rights with men by actually
drawing them into social and production activity, and
by reforming living conditions. Lenin wrote of woman that
"to effect her complete emancipation and make her the equal
of the man it is necessary for the national economy to be
socialised and for women to participate in common productive labour."[1]

It is a fact that, although in Soviet society women are
equal with men both politically and socially, there are still
some traces of inequality. For example, it is the woman who
bears the main burden of the housework, since the family
is still to a certain extent an economic unit. The Communist
Party has set the aim of completely eliminating the traces
of women's inequality in everyday life, of creating all
the social conditions for combining a happy motherhood
with increasingly active and creative participation of
women in production and social activity, in science and
art.

As we have said, a person's first notion of socialist community life, of communist morality, of good and evil, of
respect for one's fellow human beings as well as first working habits are acquired mainly in the family. The school is

[1] V. I. Lenin, *Collected Works*, Vol. 30, p. 43.

the next step in moulding the personality and arena for its manifestations. Ever since Soviet power was established the Party has paid close attention to the schools. The Party Programme passed by the 8th Party Congress set the task of "completing that which began with the October Revolution of 1917, the work of transforming the schools from an instrument of class domination of the bourgeoisie into an instrument of complete abolition of the division of society into classes, into an instrument for the communist regeneration of society". It was the schools which to a great extent moulded the generations that built and defended socialism. The new school played an important part in combating the old influence of the petty-bourgeois, middle-class families and was on the whole victorious.

Soviet public education is based on a unified state system of schools and other educational establishments, and their complete separation from the church; universal secondary and generally accessible higher education; unity and continuity between all links in the system of public education; complete equality of social groups, nations and nationalities at all stages of education; complete equality of the sexes; indissoluble ties between the schools and the life of the people, the practice of socialist and communist construction and the activity of public organisations.

The Soviet system of education and upbringing has in practice introduced millions of children of workers and peasants to learning, so that society's intellectual potential is constantly being swelled with fresh forces from the people and the personality of the working man has acquired real possibilities for the application of its talents and abilities. Moreover, compulsory education gives all school life a democratic character. The Soviet school is not a private boarding school, not a caste institution, but an organic part of society, a reflection of its structure. The schools, both secondary and higher, have played a decisive role in preparing the specialists who have provided the technical leadership for building the material and technical base of socialism.

The main factor in the successful education of active builders of the new society is the process of instruction, in the course of which pupils not only receive knowledge but are also given a dialectical materialist interpretation of phenomena and processes and shown the inevitability of the transition of society from capitalism to socialism, the beauty and justice of the ideas of communism. The combination of study with production work at school also helps to mould ideological convictions. The Young Pioneer and Komsomol organisations also play a big part in this respect. They accustom children to the life of the collective, instil habits of social work, teach them to understand their social duty and foster a sense of comradeship.

Thus, both the Soviet school and the new family, though they are very different kinds of institution, deal with the task of educating the new man.

The whole system of general and political education is permeated with the ideas of kindness and humanity, the ideas of developing the best in man: his creative abilities in work, his belief in the truth of the communist ideals, his determination to defend them, his loyalty, and so on. All culture and education are here subordinated to fostering in the growing generation the noble qualities of communist devotion to principle, humanity, and steadfastness in defending one's beliefs.

Our ideological opponents like to find a contradiction between the growth of culture among the population and adherence to the communist principle. However, they ignore the organic relation between communism and culture, the special attraction that communist ideas have for cultured and educated people. Indeed, if the Communists urge society to get rid of its parasitic elements, to place its wealth at the disposal of all its members, to employ this wealth for the development of the talents of the working people, if they seek to turn work into a great public cause, if they set the goal of establishing world peace and friendship between the peoples, then why, one asks, should these humanist ideas be repellent to people of culture and education? In the conditions of a social system in which a person's work is the only source of his well-being, and criterion of his social status, the growth of education and culture is an essential factor in the development and consolidation of the communist consciousness.

Development of Personality in the Work Collective

Whereas upbringing in the family and at school gives the personality its general orientation, its ethos, and in this sense plays a decisive role in moulding character, the work collective provides the basic sphere for the application of its abilities, the realisation of its requirements and interests and, consequently, continues to exercise a definite influence on behaviour.

"Education in the collective, through the collective and for the collective," was the slogan formulated by A. S. Makarenko. It expresses one of the essential aspects of the socialist way of life.

Characterising the role of the collective, Maxim Gorky wrote: ". . . The collective creates a person of a completely different individual mentality, more active, more steadfast, and drawing the will to act, the will to build life from the will of the collective."[1]

In society we find people assembled in various ways, in groups, associations and collectives, all of which exert a formative influence on the individual. There are both genetic and functional differences between these communities, although they have some features in common. In Soviet sociology a class, nation or family is usually accounted a social group, while political parties, trade unions, co-operatives, cultural, technical and scientific societies are regarded as associations. As for the work collective, this concept covers the collectives at industrial, transport and building enterprises, and also enterprises providing communications, trade and public services, administrative and scientific institutions, cultural and health institutions (basic collectives), and also workshops, work teams, etc. (primary collectives).

Consequently, the personality-class relationship is not to be equated with the personality-collective relationship. A person does not belong to a collective from birth. He has various opportunities (in various social conditions) for choosing his occupation and, hence, the collective in which he works; he may also transfer from one collective to another. A collective is distinguished from an association by

---

[1] Maxim Gorky, *Collected Works*, Vol. 17, p. 193 (in Russian).

the fact that its formation is directly determined by the needs of production, and work is the basis of the development and functioning of such a collective. Common tasks and close contacts in work together are the obvious attributes of a work collective.

But while it differs from the group and the association, the work collective depends entirely on them in its character. In other words, the character of the relationships within the collective depends on the development of collectivism as a principle of social relations, and these are determined by the form of ownership of the means of production that dominates society. Marx and Engels called the associations and collectives in exploitative society "illusory community" and "substitutes for the community"[1].

The whole history of capitalist society and the modern bourgeois world is the development of antagonistic contradictions between workers and capitalists, and intense competition between the owners of the means of production.

Competition penetrates even the ranks of the working class, although it is opposed by strong tendencies towards unity. The stimulus here is work together, common interests, revolutionary struggle. "The advance of industry... replaces the isolation of the labourers, due to competition, by their revolutionary combination, due to association."[2]

The socialist system makes collectivism the fundamental principle of social relations, and enhancement of the role of the collective in the formation of the socialist personality becomes one of the characteristic features of socialism in its progress towards communism.

First, the collective accustoms the individual in practice to socialist property and to work. It is here that a person acts directly as a co-owner of socialist property, the subject of the property, and as a worker, the subject of labour; it is here that he becomes the bearer of these most important functions of a member of society. A work collective under socialism is not merely a production unit performing its role in the social division of labour, it is also an ensemble of people linked together by a common status, common inter-

---

[1] K. Marx and F. Engels, *The German Ideology*, p. 91.
[2] K. Marx and F. Engels, *Selected Works*, Vol. 1, p. 119.

ests and aims, and a common duty to society. In other words, certain moral relationships which emerge as people's understanding of their social duty develop in the wake of socio-economic reforms and on the basis of these reforms.

This fundamentally distinguishes the relationships in the socialist work collective from the relationships that exist in the work collective under capitalism. The Soviet scientists, V. V. Boriskin and S. B. Slevich, made an interesting comparison between the lives of two such collectives in the Antarctic. They observed how human relationships took shape within these collectives. The constant feature of the life style of Soviet polar explorers is collectivism in discussion of all basic questions, plans and results of work. The spirit of mutual assistance, collective responsibility and socialist competition is clearly in evidence at Soviet arctic bases. "The Americans who observed the work of the Soviet polar explorers in most difficult conditions at the Vostok Station stated how surprised they were by the cheerfulness and good spirits of the Soviet people. They laughed, sang, joked, bawled encouragement at one another."[1]

At the American station elements of collectivism are also to be observed because people are disciplined by their sense of duty. But the setting up of the collective runs into difficulties rooted in the social environment from which this collective has come. People are divided by the same social antagonism that is inherent in life on the mainland, and that sooner or later shows itself within the polar collective.

With many examples Boriskin and Slevich show that the influence of production relations is "the most important cause of changes in the sphere of socio-psychological relationships. The result is that even quite small groups of people split up according to class, social estate, nation and are not free of the antagonism that springs from this soil."[2]

---

[1] V. V. Boriskin and S. B. Slevich, "Man in the Antarctic", *Priroda,* 1968, No. 12, p. 36 (in Russian).

[2] The Soviet polar explorer P. D. Astapenko, who spent a winter at the Little America V Base, writes in his book *Journey to the Back of Beyond:* "Everyone was working in one way or another but the striking thing was the absence of any uniting principle in the work of the whole collective of the station or even individual members of the crew.... It was not customary to decide or discuss anything collecti-

Second, work in a collective is the source of a person's
material well-being, the source of the development of his
abilities and requirements. The level of personal activity,
the formation and realisation of personal interests depends
largely on the work of the whole collective, the enterprise.
The coincidence of people's fundamental interests does
not rule out the possibility of divergence between general
and individual interests. Moreover, people must understand
the coincidence of social and personal interests if it is to be
realised in practice, in a person's behaviour. Therefore, collectivism in terms of actual relationships signifies that a
person should act with due consideration for the general
interests and rules of collectivism and not undertake actions
that could harm the collective as a whole. Collectivism also
presupposes that the collective should show equal care and
consideration for each one of its members.

Third, the work collective under socialism is a place not
only for production activity but also for socio-political and
cultural life. Of course, both political work and trade union
work are carried on at a private capitalist enterprise as well,
and this is quite natural, for where else would one expect
to find it but where there are masses of workers. But at a
capitalist enterprise the political and trade union work is
directed against the exploitative activity of the capitalist

---

vely.... Every crew member worked at his own risk and, only in case
of necessity, himself looked for somebody with whom to share   his
thoughts or ask advice. Such practice even in a collective of experienced
scientists is not always justified, and it was all the more unsuitable at a
station crewed mainly by young men who had only just started out in-
dependently as specialists" (*Priroda*, 1968, No. 12, pp. 36-37).

"The Japanese researcher I. Kitamura in a brochure published by
Kyoto University in 1963 gives an original picture of the development
of social relations at the Showa Antarctic base. He appraises human
relations during the first winter as 'relations of primitive communism'.
All the material values used by the base were 'public property'. When
the base had been in existence for three years the commune reached
the stage when it became necessary to introduce laws.... Prices were
fixed for everything we used. We also observed the practice of barter.
I. Kitamura calls this stage 'primitive capitalist society'. In later years
everything was regimented, even the roster for use of the bath. The
value of the things used grew. 'The author does not know,' Kitamura
writes, 'whether differences in individual well-being had increased, but
by the fifth year of its existence the group was a society governed by
law.'" (Ibid., p. 37).

and in defence of the rights of the working people and is, therefore, separated from production. In the case, when the capitalist by a system of measures seeks to reduce class conflict and win over the workers, all these measures motivate against the workers and, like other management methods, perform the function of exploiting hired labour.

In contrast to this situation, in the socialist work collective ideological, political and cultural life is closely connected with production activity, with the interests of the whole national economy, the whole country. Here manual work is practically combined with managerial work, with participation in cultural and political life. It is no accident that many foreign visitors to the USSR are astonished by the scope and intensity of Soviet people's cultural life.

Different approaches to the organisation of society determine different approaches to the problems of the collective and collectivism on the part of Marxists and their ideological opponents. Bourgeois sociologists who defend private property, naturally, concentrate their attention either on the organisational and technical or the psychological aspects of the relationships between the collective and the individual. In doing so they are unanimous in asserting that the collective is bound in some way to crush the individual, and that freedom of the individual is possible only to the extent that the individual's ties with the collective are weakened. Thus, it is argued that the basis of human solidarity is not unity of interests but mutual liking, and respect for the will of the group. According to Emile Durkheim, "a feeling of 'respect' for group dictates" is the essence of relations in the collective.[1]

The well-known American "sociometrist" J. L. Moreno holds similar views. He regards the feeling of mutual liking as the basis of the collective. The cause of all conflicts is disalignment of the two social structures: the microstructure (psychological relations between people) and the macrostructure (people's disposition in production, the family, etc.). Improvement of people's position according to their

---

[1] Emile Durkheim, *The Division of Labour in Society,* from *Modern Sociological Theory in Continuity and Change,* ed. by Howard Becker and Alvin Boskoff, New York, 1957, p. 22.

likings and inclinations is enough to dispose of contradictions.[1]

One can hardly deny the importance of mutual liking in the formation of a collective and selection of personnel for any particular post. This has always been done empirically in all social structures. It is hard to imagine a situation in which, with all qualification of two people being equal, preference would be given to the one who was antipathetic, unlikeable. The task, therefore, is to study the psychological structures of collectives and the qualities of their members systematically and by scientific methods along with their political and practical qualities.

However, no mere improvement of the organisational, technical and psychological structure of an enterprise can of itself, without the socialisation of private capitalist property, radically change the social microclimate and establish common interests between workers and employers. Evidence of this fact is to be found in the persistent strike movement of the working class in the capitalist countries in defence of their vital interests, including enterprises where the various "human relations" experts have applied themselves to "normalising" relations between the bosses and the men they hire.

Thus, although the work collective came into existence a long time ago, only under socialism, when work is obligatory for all members of society, does it become the essential connecting link between the individual and society. The socialist work collective is a group of people in direct contact with each other and performing a definite production task in the interests of society, bound together by a common goal, discipline, responsibility and unified management. The community of the fundamental interests, goals and tasks of society and the collective, the individual and the collective, society and the individual is the characteristic feature that makes the socialist work collective the focus not only of the production but also of the socio-political and spiritual life of the working people.

Karl Marx's words fully apply to the socialist work collective. "Only in community with others has each individual

---

[1] *Sociometry and the Science of Man,* ed. by J. L. Moreno, New York, 1956, pp. 248, 250, etc.

the means of cultivating his gifts in all directions; only in the community, therefore, is personal freedom possible."[1] Indeed, only the collective can create all the necessary conditions for training and educating a person, only the collective can give him moral support in moments of personal crisis.

The collective's demands upon its members, its inculcation of a sense of responsibility in each person play a tremendously important role. No specialised control agencies can replace the wealth of comradely, friendly influence that the collective can bring to bear. There is no greater power of influence on human behaviour than the power of the collective.

Performing the same educational tasks as society as a whole, the work collective has its own specific means of work and political education.

The educational function of the collective consists in the fact that it transmits to the individual some of the basic qualities inherent in our society, and also the specific features of the professions, the group psychology that have taken shape in the given collective as a result of its own history and specific situation. The collective is not only a producer. It is also an educator, or more precisely, it is as much an educator as it is the basic link in socialist production.

* * *

In the objective position of the individual, or rather, the position of all members of society under socialism there appear a number of common essential features, notably in the property and distribution relations, in the character of work, in the attitude to the state power, i.e., in those spheres of social life that decisively influence people's behaviour and personal qualities. In other words, socialism creates a new system of conditions and stimuli which shape certain social and spiritual needs, interests and goals that become motives of human behaviour.

Having thus fundamentally transformed social relations, socialism has in so doing changed not only the substance of

---

[1] K. Marx and F. Engels, *The German Ideology,* p. 91.

the influence exerted by the social environment on consciousness and behaviour, but also the mode in which this influence is exerted. Before socialism there was never a society in which all the social institutions—the family, the pre-school institutions, the school, the mass children's and youth organisations, the public, political, state and other organisations—purposefully influenced the consciousness of all members of society on the basis of general principles, norms and ideals reflecting their common interests. In short, the purposefulness, the broad scope and the intensity of social influence are essential features of the new element that socialism has introduced into the character of the interaction between the social environment and the individual.

For the first time in history it is not class, hierarchical, national, religious or any other group attributes that are of primary importance in people's social life, but the common social characteristics that belong to all social groups, all members of society. Besides particular typical groups it becomes possible for the general qualities of the integrated social type of personality to appear in the typological structure of society.

The social content of the changes that have taken place testifies to the movement of society along the path of humanisation, the humanising of conditions of life. Socialism has abolished exploitation of man by man and has set all material and spiritual wealth to serve the interests of the working man; work is becoming not only a means of livelihood but also service to society; human relations are characterised by social homogeneity, planning, collectivism and fraternal mutual assistance.

In other words, the historical transformation of society has been accompanied by intensive development of socialist, general Soviet features in the position of the individual.

Not only the content of the social experience that a person assimilates, but also the character of a person's activity in assimilating this experience, the system of interaction between the individual and society, have changed. Thanks to the planned development of the economy and the clarity of the ideological aims, social relations and processes are becoming intelligible to the members of society. What is more, the socialist organisation of social labour, the rules of socialist community life stimulate people to be active in the name of social interests, make the worker see in his work a social purpose and a means of becoming involved in social interests. The individual acquires far wider opportunities for active participation in social and public life than under capitalism, his personality tends to become more social and qualitatively new conditions and possibilities are created for each man to consciously shape his own essential being.

While regarding socialist society as a new environment of the personality, and also a new character of the interaction between society and the individual, we must not forget that the "birthmarks" of capitalism retain a distinct hold within the new system of relations and exert their influence, that the capitalist world, imperialist reaction, are making tremendous efforts to check the development of the new society. Moreover, the formation of the new society inevitably poses intricate problems and this entails mistakes, losses, and so on. But this in no way overshadows the fact that socialism is a major historical advance in forms of human community life, in the discovery of fresh possibilities for the development of man in general and the human personality in particular.

CHAPTER FOUR

SOVIET MAN AS A SOCIALIST TYPE
OF PERSONALITY

A person's image is the image of society. The formation of a new type of person is the natural result of the establishment of socialist social relations in our country, of the educational work of the Communist Party and the Soviet state. Summing up the fifty years of development of socialism in the USSR, the Central Committee of the Communist Party of the Soviet Union stated in the theses passed at the Central Committee Plenary Meeting in June 1967: "Economic and political transformations have entailed profound changes in social consciousness, with the result that the ideological unity of Soviet society was established. Marxist-Leninist ideology became a powerful motive force of social development, an important factor in rallying the Soviet people, and a source of their socio-political and labour activity. New generations have been brought up in a spirit of wholehearted loyalty to communist ideals, convinced of the justice of our great cause. The character of Soviet man was forged, the character of fighter, revolutionary and conscious working man."[1]

The characterisation of a social type always requires elucidation of its general features, its identification with a particular social group. But this elucidation should be of personal features and not of the environment, that is, of the characteristic features of consciousness and behaviour inherent in the given social type of personality, which in its

---

[1] *50th Anniversary of the Great October Socialist Revolution,* Moscow, 1967, p. 46.

own specific way embodies the features of a definite social group.

Since we are discussing an extremely broad formation of types on the scale of the entire society, we must obviously concern ourselves only with the main, fundamental peculiarities of the social content of the personality, with those features which give an adequate characterisation of the social type but at the same time do not exclude the immense diversity of the particular and the individual in people's consciousness and behaviour. If individual existence is the mode of existence of the general, the conditions and directions of the development of individuality, the nature of this individuality are an indispensable characteristic of the personality and, therefore, a component of the problem of the development of personality.

And finally, since we are discussing the new personality, it is clearly essential to find out what exactly distinguishes the features of this personality from the social types of previous history.

1. SOCIALIST ETHOS OF THE PERSONALITY

Ethos, as we stated in the first chapter, is the generalised indication which allows us to elucidate what is typical in personality, because it is here in the specific forms of the individual consciousness that what a person absorbs from his environment and what he realises in his activity is expressed. Characterising the basic qualities of the type means characterising the basic elements of tendency.

Socialist society as a complex of economic, social, political, cultural and ideological-moral conditions, by means of developing the forms of collective production, economic and moral stimulation of a socialist attitude to work, propaganda of the scientific Marxist-Leninist world view and communist moral principles and norms, and also by means of compulsion if necessary, inevitably conditions the activity and behaviour of its members in a socialist spirit and, consequently, the evolution on this basis of definite qualities of a socialist ethos, or orientation, of the personality. "The moulding of the new man," states the Programme of the CPSU, "is effected through his own active participation in communist construction and the development of communist principles in the economic and social spheres, under the influence of the educational work carried out by the Party, the state and various social organisations."[1]

Thus, the consciousness of separate individuals does not merely register the presence of principles and forms of organisation of socialist society, but accepts them as a right and just system. Knowledge becomes approval of the socialist principles and norms of social organisation, becomes ideological convictions that guide people's actions towards consolidation and development of socialist society.

Adherence to the Communist Principle, Priority of Social Interests

The first group of the features of the new personality is related to its attitude to society as a whole. The most essential characteristic of the worker's position in socialist production consists in the fact that the social interest acts objectively as the interest of all members of society. This is due to the fact that the product of the worker's labour, being social property, is a means of satisfying the needs of members of society and the development of their abilities. Historically social property arises after the setting up of the dictatorship of the proletariat, and its appearance, although conditioned by the development of the productive forces, is at the same time the realisation of socialist ideas. It is natural that the interest of society should be related in the working people's consciousness not only to social property but also to the socialist state and the ideology of communism in general.

The founders of scientific communism stated quite definitely that under communism social interest should become the interest of members of society. Communism is a society in which "the interest, good, happiness of each individual is indissolubly connected with the good of other people"[2], a society "in which community of interests is elevated as the basic principle, in which social interest is no longer distinguished from the interest of each individual person".[3]

---

[1] *The Road to Communism*, Moscow, pp. 563-64.
[2] K. Marx and F. Engels, *Works*, 2nd Russ. ed., Vol. 2, p. 535.
[3] Ibid., p. 538.

It may be asserted that socialism in principle already solves this problem, although needless to say non-antagonistic contradictions between society and the individual continue to exist. The basis of this solution is the community of fundamental interests of classes and social groups. But social, public interest, having become the general interest for all groups, is thereby the interest of each individual person, and acknowledgement that the social interest comes first is the main characteristic of the consciousness of the new personality.

Already today in socialist society everything that corresponds to the interests of society also serves the interests of the working people. Social property offers wide scope for the development of the productive forces and thus accelerates the all-round progress of society. The rapid growth of production creates material and spiritual conditions for the development of the members of society. Planned organisation of the economy rules out unemployment, ensures constantly increasing material well-being, gives people guaranteed prospects in life, makes the aims and problems of economic development intelligible to the working people and thus creates conditions for their conscious participation in production, in all social life. The socialist principle "From each according to his abilities, to each according to his work" is addressed directly to the individual and stimulates the emergence and development of a person's abilities and gifts. Socialism has directed all the resources of culture to the service of the working people's interest, to the development of their abilities and talents. Steady growth of the material well-being and cultural level of the people is in socialist conditions a law of development of society. Socialist democracy brings into the management of public affairs millions of working people.

In these conditions concern for the public good becomes the most personal concern of all members of society. Personal needs and interests become organically linked in people's consciousness with the interests of society, with ideological and political interests. The establishment of communist relations, the communist ideology becomes the working man's own affair, his highest interest and ideal.

Thus, *the socialist personality emerges as a high-princip-*

*led personality, placing the social, the public, interest first,
and sharing the aims and principles of the communist ideology.* From this spring such features of the personality as a
developed sense of being the master of one's country and of
its wealth, a consciousness of the dignity of the man of toil,
optimism and purposefulness, confidence in the future, political activity, initiative at work, and so on.

A person in bourgeois society, besides the unemployment
and material hardship which he quite often experiences,
knows yet another misfortune—the feeling of hopelessness
and loneliness. The idea of loneliness and neglect, of general hopelessness, as the expression of the actual feelings of
certain groups in the West, runs right through many works
of literature and art. Socialism has brought people the prospect of development, the sense of faith in the future. The
great aim of building socialism and communism, of the planned, conscious improvement of social life draws all members of society into its realisation, and this generates great
energy on the part of the masses.

The American billionaire and diplomat Averell Harriman in a book about his visit to the Soviet Union *Peace with
Russia?* gives his impression of Soviet workers: "I was
struck by the interest and pride I found on the part of individual workers in their own contribution to the national
goal."[1]

This interest and pride of Soviet workers exist not only
because, as a rule, they are well informed about the general
state of affairs at their factory and in the country as a whole,
as Harriman writes, although this is an important factor, but
also because this is one of the expressions of the character of
socialist relations in socialist society. The essence of these
relations is that every Soviet person is master of all the
wealth created by the labour of all members of society
and bears a certain degree of responsibility for the general
state of affairs, for the good of his or her country and
people.

When speaking of the Soviet workers' and in general the
Soviet people's attitude to work and sense of ownership, we
do not always think deeply enough of the new meaning of

---

[1] Averall Harriman, *Peace with Russia?*, New York, 1959, p. 86.

this concept. But the concept of "owner" in socialist conditions is quite different from what it is under capitalism. Of course, when we speak of a "sense of ownership" or an "owner's attitude to affairs", we are stressing the unity of the personal interest and the work that the person is doing. But the concern of the small peasant or craftsman for the prosperity of his enterprise is one thing, and the concern of the worker at a socialist enterprise for the state of affairs at that enterprise is quite another. Here each person is rich not by the amount of goods he has managed to accumulate but by the wealth of the whole country. The sense of being the owner of one's country and one's production is inseparably connected with the notion of socialism as a just society with its achievements, principles and rules. This feeling constantly increases in proportion to the general success of communist construction and the success of educational work.

Of course, not everyone has this feeling to the same degree. Some people do not have it at all. But the point is that the system of relations between people under socialism is such that it inevitably gives rise to a mass awareness and concern for the common good, to adherence to the communist principle.

Throughout the history of the construction of socialism Soviet people have displayed genuine enthusiasm and concern for the common good. Back in the years of the Civil War the workers began doing voluntary unpaid work on Saturdays, the so-called *subbotniks,* as a contribution to the fund for the defence of the young Soviet republic. During the first five-year plans this enthusiasm of the workers showed itself in a mass movement of shock-workers. Huge factories grew up in a very short time thanks to their devoted labour. The Land of Soviets acquired its own heavy industry. During the Great Patriotic War (1941-45) Soviet people displayed unprecedented heroism on the home and fighting fronts, defending the cause of socialism. After the war they performed another great feat in restoring the socialist economy destroyed by the war and got it moving again at a rapid pace. In all matters, great and small, Soviet people have shown unity of will and aspiration, iron discipline and organisation, and the ability to place social interests before their own personal interests.

Work for Society as the Highest Meaning in Life

Another set of attributes of the socialist type of personality is connected with a person's attitude to his own activity, his own labour, with the understanding of its social significance. The new attitude to work is, perhaps, the most striking and significant expression of the changed essence of man, because "free, conscious activity is man's species character".[1]

Work under socialism acquires a new meaning. It is no longer merely a means of livelihood but has also become a means of contributing to the common weal, of serving the people and socialism. From being a narrowly private matter the ordinary everyday toil of the peasant or the factory or office worker becomes a variety of social activity in which he reveals his abilities, displays his energy and initiative as master of the job he is doing. Such an attitude to work is developed by educational means, encouraged by state awards, and heightened by art.

Under such conditions an interest in the content, the result of one's own labour activity is bound to flourish on a mass scale. A person does not merely set out to earn money. He is concerned about general questions of production, the success or failure of his workshop, enterprise or institution. Whereas of the worker under capitalism Marx said, "The worker only feels himself outside his work, and in his work feels outside himself,"[2] one may say of the worker in a socialist enterprise that he feels at home even when he is working. The working man in socialist society lives a life that is full of real significance when he is working. The time scale of his life is expanded, as it were. *Work at a socialist enterprise is regarded by the individual as serving the good of the people, as the highest meaning in life.* Here we have yet another basic characteristic of the socialist type of personality.

As the character of work and the worker's attitude to work have changed, so has his attitude to culture and education. The prestige of knowledge, of science, the prestige of the scientist, the educated man in the eyes of the people has

---

[1] K. Marx, *Economic and Philosophic Manuscripts of 1844*, p. 75.
[2] Ibid., p. 72.

risen tremendously. Education and study have become an important need of the working people. An intensive spiritual life has become a characteristic feature of Soviet reality, and the urge to acquire knowledge, culture and a wide range of intellectual demands, an inseparable feature of the new personality.

Before socialism appeared on the scene the work of only a few "lucky" categories—writers, scientists, artists, actors, and the like—could be creative and inspired, could lay claim to social recognition. Capitalism is able to achieve high productivity of labour and make complex machinery, but it can never eliminate the humiliating position of the working man who has to work for his capitalist boss, and, consequently, it cannot evoke such interest among the workers in the results of the production activity as exists under socialism; nor can it create conditions for labour activity through which the high moral qualities of the personality become manifest.

Under socialism already in the immediate process of production, i.e., even before they emerge into the sphere of political and legal relations, conditions are created for the moulding of certain ideological and moral attributes of the personality, because work itself, its organisation, its problems and joys acquire moral aspects as well as the usual technical and organisational features.

Some years ago the author was studying the behaviour of workers in the immediate process of production. Some of the notes he made of the time refer to the above-mentioned qualities of the workers. A meeting of the shift workers of No. 1 weaving shop of the Frunze Textile Factory in Moscow was attended by assistant foremen, weavers, fillers and cleaners. This particular shift had a fairly good reputation on all counts at the factory, but at the meeting all the speakers talked mainly about shortcomings, i.e., about the things that were hindering their work. The assistant foremen came in for most of the criticism. "The assistant foremen," cleaner K. stated, "are slack in checking up on the cleanliness of the looms, so sometimes we have a dirty warp to work on. On the whole our assistant foremen have been rather lackadaisical lately." There was also some criticism of the spinners, who had representatives at the meeting, for too long bobbins, which slowed down the work in the weaving department.

12*

Then an argument began, quite a fierce argument and one that could fairly be called constructive. It was about the reasons for the "knocking" of the shuttles. Various suggestions as to the cause were made. The shift foreman was also criticised for not having got rid of this defect. Weaver M. proposed that there should be more pooling of experience in the shop. "We pool experience between factories, but in the shop things are just allowed to take their course," she said. I shall always remember the plain but significant words spoken by weaver F. At first she spoke of the poor supply of woof, and of how they ought to ask the director of the factory to attend one of their meetings, and then she said: "At one time our shift was among the lagging ones. But that time has passed. Although there are still a lot of shortcomings, our collective has become united and the foreman manages the shift well. Now you work and feel that you want to work even more and better!"

The speeches made by F. and the others evinced an all-round interest in production as a whole, a wide horizon and collective responsibility for the common cause, high standards and a proprietary attitude towards everything concerning the factory. The joy of work has not been destroyed by the modern automatic weaving loom; such joy still exists. But it exists only when the worker at a socialist enterprise feels himself to be the true owner of his people's enterprise.

The new attitude to work, the features of the new working man show themselves most vividly, fully and persistently in socialist competition, particularly in its highest form—the movement for communist work. The participants in this movement see the task of raising labour productivity through the prism of the tasks of communist education.

Let us take one document that characterises the communist work movement. It consists of the "commandments" drawn up by the workers of the Moscow-Sortirovochnaya Depot, when the movement was in its infancy. They run as follows:

"Let us imagine that the dream has come true and tomorrow we enter communism.

"This means: never refusing any kind of work, profitable or non-profitable, easy or difficult, and setting about it with a will. In other words, treating work as a need and a joy.

"Let's achieve the highest productivity of labour!—that is our slogan.

"Be efficient at every job. Think of the best way of doing it. One for all, and all for one.

"We consider:

One shirker is a disgrace to the whole team;

one man missing work is a stain on all the others;

one man producing defective goods is a disaster for the whole collective.

"Don't lock away your knowledge and experience in a money-box, share them with everyone. If you see that your neighbour is lagging behind, lend him a hand. If there is something you can't do yourself, don't be too proud to ask a comrade.

"When you have done your stint, don't waste time. School, technical college and institute are waiting for you. If you have a minute to spare, spend it with a book. Study so as to be able to bring even more good to your people.

"Make yourself cultured. Give up swearing, rudeness and drinking. Never turn a blind eye to facts of hooliganism, drunkenness and unculturedness. If someone is harmed in your presence, you are to blame as well.

"Respect age in the street and in the family, be polite, cordial and tactful.

"If you break these rules, there is no place for you in a communist work team."

These "commandments" show deep respect for the beauty and dignity of the human personality and an indomitable desire to live and work in the communist way.

The obligations undertaken by the initiators of the new movement were divided into three sections. The first section dealt with ways of raising labour productivity, improving economic indices and technology. One particular proposal was to produce such high quality work that it could be delivered with the guarantee stamp of the workshop instead of being passed by an inspector from the Ministry of Railways. The second section dealt with matters that are not included in a worker's actual duties, but which would promote a general rise in productivity, such as acquiring a new skill in locomotive repair without interrupting one's regular work, helping to repair farm machinery belonging to the collective farm patronised by the depot, doing eight hours work a month to help build a block of flats for the staff of the depot, training a group of pupils from the secondary school patronised by the depot in the trade of diesel locomotive repair, third class. The third section dealt with such matters as raising the educational and cultural level of the workers. Every worker was to be educated up to secondary school or secondary technical school standard within three to five years.

From these "commandments" it can be seen that the workers have right from the beginning set themselves two aims: raising of the productivity of social labour and education of a new kind of person. As mass-scale experience showed, this example roused a wide response among the advanced workers, collective farmers and state farm workers.

Ideological motivations in work and activity in general produce a powerful effect in actual work results and in initiative at work. The actual work indices of Communists, communist-way workers, Komsomol members and active social workers are higher than those of other workers. On the other hand, work motivations are to be classified as follows: first come ideological motivations, second comes work orientation, third comes promotion at work, and fourth wage orientation. Hence one may draw the conclusion that if this tendency is confirmed in more representative inquiries, we shall find it empirically established that there is a tendency for work to turn gradually into a vital need, because interest in maintaining work activity is becoming the dominant orientation of the workers in the structure of work motivations.

There are, of course, still many problems in the sphere of labour. These include: low level of skill of certain categories of workers, lack of interest in work among the unskilled trades involving heavy monotonous work, violations of labour discipline, lack of information on production at some enterprises, fluidity of labour, and so on. These and other phenomena hold back the development of production and hinder progress in work education. However, the results already achieved in building a new attitude to work offer assurance that these problems will be successfully solved.

Collectivism, Fraternity, Internationalism, as Attributes of the New Personality

Yet another group of features finds its expression in the attitude adopted towards other people. It should be noted that before, when we were talking about adherence to principle and attitude to work, we also had in mind relations between people. But whereas we were then discussing relations concerned with social interest, with one's own activity, we are now examining those relations that take place entirely between people.

The essence of this aspect of the personality's general orientation or ethos is expressed in the fundamentally different relations that exist between people under socialism and under capitalism. In bourgeois society there is a constant insoluble conflict between the goals proclaimed by society and the norms by which members of society are guided in attaining these goals. The social nature of the capitalist's wealth, the antagonistic interests of social groups and the constant need to protect these interests lead to endless conflict between classes and nationalities, and hence to conflict between the proclaimed goals and actual norms.

Some American sociologists and publicists have noted in capitalist society the existence of two different sets of rules or codes of conduct. Max Lerner, for instance, defines them as the "operative" and the "formal" codes. The operative code consists of the goal-norms, the principles and motives of individualism and their actual realisation in bourgeois society. The formal code is made up of the officially proclaimed restrictive norms and various moral categories that support them, such as the categories of "duty", "honesty" and "respectability". The operative code is the one that is actually practised, while the demands and behests of the formal code are merely proclaimed. The conflict lies in the clash between the goal-norms (in this case, the principles of individualism) and the restrictive norms, the laws, rules, prohibitions and regulations of society. Under such conditions hypocrisy becomes a natural and typical fact of bourgeois ideology and morality, a quality of the bourgeois personality, a quality of bourgeois institutions, the state, the schools, the churches, and so on. Hence the possibility and necessity of amoralism, crime, anomie, and the social sickness of the personality connected with them.

The psychology of bourgeois individualism makes its basic principle the isolation and juxtaposition of private interest to the interest of other people, the interests of society. This interest is understood as the acquisition of wealth by any means. With the bourgeoisie in mind Engels wrote: "...Wealth, more wealth and wealth again; wealth, not of society, but of this shabby individual was its sole and determining aim."[1]

In conditions of capitalist relations the preaching of extreme individualism and even actions of an egoistic nature are not punished by official society (although they may be condemned by progressive elements). The enrichment of some at the expense of labour of others, at the cost of ruining and impoverishing others is officially recognised as a legitimate phenomenon. The profiteering that is punished in socialist society under articles of the Criminal Code, is in capitalist society regarded as a perfectly normal expression of private enterprise. Of course, certain abuses at various times and in various countries are subject to legal action, but their general moral basis is the same as that of the stock exchange mechanism and the speculation in stock and shares. Naturally, individualism and egoism form the keystone of all bourgeois philosophical systems, while propaganda of racialism, war, fascism and other misanthropic ideas that destroy the personality is allowed and even encouraged under the pretext of "freedom" of the individual.

In socialist society the principles proclaimed for the whole of society—democracy, collectivism, internationalism—are the guiding principles of the activity of all institutions and citizens. The activities of the state, the departments of the administration are in all their main and basic parameters merged with the aspirations of the general public. The democratic spirit of socialist society permeates both the system of administration and the way of life as a whole. Hence profound respect for the working man, the democratic spirit, collectivism and internationalism emerge as vital attributes of the Soviet person.

---

[1] K. Marx and F. Engels, *Selected Works*, Vol. 3, p. 209.

For thousands of years generation after generation of mankind have dreamed of fraternal relationships between all the members of society. Nearly two thousand years ago the Christian religion proclaimed that all men are brothers and should love one another as brothers. But this gospel was powerless to create love between the exploiters and exploited, between slaves and slave-owners, oppressors and oppressed. The French bourgeois revolution declared the slogan of fraternity among nations, but the bourgeoisie brought not fraternity but a whole epoch of bloody conquests, murderous colonial and imperialist wars for purposes of expansion and robbery. The ideas and slogans of fraternity between men and nations turned out to be an unattainable goal.

It is primarily the working class that is destined to bring about true fraternity of the peoples, the working people of all nations. This is because of its social position. The brotherhood of the workers forged in revolutionary struggle in the conditions of capitalism gradually becomes the norm of human relations already under socialism, and then becomes established in all spheres of life under communism.

Communism, collectivism, fraternity are organically interconnected and interdependent concepts. The realisation of one of these ideals is inconceivable without realisation of the others. As a feature of the new social relations fraternity manifests itself in collectivism, in creative competition, in comradely help and mutual criticism.

Fraternity, comradeship extend to the relations between nations since national distinctions do not at once disappear but continue to exist for a time even at the highest stage of communism. Fraternal relations between nations are what we mean by internationalism. Just as fraternal relations presuppose friendship and mutual assistance between all people, so does internationalism signify close co-operation between the people of all nations, the unity of their economic interests, ideological-political views, social goals and ideals.

People, naturally, regard the institutions of socialist society—the state, the Party, the Komsomol, the trade unions—as their own organisations, and their activity as activity in the interests of the working man. The criteria of a man's personality are his adherence to the communist principle, his work, knowledge and moral qualities, regardless of his material position, origin or nationality. *Consequently, the consciousness and behaviour of the socialist type of personality is characterised by such features as collectivism, fraternity and internationalism.*

Thus, the general orientation, the socialist ethos of the personality, taken in its most essential features, consists in recognition of the goals and principles of the communist ideology and the priority of social interests; awareness that work for the good of society is the highest meaning in life, a means of asserting one's own worth, developing one's abilities; and acceptance of fraternity, collectivism and internationalism as the basic norms of human intercourse.

The appearance and development of these general features of the socialist type of personality by no means contradict the Marxist-Leninist proposition on the decisive role of social groups, or classes, in the formation of types of personality. The historically new community that has taken shape in the USSR, the Soviet people, while retaining certain differences between classes and nations, is so firmly united by common interests, goals and ideals, and its influence on the personality is so intensive and homogeneous, that it forms on a mass scale the essential features that are the qualities of the unified socialist personality.

While new features of the personality are formed, many old habits, customs, traditions are retained. In life this sometimes appears to be an intricate, often unexpected and contradictory intermingling of the progressive and the obsolete. Nevertheless, the steadily growing new attributes are the stronger. Lenin pointed out that the real social intentions and feelings of real individuals may be judged by the social actions of these individuals, i.e., by social facts.[1] The mass nature of the process—successful development of the socialist personality—is primarily measured by the masses' practical support of the basic principles of the socialist system, the Party's policy and the moral norms of socialism.

---

[1] V. I. Lenin, *Collected Works*, Vol. 1, p. 405.

2. COMBINATION OF THE GENERAL
AND THE INDIVIDUAL IN THE SOCIALIST TYPE
OF PERSONALITY

While creating common conditions of existence and integrating people's consciousness in a certain way, socialism at the same time introduces something new into the development of individuality as well. Differences between people are inevitable. What is more, they are essential as a mode of existence of the general, as a manifestation of people's talents and abilities, and also (to a certain extent) as a condition of the stability and unity of society.

Character of Integration of the Personality
Under Socialism

The general features of the socialist personality that we have just mentioned are, of course, schematic in character, and every scheme or outline suffers from lack of fullness. But definition of the general features of the development of the socialist consciousness, the socialist type of personality is an important task of the science of the new society, because this is how we detect the general effect produced by changes in the social conditions of life and by educational work. Only such an approach can provide a general conception of the socialist personality, which in its turn supplies the key to the solution of many particular problems.

The conception of the socialist type of personality that we have outlined is free from any normative approach. We have taken as the foundation of its attributes the basic relationships of the individual (to society, to work, to other people), from which there develop systems of specific qualities that constitute the essence of an ethos of the personality. Moreover, it does not always happen that certain features stem from one particular relationship. Collectivism, for instance, is formed under the influence of all the three spheres of relationships.

Such an approach to the characterisation of the socialist type of personality makes it possible to deal with the features of more than one level of consciousness, feelings, emotions, ideas, theories. A person's relations to the world and hence, the features of his personality, show themselves at all levels of consciousness—in the sphere of feelings and emotions, and in the sphere of theoretical consciousness. For instance, one can speak of collectivism and internationalism both as systems of opinions and as feelings, whereas hatred is only a feeling.

It goes without saying, that the above-mentioned systems of features are of a general character and only in this sense provide a characterisation of the social type. But on this basis it is possible and necessary to specify the features to be found in various aspects of a person's activity and behaviour. Thus, Soviet patriotism is a manifestation of love for the socialist Motherland. At the same time it is one of the concrete manifestations of communist adherence to principle. Internationalism, discipline and organisation, social optimism, etc., are also manifestations of adherence to the communist principle. Consequently, the three above-mentioned spheres of relationships and activity provide a basis for systematising the various features of the personality in three fundamental groups, and this is of both theoretical and practical significance.

The content of the general features that create the new type is decisively important to an understanding of the character of the integration of personal features under socialism. Such essentially important phenomena as ownership of the means of production, attitude to work (the obligation to work), the principle of distribution, power and ideology, which previously served to divide people, have now become species attributes uniting people as a type. Therefore, despite the surviving difference in status, work, and so on, the social content of the roles performed has become much more closely aligned, since all social groups, work collectives are tackling general tasks the purpose of which is to perfect social life on communist principles. Unprecedented aspects of socio-political participation have appeared in the activity of the broad sections of the working people; new ideological and moral principles are being established (to varying extents and with varying success) in labour, social work and everyday behaviour.

A characteristic feature of the new type of personality is the depth, stability and intensity of its communist ideological and moral attributes. Of course, history has recorded in-

stances of great self-sacrifice in the name of ideological principle, great courage and heroism, devotion, purpose and energy. But these manifestations of lofty moral features came
only from advanced revolutionary fighters. Socialism, however, elevates these best features of forward-looking people
into standard behaviour for all members of society. The concepts formed long before socialism, which we employ to characterise the new man (devotion, courage, energy, etc.) express people's attitude to new historically unprecedented social institutions, such as social, public ownership of the means
of production, work at a socialised enterprise, the socialist
state, and so on. And all this forms a totality of personal
characteristics that really do amount to a new ethos of the
personality.

This new position and new ethos of the personality radically alter the relationship between a man's personal aspirations and his social activities. The individual, personal life
is raised to a far higher social level. The individual in socialist society, having become committed to the interests of the
whole people, enters widely into social life. This brings him
into the big world of concern for the fate of society, gives
him new energy, abilities and talents. Commitment to the
common cause provides the wings on which a person's spiritual life soars to new heights. Mass political and labour activity is one of the characteristic features of Soviet life and
"a person whose collective perspective predominates over
the personal is already a person of the Soviet type".[1]

The American publicist Albert Kahn believes the creation
of a new kind of person to be the most astonishing achievement of Soviet society. He argues against those who assert
that it is impossible to change human nature. He writes that
in the Soviet Union there are egotistical and narrow-minded
people, bureaucrats and hooligans. But the overwhelming
majority of people whom I met, he writes, are representative
of the new society. No one can argue today about whether
it is possible to change human nature. Life itself has answered that question. For all who have eyes to see, will see
quite clearly that the thing that through the ages has been

---

[1] A. S. Makarenko, *Pedagogical Works,* Moscow-Leningrad, 1948,
p. 180 (in Russian).

known as "human nature" *has* changed in the Soviet Union. In this country man is changing himself in the process of changing society. A man of a new mould now walks the earth.

What features predominate in Soviet people? They are kind but they are also strong. They are confident but also modest. They have a deep sense of patriotism but at the same time they are infused by a spirit of universal brotherhood. They aspire eagerly to knowledge, have a profound respect for science and regard work as a noble occupation.

They are people who speak for peace not only because they have experienced the horrors of war but also because they admire the beautiful and value life.

Albert Kahn notes such features as Soviet people's pride, but it is pride of a special kind, pride in the successes of society, their enthusiasm for work, their fraternal attitude to all working mankind. He also notes Soviet people's modesty. The average Soviet citizen is not aware of the fact that he is a person of a new mould. He, probably, never considers how different he is from people living in capitalist society. Educated in a new world, he finds it hard to imagine the old world, where the human spirit is so often crushed, where there is ceaseless friction and struggle between people and where ruthless exploitation of man by man is always present.

The world is witnessing a deep-going process in which not just a few individuals or certain narrow sections of the population but an ever increasing mass of the people is taking a more and more active part in all spheres of social life, in which man is freeing himself from the narrow circle of a restricted life, in which man's interests, horizon, aspirations and deeds have marvellously widened and rank-and-file workers regard the fundamental problems of communist construction as their own intimate concern. The essence of Soviet man lies in the tremendous expansion of the framework of his interests. Many of the problems on which the whole country is working have become his closest concern. The questions of the life of the collective in which he works, the town where he lives, of the whole country worry him no less and sometimes more than his own purely personal domestic problems. His whole inner life is illuminated by the high social ideals. With this are connected many of his other splendid features: devotion to the ideals of communism, an urge to acquire knowledge, a creative attitude to work, discipline and organisation, patriotism and internationalism, confidence in the future, and so on. Very little is needed for a man to live only for himself, but to live for oneself and for others a man needs a great number of good attributes, strength and abilities. Not for nothing is it said that man is rich not in what he himself possesses but in what he gives to others.

All this goes to show that under socialism a qualitative change has occurred in the historical development of the personality, that a new, incomparably higher level of the integration of the personality (spread of the communist world view and communist morality) and socialisation of the personality (drawing individuals into social life) has been achieved. There can be no doubt that in the conditions of socialism the mass of the working people has been integrated on the basis of Marxist-Leninist ideology, which in general indicates the appearance of certain common features of the personality of the socialist type.

Dialectics of the General and the Personal Under Socialism

But may not the development of social homogeneity lead to a levelling of people's needs and abilities, their personal interests and to monotony in life in general?

The personality and personal life are always autonomous to some degree or another. The personality is always a separate individual, a biological individual and a special social phenomenon, and as such it has its own system of personal needs and interests whose satisfaction is the primary condition of the existence of this person, this personality, this individual. The personality has its own unique history of cognition and experience, which places a unique individual imprint on the development of feelings, knowledge, abilities and needs. In short, its individual peculiarities may be the measure of its social development, the form of embodiment of sociality, since it is only in the individual that the general exists.

But since the measure of a person's sociality is expressed in his individual peculiarities, the development of society depends not only on what gives people certain common features but also on the conditions that breed individuality. Despite the increased significance of teamwork, collective effort, in our day both in science and production, we must not forget the simple truth that fruitful ideas, solutions, discoveries or at least their elements are generated in the brain of the individual.

The development of the individual's abilities benefits not only the individual himself. It is an essential condition for the further progress of socialist society, for its development into communist society. The growth of production, the solution of social problems, the level of scientific and artistic creativity directly depend on the worker's initiative, skill and ideological orientation. In other words, the posing and solution of current problems, the intensity and level of creativity depend on the worker's conditions of work and rights, on the degree of freedom of thought and action of separate individuals. Without creative discussion of scientific and practical problems, without criticism and self-criticism there can be no successful movement forward.

The objective basis for this diversity in human life is the process of increasing differentiation of production, scientific knowledge, social activity, and so on. Since the life of every individual is a unique story, combining all the variety of his experience, knowledge and interests and beliefs, a unique individuality is formed which is an attribute of the human personality.

As a result of the diversity of conditions of life every given type of social relations creates a whole system of types of personality, a diversity of individualities. The very reason why society creates this diversity is because it needs it. The development of individuality, the development of a great variety of individualities on the basis of a definite level of integration of society is one of the conditions of social progress.

It is a general law that with the transition from one socio-economic formation to another the autonomy and the freedom of the individual increase. History shows that the meaning of the word "personal" changed. It was the slave's personal affair whether he chose between life and death, although in life he had very little personal choice. He could choose neither his master nor his work. Even the choice between life and death was very often not his to decide. The serf was a good deal more often able to arrange his personal affairs because he was freer than the slave. The sphere of his personal life that was independent of the master had widened. But for him as for the slave the possibility of moving from one place to another depended on the master. He could fall in love, but could marry his beloved only with the consent of the landowner. The worker in capitalist society becomes personally a free man, although he is dominated by economic compulsion and the political power of capital in all their grim and lack of prospects.

Under socialism the public interest becomes the content of the interest of the individual, but purely personal interests are also developed.

Despite the allegations of the anti-Communists that socialism crushes diversity in the name of the universal, reality paints a different picture: living accommodation and correspondence are strictly protected by law; moral standards do not permit interference in matters of love or friendship, society fosters respect for personal tastes and opinions. If these standards are violated, such violations are invariably condemned. It is characteristic that respect for personal life in the USSR is noted also by observers from abroad. For instance, the French writer Pierre Pathé has noted that in the Soviet Union people show far more respect for private life than is shown in the West.

Genuine respect for the individual, attention to his personal interests has nothing in common with allowing certain individuals to do as they like without respecting the interests of other people. Socialism differs from capitalism on this plane in that by restricting the arbitrary action of individuals it frees people from blatant interference in their personal lives.

In the USSR capitalist private property has long since been abolished, but the economic and cultural life of the towns and villages which for decades has been developing on the basis of public ownership of the means of production is far more varied, intense, meaningful, interesting and spiritually satisfying than the life of bourgeois society. This is acknowledged by many observers from abroad. Socialism creates practically unlimited and constantly expanding opportunities for creative activity on the part of millions of people, for development of their interests, requirements and abilities.

While increasing the variety of forms of social initiative and creating the necessary conditions for its application, society cannot, of course, remain indifferent to what its members do, what the aims of their activity are, how they make use of public funds and conditions of labour, etc. The interestedness of any society in the activity of its members ultimately manifests itself in the fact that every social system develops and encourages certain forms of activity and, consequently, creates its own characteristic types of abilities and requirements.

When speaking of diversity one must also bear in mind the content of this diversity. One cannot say, for instance, that contemporary bourgeois society suffers from monotony. But the "variety" that we observe in the spiritual life of the ruling classes of the capitalist countries is ultimately governed by the race for profit, the struggle for power, for domination over others, for robbing other countries and peoples. The bitter fruit of all this in spiritual life is zoological individualism, chauvinism, racialism, the gangster cult and other similar means of corrupting people's consciousness. The "principle" that demands tolerance of the worst solely on the grounds that its presence makes for variety signifies, of course, defence of everything ugly, obsolete and reactionary.

Such "variety" is eliminated under socialism. Socialism encourages a variety of abilities and forms of activity that serves man, develops his high moral qualities, his intellectual and physical gifts.

Socialism has, indeed, produced people of extremely varied occupations, inclinations, enthusiasms, tastes and likings. But all the same they are devoted to communism, love their country, its glorious history, value culture and take pride in its historic mission.

An orientation towards social interests is a characteristic feature of the socialist personality, and this has a beneficial effect on the personality itself. However, the interaction between the general and the individual encounters difficulties even in socialist conditions.

Everyone has a good many interests connected with the satisfaction of his material and spiritual needs, development of his energies and abilities and preserving his own life. Actions connected with such personal interests are rightly described as the individual's personal affair since the individual himself, and he alone, can decide whether or not to perform such actions, although a particular decision, being determined by the environment, by its previous influence, may to some degree effect the people around him. Take such decisions as whether to go to the cinema or not, whether to read a particular book or not, make friends with a person or not, go to work tomorrow or not, buy a certain suit or not, join the Komsomol or not, remain in the underground in the enemy rear or not—all such decisions rest with the individual. The social significance of these actions, however, is by no means equal, particularly in varying situations.

The mere fact of drinking water or going to sleep cannot harm anyone else in itself, although even the satisfaction of the most elementary needs is always connected with other people. There are situations, however, (falling asleep on sentry duty, for instance) when sleep may prove disastrous for oneself and one's comrades. By joining the Komsomol or remaining in the underground behind the enemy lines, a person enters a circle of intensive social life, involving numerous mutual obligations. And although there is a great difference between actions of the former or the latter kind, a person is obviously dependent on the people around him in both cases. A person's interests are shaped and satisfied only in connection with other people and with other people's help. Therefore, actions designed to satisfy an individual's needs are formed in a definite way and, as a rule, have a definite orientation and definite social consequences. Hence, the personal never remains purely personal, but is in one way or another connected with society.

The personal remains personal as long as it does not conflict with the interests of society, of the group, i.e., as long as it is approved by society, and thus once again is not an entirely personal matter. For other people, for society, the behaviour of the individual continues to be entirely his personal affair only as long as it does not affect other people,

13*

the interests of society. The degree of effect exercised by the
personal on the social gives us the sole criterion by which we
are able to distinguish the "personal" from the "social".
Consequently, the attitude of the people around one to one's
actions depends on the extent to which these actions correspond to or contradict the predominant norms and morality.
The boundary between the "personal" and the "social", the
content of personal interests differs in different social situations.

It would be naïve to assume that the interests of socialist
society and the interests of the individual coincide in all circumstances. But this divergence is quite different in socialist
conditions from what it is under capitalism. Insofar as the
social interest objectively becomes the interest of the individual the contradiction between personal and social interests
emerges as a contradiction between the individual's own interests, non-essential or essential, temporary or permanent,
immediate or long-term. A person must, of course, always
be involved in the circles of these alternatives. Depending
on his general orientation, level of knowledge, willpower,
and the nature of circumstances, he at any given moment
may prefer one or another decision, choosing the decision
that is more or less pleasant or perhaps totally unpleasant
for himself. But since under socialism the circle of personal
interests is considerably widened, the character of this choice
is also fundamentally altered. Whereas under capitalism the
interests of the capitalists are everywhere disguised as the
interests of society and the social (or "public") interest is
imposed on the individual, under socialism the individual,
while giving preference to social interests, makes this choice
in the framework of his own interests.

Needless to say, even under socialism situations involving
conflict are possible, when, for instance, out of egoistic considerations preference is given to personal desire to the de-
triment of society, but this does not change the fundamentally new order of things. At the same time we must note situations that involve conflict of another kind, when the individual finds himself in a dramatic situation owing to certain
misconceptions of personal interest.

In such cases a person acts against his own interests, although he is entirely convinced that his real interests lie pre-

cisely in this course of action. There would seem to be three cases of this kind:

(1) A person sees an interest that is alien to him as his own. Lenin's article "In the Servants' Quarters" examines the psychology of the lackeys, guided by the interests of their master. In socialist society certain individuals may also see alien interests as their own, all the more so because bourgeois propaganda, sometimes not unsuccessfully, presents the selfish interests of imperialism as the interests of the working people of the socialist countries.

(2) A person misunderstands his own interests or the means for satisfying his needs, i.e., an illusory interest is created that actually contradicts the interests of the given person.

(3) Existence of wrong needs, detrimental to man, his morality and spiritual and physical development, which the individual regards as an interest of vital importance to himself.

All these cases occur because reality itself offers opportunities for the divergence of interests and the individual becomes disoriented in life. The solution to them comes gradually, through a whole set of measures—improvement of living conditions, education, prevention, and so on.

Personal Freedom and Responsibility under Socialism

Yet another aspect of the problem of combining the general and the individual lies in the development of the individual's freedom and responsibility.

Freedom is one of the supreme values of human life. If what we mean by freedom is the conditions, the possibilities for activity, the realisation of aspirations, manifestation of abilities and satisfaction of needs, even ideological adversaries representing different classes would accept such a definition. But at the same time it is a well-known fact that freedom has always been and still is the subject of intense political and ideological dispute. Philosophers have striven to reveal its meaning, poets have sung its praises, the exploited and oppressed have engaged in mortal struggle for its sake. Freedom, or to be more exact its interpretation, has always served as a weapon for the defence of certain interests, and the struggle of the interests of various classes, groups and individuals constitutes the essence of the antagonisms that have existed throughout the history of society.

In bourgeois society freedom of the individual is bound up with property. Marx and Engels pointed out the identification in bourgeois literature of private property with freedom. For the bourgeois ideologist, they wrote in *The German Ideology*, "the 'Ego' (*moi*) includes 'mine' (*mien*)", and this philosopher finds a natural basis for private property in the fact that "nature has endowed man with an inevitable and inalienable property, property in the form of his own individuality"[1]... "For the bourgeois it is actually the case, he believes himself to be an individual only insofar as he is a bourgeois."[2] In such conditions the freedom of the individual is bound up with his property and appears to him to be an accident (since the fact of the given individual's possession of property is in itself accidental). "This right to the undisturbed enjoyment, within certain conditions, of fortuity and chance has up till now been called personal freedom."[3]

The word "freedom" may imply quite different meanings. As an illustration of the essence of bourgeois freedom one may cite the example that Marx himself once gave. "A Yankee comes to England, where he is prevented by a Justice of the Peace from flogging his slave, and he exclaims indignantly: 'Do you call this a land of liberty, where a man can't larrup his nigger?'."[4]

Marx and Engels stressed that in their teaching they had no intention of abolishing freedom and the individual. It was a matter of abolishing the state in which they exist in bourgeois society, where only capital possesses independence and individuality, while the working man is deprived of independence and depersonalised. It is to this depersonalisation of the working man that the Marxists-Leninists are opposed.

Socialist reforms radically alter the character of individual freedom in all its aspects and manifestations. Only

---

[1] K. Marx and F. Engels, *The German Ideology*, p. 246.
[2] Ibid., p. 247.
[3] Ibid., p. 92.
[4] Ibid., p. 225.

when people are equal in the main—in their relationship to the means of production and to state power,—when they are united by common goals and intentions, when their relations are characterised by socio-political and ideological unity, only then do the class barriers collapse that have limited freedom of the individual, only then are favourable opportunities created for the free expression of their aspirations, for participation in the management of social, public affairs.

Freedom has various aspects: economic, social, political, ideological, moral, and so on, i.e., as many aspects as there are aspects or spheres of human activity.

The basis of individual freedom lies in *economic* liberation of the working people from capitalist exploitation, because there is not and cannot be real individual freedom for the working man if his life and activity are determined by the selfish interests of the exploiter, if the private capitalist economy is periodically shaken by crises and constantly reproduces a reserve army of unemployed.

The individual in socialist society is free of economic crises and unemployment. The planned growth of the national economy ensures a steady rise in the well-being of the whole people, for improvement of the people's standard of living is the supreme aim of the Communist Party and the socialist state. This freedom rests on the banishing from society of another freedom—the freedom of private property, the freedom to exploit.

Socialism guarantees broad *social* freedoms. The highest freedom of the individual is the freedom of labour activity, the guarantee given to every member of society of his right to work. The individual is presented with a wide choice of activity, freedom to develop and apply his abilities. Free education and health protection, social insurance in old age and sickness, enormous housing and cultural construction— all this offers a person tremendous scope for fruitful activity for the good of society and in the interests of his own personality. The Soviet state spends huge amounts on social and cultural measures.

Socialism opens up genuine *political freedoms* for the working people. Above all people are released from the political pressure of the bourgeois state, from the combinations and manoeuvring of bourgeois parties hostile to the people, from rigged parliamentary elections, from downright political blackmail and compulsion. The activity of any individual directed towards benefiting the people or protecting the rights and freedoms of other individuals coincides with the direction and purpose of Party and state and receives their support. Such great gains of political freedom as free discussion and participation in the solution of questions of social and state life, in administering the affairs of society and the state have for long been part of the Soviet person's life.

Freedom is essential to the individual not only for the expression of his will and development of his abilities. In life one has to wage a struggle against everything that is alien to socialism: bureaucracy, the psychology of the private property-owner, ignorance, and so on. Freedom in the political sphere is asserted in struggle. State compulsion, political persuasion, criticism and self-criticism emerge as instruments for correcting shortcomings, as work to create conditions for freedom of the individual.

In the field of *ideological life* socialism liberates people from the corruptive influences of anti-humanist ideas and doctrines and makes it possible to concentrate all the creative energy of the personality on evolving a noble, profoundly humanistic culture—sociology, natural science, art, the development of a scientific world view in all citizens, creation of a whole man, a personality, that combines lofty motives with practical action. In this field, too, of course socialist freedom rules out all misanthropic ideas and society wages an irreconcilable struggle against them.

The benefits that socialism has provided for the individual evoke a mighty wave of enthusiasm, of creative initiative and activity on the part of the masses in pursuing the aims of the whole state. Collectivism becomes the basic moral norm of socialist society. The individual in socialist society is released from such individualistic principles of morality as "man unto man is a wolf" or "each man for himself and only God for all". They are being steadily replaced by such principles of communist morality as "each for all and all for each", "man unto man is a friend, comrade and brother". This is what *moral* freedom means under socialism.

Freedom of the individual under socialism, as distinct from the accidental character of bourgeois freedom, acquires the character of a law. It moves into the sphere of practical activity for the good of the people, the development of one's own abilities as a member and worker of socialist society.

The free development of the working man under socialism cannot fail to influence the consciousness of the working people in the imperialist countries. The exploiters find it increasingly difficult to hold power solely by means of force, and they try to use the working people's desire to develop freedom and democracy. But the people's interests are organically alien to the imperialists; they have neither the desire nor the ability to give the working people genuine freedom. Hence the illusory nature of the notions of freedom that are cultivated by bourgeois philosophers and sociologists.

One of the most widespread conceptions of freedom is founded on the extremely old assertion that true freedom is absolute untrammelled freedom of the will. According to the existentialists, man's existence is freely formed by him according to his own design. A man may be free only in the sphere of his subjective aspirations and, consequently, can be responsible only if he makes a moral choice in complete isolation, obeying his own "absolutely free" idea. The magazine *Amerika* (official American Russian-language magazine published and distributed in the USSR by the US Government) asserts: "Self-will may, of course, be a very dangerous factor. Nevertheless this is where the very essence of human freedom lies." But this does not prevent the US police and army from dealing ruthlessly with the "self-will" that the American Negroes, for instance, display in the struggle for their fundamental interests, or that was displayed by the Americans who protested against the war in Vietnam.

The theoretical inconsistency of the "absolute freedom" theory has frequently been proved. But it still enjoys a certain amount of influence. The point is that freedom of the will is one of the basic manifestations of vital activity. It signifies a person's ability to act in accordance with his own decisions. But as interpreted by the idealists, actually existing phenomena are distorted and carried to the point of absurdity, thus becoming their opposite. Freedom of the will is thus transformed into unlimited individual license, absolutely independent of society, of the people around one, that is to say, it is transformed into a fiction, for such unlimited will never has existed and never will exist anywhere, except perhaps in the overexcited minds of the anarchists.

Indeed, man always has to make a choice when taking a decision. But in making his choice he does not isolate himself from other people, from society, but rather establishes new contacts with them. Every person's interests, goals, motives are shaped under the influence of his environment and, consequently, freedom in general is possible only thanks to close links with other people, otherwise it loses all meaning. Living in society, a person belongs to a definite social group or collective, is connected with it by common interests, and cannot fail to take these interests into consideration when making a choice. Finally, the objects of choice are also placed before the individual by social conditions. As Lenin wrote, "One cannot live in society and be free from society."[1]

Thus, the claim that freedom is the unlimited will of the individual obviously conflicts not only with logic but also with social practice. But this subjectivist interpretation of freedom suits the ruling classes of bourgeois society very well. The political purpose of the theory of absolute freedom of the spirit lies in diverting the working people from the real economic and political problems, diverting them from the tasks of the class struggle and preventing the individual from understanding his true interests.

The Marxists do not deny free will. They only stress its connection with necessity. "Freedom of the will, therefore, means nothing but the capacity to make decisions with knowledge of the subject."[2] In this sense real freedom is conscious necessity.

But the cognition of necessity is only the first condition of man's free action. Necessity cannot be reduced to mechanical determinism, in other words, the objective laws determine man's behaviour in different ways. Successful action entails creative search and the choice of the most effective solutions, and in this sense necessity presupposes a certain freedom of choice. The more deeply a person penetrates into the essence of the objective processes, the clearer the situation becomes, the freer he is in his decisions, and the wider his choice of

---

[1] V. I. Lenin, *Collected Works*, Vol. 10, p. 48.
[2] F. Engels, *Anti-Dühring*, 1969, p. 137.

solutions. And vice versa, the more limited his grasp of the situation, the less free he becomes.

Freedom of the individual implies both the quality and the conditions of his activity.

Freedom of choice does not necessarily imply freedom of action. One may take a certain decision, but if the actions designed to realise it are limited by social conditions, that is where freedom ends. If the interests of the individual and his activity do not coincide with the dominant interests of the classes or of society as a whole and come into conflict with them and with the corresponding moral norms, the state, which guards these dominant interests, restricts the activity of the individual.

The key to understanding what freedom and responsibility actually mean lies in examination of the social system, the interests of classes, of social groups.

While private property and the power of the monopolies continue to exist in the world, there is not and cannot be freedom for all people. The Marxists-Leninists' basic approach to the problem is to answer the questions: freedom for whom? freedom for which class? freedom in what? It is the opposition between the class interests of the capitalists and the working people that contains their opposite understanding of the essence of freedom. "People," Lenin wrote, "always have been the foolish victims of deception and self-deception in politics, and they always will be until they have learnt to seek out the *interests* of some class or other behind all moral, religious, political and social phrases, declarations and promises."[1]

Freedom, like interest, cannot be understood without considering the link between the individual and society: interest characterises the general orientation of the individual's activity, while freedom indicates the possibilities, the limits of this activity. To the extent that personal interests are in conflict with the interests of society, social groups or separate individuals, so is the freedom of the individual restricted. And vice versa, if the interests of the individual coincide with the interests of society and other people, his activity acquires scope and support.

---

[1] V. I. Lenin, *Collected Works*, Vol. 19, p. 28.

Freedom is inconceivable outside revolutionary practice aimed at creating favourable conditions for man's life and labour activity. When revolutionary fighters act in the name of freedom they usually present specific economic and political demands and work for their realisation. In doing so they achieve only that degree of freedom that the existing conditions of the material life of society allow. Freedom, Engels wrote, "consists in the control over ourselves and over external nature, a control founded on knowledge of natural necessity; it is, therefore, necessarily a product of historical development."[1] Concretising this general philosophical proposition, Engels showed that the winning of freedom coincides with the task of the revolutionary transformation of capitalism into socialism in the interests of the working class and all working people. "To accomplish this act of universal emancipation is the historical mission of the modern proletariat."[2] In the socialist revolution the revolutionary activity of the proletariat based on the knowledge of the laws of social development coincides with the objective development of historical processes. Consequently, the truly free activity is activity which evolves in accordance with historical necessity. It is revolutionary practice that is both free activity and the condition of the further development of freedom.

Freedom inevitably generates the problem of responsibility. The advocates of absolute freedom of the will maintain that acknowledgement of determinism removes the problem of responsibility. Since man's actions are conditioned by external circumstances, he cannot be responsible for them.

Necessity, however, presents man with the opportunity (and inevitability!) of choice, the material, so to speak, for the solution of this or that problem. In the framework of general dependence on objective conditions a person takes a decision according to his own will. So the question is bound to arise as to how far a person's decision coincides with or contradicts certain social interests. Only through knowing and considering objective conditions is a person able to approach a decision, to determine its correctness or incorrectness. Lenin stressed that "only the determinist view

---

[1] F. Engels, *Anti-Dühring*, p. 137.
[2] Ibid., p. 338.

makes a strict and correct appraisal possible instead of attributing everything you please to free will".[1]

Two people may with equal correctness appraise all the arguments for and against in a given situation, but their decisions and actions will differ according to their beliefs. In other words, in any given situation a person chooses a certain position out of a number of possible positions, and this position is determined mainly by his socio-class interests.

In taking a particular decision or performing certain actions a person makes a certain moral appraisal of phenomena and human actions. Consequently, acknowledgement of the determinacy of actions does not imply denial of the individual's moral responsibility.

The difference between the subjectivists (in this case, the existentialists) and the Marxists is that the former place responsibility entirely on the individual and transfer the criteria for appraisal of behaviour to the sphere of the subjective, while the Marxists, without releasing man from personal responsibility, show the objective conditionality of his decisions and see the criteria of behaviour in correspondence of the decisions taken to the demands of objective reality.

The possibility of divergence between objective purpose and personal aims is a question of to what extent a person carries out the moral demands of society, i.e., a question of the correspondence of action to duty from the standpoint of possibility. Is a person in general capable of performing the demands made upon him? To what extent has he correctly understood and interpreted them? Should a person answer for the consequences of his actions? Can he foresee them?

Reality is full of contradictory processes, phenomena and situations. Of course, a person acts as the circumstances of life dictate, but he does so in accordance with his convictions and moral rules under the influence of circumstances and to the extent that his strength of will permits. The object of a person's attention and activity, the character of the motivations and social control—these are the factors that predetermine the content and level of the individual's free behaviour.

---

[1] V. I. Lenin, *Collected Works*, Vol. 1, p. 159.

If freedom signifies the possibility of choice, responsibility is the evaluation of choice, decision, action, evaluation of the benefit or harm they may bring to society. Being responsible means foreseeing the consequences of one's actions, being guided in one's actions by the interests of the people, of the progressive development of society.

Freedom presupposes responsibility and responsibility in its turn is the condition of freedom. Freedom is inconceivable without responsibility, just as responsibility is the essential condition of freedom. Freedom is never abstract and unlimited. Truly free activity is always purposeful and always takes place in a definite framework. Hence every free action is at the same time a responsible action. The wider the framework of the individual's free activity, the greater the amount of his responsibility. Violation of laws, ignoring of social interests and irresponsible behaviour encroach upon the freedom of other people. Voluntarism in politics looks outwardly like extremely free activity. In fact, however, it implies underestimation of objective processes, arbitrariness and the violation of freedom. On the contrary, only responsible behaviour promotes the development of freedom in society.

The interaction of freedom and personal responsibility has altered considerably with the change in the character of democracy under socialism. The man of toil is beginning to feel himself master of life and to find his way more easily in the complexity of social life.

Under socialism the liberated masses of the people take upon themselves responsibility for the fate of their country. Whereas the servants of the exploiting classes are primarily responsible to their class, to the state that guards the interests of the ruling class, the representatives of the working people in socialist society are responsible to the people and their state. The socialist state, which has no other interests but those of the people, concerns itself for the good of all members of society.

All this was bound to have an effect, and did have the effect of developing among the Soviet working people a high sense of responsibility, of making them more active. Their high degree of consciousness displayed itself in the broad development of socialist competition, in mass heroism during the Great Patriotic War, in the development of feelings of collectivism, patriotism and internationalism.

This has exploded the thesis of the opponents of Marxism who maintain that the Marxists' acknowledgement of the determinacy of human actions frees a man entirely of all moral responsibility for his actions. The mass dedication of Soviet people testifies to their high sense of responsibility towards society, towards their comrades, towards themselves for everything they do. It would be hard to find moral appraisal playing such a great part anywhere as it plays under socialism. "The Soviet system has brought up the working people in the spirit of devotion to the cause of socialism, of collectivism and developed the feeling of being master of their country. But to be master means that, alongside great rights, you also have great duties. It means to bear high responsibility not only for one's own personal work and behaviour, but also for the affairs of the collective, the enterprise, the entire country. The development of these qualities, which must be inalienable traits of the inner world of every Soviet citizen, is one of the most important tasks of the Party in communist construction."[1]

3. CRITICISM OF BOURGEOIS CONCEPTIONS OF SOVIET MAN

The Soviet Union's successes in moulding a new kind of person, and their acknowledgement abroad, confronted the anti-Communists with a knotty problem. They had to explain the behaviour of Soviet people. They had to produce their own theories about the Soviet people's dedication to the ideas of communism, the socialist system and the policy of the Communist Party. All such theories had to perform at least two functions. They had to prove the general unreality of the idea of making a new man and also provide a commentary on the way of life, the image and behaviour of Soviet people.

There exist a whole series of bourgeois conceptions of the Soviet man that in one way or another seek to perform these

---

[1] L. I. Brezhnev, *Fifty Years of Great Achievements of Socialism,* 1967, p. 52.

functions. The fact that there are so many of them is, on the
one hand, a tribute to the needs and moods of various sections of the bourgeoisie and, on the other hand, a testimony
to the general failure to discover a convincing explanation
of a phenomenon that is capturing the imagination of increasing numbers of people in the bourgeois world.

The Conception of the "Collectivised Soul"

Many Sovietologists make no attempt to deny that the
cause of Soviet people's activity and organisation is the influence of the communist ideology. What is more, they attribute the critical condition of the bourgeois West to the
lack of any positive ideological programme on the part of
the bourgeoisie and the fact that the Communists have a
carefully worked-out and goal-oriented programme. Thus,
a West German anti-Communist believes that "The East
led by the Soviet Union has built up definite positions and is
moving ahead.... Success is possible only if the West produces the one strong and positive idea that can be set up in
opposition to the East."[1]

The conception of the "collectivised soul", stemming from
the open or tacit admission of the decisive effect of the communist ideology on Soviet people, consists in the assertion
that owing to the domination of a unified ideology socialism
destroys the freedom of the individual and the individual
personality itself. A *Handbook on World Communism*, issued in West Germany, informs us, for example, that "the
individual today is always regarded and used by the Communists as an instrument, as a means for achieving the aims
of the Party."[2] And even the direct lie is not considered too
shameful. The individual has no freedom to choose his profession, writes Klaus Mehnert, and must carry out the instructions of his superiors.[3]

The Soviet person has no morality—such is another
"truth" which the anti-Communists use to frighten the bour-

---

[1] R. Kinsky, *Naturgesetzlichkeit der Gesellschaftsordnung*, Nürn-
berg, 1961, S. 5.
[2] *Handbuch des Weltkommunismus*, Freiburg-München, 1958, S. 631.
[3] K. Mehnert, *Der Sowjetmensch*, Stuttgart, 1959, S. 107.

geois philistine. Since communism repudiates religion, it also repudiates the moral values of the West, which are based primarily on religion. The Soviet social system is said to be opposed to the family. The family is presented as something hostile to communism, as a stronghold of the old morality and old habits.

Out of these "basic" precepts methodological principles have been evolved that are used for explaining everything connected with the USSR and socialism in general. The idea that propaganda is bound to be "one-sided", as students of bourgeois propaganda delicately put it, is elevated to standard practice. Philosophically speaking, such propaganda is based on the so-called stereotype principle, proposed by Walter Lippman as long ago as 1922 in his book *Public Opinion.* According to this principle, the purpose of propaganda is to make the individual perceive the world through "imagination" and not through actual knowledge. Stereotypes, according to Lippman, enable a person to conceive an opinion about the world before he has seen it, and to imagine most things before he experiences them. Such "preconceptions" deeply govern the whole process of perception. In the form of preconceived, programmed stereotypes they mark out certain objects of surrounding reality as familiar or strange, emphasising the difference, so that the slightly familiar is seen as very familiar, and the somewhat strange as sharply alien.[1] Emory S. Bogardus believes that this method expresses the very essence of propaganda today, which he defines as "a one-sided presentation of an idea or a programme signifying that it is major truth. It is a part of the truth presented as the whole truth, and here is where deception enters as an integral part of a great deal of propaganda."[2]

The following facts illustrate how this is applied in practice. In some schools in the United States a course of anticommunism was introduced. The organisers were extremely anxious to make sure from the start that the teaching of anticommunism did not work out as propaganda of communism.

---

[1] W. Lippman, *Public Opinion,* New York, 1945, pp. 89-90.
[2] Emory S. Bogardus, *The Making of Public Opinion,* New York, 1951, p. 149.

One of them, David Mallery, in the book *Teaching About Communism* insists: "The presentation of the anti-communism course must be very firm and positive, permitting no challenge from any student to the basic proposition that communism is wrong and our way of life is the only way. Stated differently, academic freedom should not permit academic discussion of whether we are right in this course.... The stressing of both sides of a controversy only confuses the young and encourages them to make snap judgements.... They should be taught only the American side."[1]

There have been well-known cases of quite shameless distortion of history all for the sake of presenting Soviet people as lacking in a "human face".

Crude distortion and falsification do not always work and are powerless against facts, against truth. Therefore, they have to be accompanied by misinformation dressed up in the garb of scientific criticism.

The Slavophile Variant

Another explanation of the Bolshevik type of personality that is given wide currency in the West is the "Slavophile variant", the stressing of the mysteriousness, the peculiar nature of the Russian soul with its eternal messianistic aspirations. We cite some examples of these assertions. Hans Kohn, for instance, writes that extremism, messianism and totalitarianism are deeply inherent in the Russian people. Stuart R. Tompkins maintains that "the Russian mind", as distinct from the national qualities of the peoples of Western Europe is ingrained with fanaticism, intolerance, the habit of obedience and at the same time anarchism.[2]

It is characteristic that a considerable part in spreading these ideas was played by émigré circles of so-called "Eurasian School", which took its cue from Dostoyevsky and other Slavophiles.

---

[1] David Mallery, *Teaching About Communism*, Boston, December 1962, p. 7.

[2] S. Tompkins, *The Russian Mind from Peter The Great Through the Enlightenment*, Norman, 1953, idem, *The Triumph of Bolshevism: Revolution or Reaction?*, Norman, 1967.

In *Crime and Punishment* Dostoyevsky propounds the idea that there is no essential difference between revolutionary violence and crime and hence between the revolutionary and the criminal. In *The Possessed,* written after the famous Nechayev trial, he embodies this idea in the concrete image of the criminal adventurer Pyotr Verkhovensky. Dostoyevsky himself wavered between the desire for a "harmonious future" and the fear of it. He was also pursued by tormenting doubts concerning the socialist revolutionary path to this harmonious future, imagining that it would involve crude violence and cruel egalitarianism without consideration for the human personality and boding ill for the future promised by socialism.

It is no accident that the bourgeois Sovietologists have for many years lauded *The Possessed* as a "revelation about the Russian revolution" and a prophesy of the events of the 20th century. For instance, the former contributor to the reactionary Russian almanac *Vekhi* F. Stepun seeks to give "scientific" grounds for the "internal kinship" between "Nechayevism" and Bolshevism. He maintains that Lenin considered that the ideal for Communists should be "blind obedience" to the will of the leaders, and that he would rather have a hardened criminal on the barricades than a convinced Social-Democrat.

The apologist, unscientific character of the anti-Communists' allegations inevitably comes to light when they are compared with the historical reality, the way of life and behaviour both of the older generations of revolutionaries and the Soviet people of today. No one will deny that the Russians, like any other people, obviously, have their national peculiarities. But it is also obvious that in any people there are different classes, different cultures, different types of morality and, consequently, extremely different types of behaviour.

Maxim Gorky protested against distortion of the image of the Russian people. Gorky disliked the pathological eagerness with which Dostoyevsky scoured the dark corners of the human mind. "...Fyodor Karamazov, the 'man from underground', Foma Opiskin, Pyotr Verkhovensky, Svidrigailov are not all that we have amassed in life. Something more than the bestial and the thievish burns within us!" Gorky wrote. "But Dostoyevsky saw only these features...."[1]

In his own works Gorky gave us a vast assortment of characters, but he always had a liking and a keen eye for any new type of human personality. With joy and excitement he noted that "a new type of person is coming into life straight from the very mass of the Russian people, a person of cheerful spirit, full of an ardent desire for culture, a person healed of fatalism and pessimism, and, therefore, capable of action."[2] Gorky linked the awakening activity of the Russian people with the spread of revolutionary ideas. Arguing against those who maintained that "the Russian people have many superstitions but no ideas", he emphasised: "...An idea is being born in the Russian people and it is the very idea that may straighten them, namely, the idea of taking an active attitude to life, to people, to nature."[3] There is every reason to regard Gorky as the first writer, the first artist to perceive and recreate Russia's new man— the type of the proletarian revolutionary, a type comprising a great variety of individuals.

The Eclectic Variant

The advocates of this conception of the Soviet man also believe that the communist ideology is accepted by the population of the Soviet Union, but at the same time deny that it has had any serious effect on their personal make-up. This approach we find most fully expressed by Klaus Mehnert. He writes: "No one will deny the fact that the Russian of today, or the person now living in the Soviet Union, in short, the Soviet man, in the particular sense in which the term has been used in this book, is no longer the Russian as our fathers used to conceive him (often, of course, with a touch of the romantic). Many of his 'typical Russian' features have retreated into the background and some of them have turned (particularly in the upper strata) into their opposite. The wild valour has been curbed, the uncalculating impetuosity and impulsiveness have given way to the disci-

---

[1] Maxim Gorky, *Collected Works*, Vol. 24, pp. 147-48 (in Russian).
[2] *M. Gorky on Literature*, Moscow, 1955, p. 116 (in Russian).
[3] Ibid., p. 115.

pline and stability of modern working life, irrationalism has been replaced on a broad scale by a persistent striving for prosperity, by faith in technical progress, religiosity has been confined within church walls and sects."[1] But Mehnert has not been able to find "typical Bolshevik" features among the majority of Russians. However, he is compelled to admit in the same book that "these people" approve of public ownership, bringing the individual into the collective and the idea of transition from capitalism through socialism to communism. And yet. . . they are not Bolsheviks! How does Mehnert get out of this muddle of his own making? It turns out that what he means by the features of the new personality is not its socialist consciousness but the "cold-blooded, calculated dedication of fanatics, for whom the aim justifies the means".[2] Mehnert is not in the least worried by the fact that the Communists themselves understand their task in quite a different way. His repudiation of the new man consists in introducing his own interpretations, on the one hand, and, on the other, in creating an antithesis between communist ideology and humanity.

Here are some examples. Commenting on the fact that in the USSR on March 8 it is the custom for men to give women presents and wish them happiness, Mehnert writes: "Originally this holiday was a purely political day of struggle for international socialism. . . . Demonstration in defence of women's rights and revolutionary campaign speeches were its characteristic features. . . . But today? In the consciousness of the people March 8 is almost devoid of political character. . . . I find it reassuring that the Russian people have not lost the ability to convert the political into the human."[3] Perhaps without realising it himself, Mehnert points out one of the strongest sides of the Communist Party's ideology and policy—its profound humanity. Surely, it is an excellent thing that the Communists are able to combine organically the human and the political! And this ability, obviously, springs from the essence of their teaching. In another part of his book Mehnert tells how he visited a literature lesson at a Soviet school and talked to one of the

[1] Klaus Mehnert, *Der Sowjetmensch*, Stuttgart, S. 451-52.

[2] Ibid., S. 452.

[3] Ibid., S. 355-57.

teachers. He asked her what she regarded as the true aim of education. "In preparing good citizens for our socialist Motherland," she replied. "That is just the answer I was expecting," Mehnert told her, "because that is the task you have been set by the state. But I have the impression that what you really like is not this political task but educating people in general.... I reached this conclusion during the literature lesson at which you spoke with such fervour of the human problems in the novels of Dickens." She smiled: "Yes, I like the great novels of world literature and I know of no better way of developing the human personality than reading them.... From our point of view, in a socialist country a human feeling and a civic feeling are identical." And Mehnert sums up. "Once again she had remembered the official opinions that it was her duty to defend."[1]

This is a strange way of looking at things. Mehnert simply cannot imagine that the person he is talking to could be sincere, that she might actually believe in and deliberately defend a point of view that is not to his liking. If she had agreed with Mehnert, then, no doubt, we should be told that she was stating her "own" views. She is wrong not because she is really wrong but because her statement contradicts Mehnert, who in general rules out any possibility of unity of the human and the communist.

The acceptance of communist views does not yet make people into Communists, and the changes that have occurred have not spread fanaticism—such is the shaky foundation of Mehnert's conception. Contact with the reality quickly reveals its groundlessness. Many observers have noted in Soviet people this irresistible quality of combining a simple modesty and sociability with ideological firmness and collectivism.

The attempt to dispose of Soviet man by creating an antithesis between communist ideology and humanity, by arguing their incompatibility, is only a variation of the old and fairly well-known trick. If you want to discredit your opponent, prove that his intentions and actions are hostile to humanity, that they run counter to all man's cherished notions.

---

[1] Klaus Mehnert, *Der Sowjetmensch*, S. 352.

The Concept of Original Sin

The next conception of Soviet man attempts to ignore the very fact of people's attitude to communist ideology. Its advocates may even note the "victory of ideological education" or totally deny its significance because the only thing that really matters from their point of view is the presence in society of criminal elements, of idlers, of property-owning ambitions; and if there are such elements, there can be no question of the existence of a new kind of person.

Ulpese A. Floride, an Italian Jesuit and active propagandist of Catholicism, asserts in his book *The Soviet Union's Dilemma* that the "changes brought about by the Communists in the economic structure have not improved people and not led to the establishment of the kingdom of justice and honesty". To prove his point he cites the fact that there are still people pursuing their own profit in socialist society. The fact that measures are taken against criminals and idlers he uses to support the conclusion that the Soviet Union is still far from producing a new man, ready to enter the age of communism. In short, the author entirely ignores any positive advances.

Mehnert, for example, in seeking signs of opposition to the Soviet Government, does not disdain to use street incidents and quarrels. He had the luck to observe someone riding on a tram without buying a ticket, then he saw someone breaking the traffic rules, a young man crossing the street in a wrong place. Rejoicing over the altercation between the offenders and the "representatives of authority"—a ticket inspector and a militiaman—he presents this as a conflict between the people and the state![1] There, you see, despite all the social conditions, man still seeks to satisfy his base vital instincts. "Even if a classless society came about, it would be a society of the sinful...."[2]

The overthrow of the new man is here based on Freudian teaching on man's congenital asociality, on the unalterability of his egoistic nature. A thorough critical analysis of Freud's teaching, and also of modern psychoanalysis in general, is to

---

[1] K. Mehnert, *Der Sowjetmensch*, S. 397-98.
[2] *Marxismusstudien*, Tübingen, 1954, S. 231.

be found in Harry K. Wells's *The Failure of Psychoanalysis.*[1]
The question of the correlation of the social and the biological in man has recently been widely discussed in Soviet
studies. It does, indeed, require further investigation and
elucidation, but this fact does not alter the postulate on the
determining role of social conditions in forming the ethos,
the general orientation of the personality.

The Propagandist Variant

Finally, there is the propagandist explanation of the attraction exercised by the Soviet person which is kept mainly
for internal consumption. Without bothering themselves at
all about the real state of affairs in the Soviet Union, the
enthusiasts of this point of view brand any influence of socialism as propaganda. Frederick G. Barghoorn, Professor
of Political Science at Yale University, in his book *Soviet
Foreign Propaganda* observes: "The public tendency, as well
as that of some experts on communism, is to attribute the
growth of communist power exclusively to communist cun-
ning. . . ."[2]

The propagandist variant fails to satisfy any serious demands. The same Professor Barghoorn warns: "The danger
in being guided by estimates of Soviet propaganda influence
such as the foregoing, is twofold. On the one hand, excessive
emphasis on the role of propaganda in Soviet policy can
blind one to the importance of such factors as education and
scientific research that enable the USSR to build the power
which makes its propaganda impressive. Perhaps more important, the alarmist view of Soviet propaganda may lead
us to think that all that is required to combat communist influence is American counter-propaganda."[3]

Barghoorn draws attention to the fact that there are objective conditions for the success of Soviet propaganda. He
maintains that the world's social difficulties are responsible
for the influence of communist ideology.

---

[1] Harry K. Wells, *The Failure of Psychoanalysis,* Moscow, Progress
Publishers, 1968.
[2] Frederick G. Barghoorn, *Soviet Foreign Propaganda,* Princeton,
New Jersey, 1964, p. 308.
[3] Ibid., p. 318.

Joseph M. Bochenski proposes that in order to liberate people from the influence of communism "the main thing is to destroy the Communists' ideology", and to this end the level of "Sovietology" must be raised. He is disturbed by the fact that among the anti-communist Sovietologists "a great number of cranks and amateurs have appeared who produce work of extremely doubtful value."[1] Bochenski dubs many of his colleagues pseudo-Sovietologists and tries to classify them. His classification is interesting: "These people may be divided into the following five classes: (a) scholars who are specialists in certain disciplines but have no training whatever in Sovietology; (b) Marxologists, who, nevertheless, have no training in the development of the 20th century, particularly of communism; (c) ex-Communists without any scientific training; (d) people who although they may have lived for a time in the Soviet Union and other communist countries, nevertheless, have no knowledge whatever in this field; (e) politicians, journalists, church representatives, etc., who cannot claim even the modicum of knowledge possessed by the other four groups."[2] It would be hard to add anything to this vivid characterisation.

Bochenski does not agree with those who claim that the strength of the "free world" lies in the fact that it does not stand for any particular ideas, that its doors are always open for all ideas, while it never attaches absolute value to any of them. Such scepticism, Bochenski declares, always loses in competition with communism. He proposes looking for a "middle" course. What is needed in the fight against communism is a positive spiritual principle. It should contain its own, perhaps, only a few fundamental norms and values, which would, nevertheless, (!) not constitute a system of views. These propositions and values must be accepted as absolutes and not placed in doubt.

What are these values? There are five altogether: (1) the scientific idea, man's scientific authority; phenomena of people's inner spiritual world; divine authority also

---

[1] Joseph M. Bochenski, "Sowjetologie", *Aus Politik und Zeitgeschichte,* Beilage zur Wochenzeitung *Das Parlament,* Bd. 11/62, 14 März, 1962, S. 111.

[2] A whole series of other authors write critically of the work of Sovietologists.

legitimate; (2) the humanist idea: complete free unfolding of all the abilities of modern man is the greatest value on earth and the supreme aim of any policy; (3) the social-democratic idea: every person has certain inherent and inalienable rights, and all people in this sense are equal; (4) the politico-democratic idea: of all the political regimes we have experienced the least bad is the democratic-pluralist system, i.e., capitalism; (5) the economically pluralist idea: of all the economic systems tested by life the pluralist (read, capitalist—*G. S.*) has advantages over the monopoly of the means of production (read, socialism—*G. S.*).

And that is all. We are confronted with an incredible mixture of the most varying points of view and ideological trends. All his life Bochenski has been criticising the Communists for allegedly encroaching on individual freedom, but here he demands that people should accept his recommended values as absolute and not subject to doubt.

Imperialism's lack of any positive programme is by no means due to insufficient intellectual ability on the part of its ideologists. It is an organic fault in the capitalist system. The development of the "social order in the world" is tending more and more towards collapse of the capitalist system and its ideology, towards the growth of socialism and the socialist consciousness of the masses. More and more people are beginning to understand that what matters is the real processes that are taking place in socialism and capitalism, and that propaganda is secondary. The Communists may rightly take pride in the fact that they are able to put across their ideas to the broad masses of the working people, because they are bringing them the noble ideas of humanism and truth. The true causes of socialism's increased prestige and the growing interest in the socialist way of life and the new people are the successes of socialism, the deeply humanistic content of its ideology, the economic and cultural achievements of socialism and the strength of the USSR and the countries of the socialist community.

Bourgeois ideologists have been extremely active in evolving various conceptions of the Soviet man. No matter how different they may be, all the conceptions have the characteristic feature of speculation on actually existing problems, the effort to use truth to manufacture half-truth and half-truth to produce thoroughgoing lies. On the other hand, all these conceptions are basically designed to justify bourgeois values.

* * *

The socio-historical needs of society's movement towards socialism and communism, which have found expression in real social forms and institutions, in ideological and moral values, have become the needs, interests and motivations of people. There is every reason to assert that these people are personalities of a new social type.

It must be emphasised that we are speaking of the appearance of a special social type and not of just, say, a class type. The features of the Soviet man are moulded on the basis of the ideology of the working class and in its image and likeness, but he is a type which has formed through the transformation of certain features that were once special class features into features of the whole people, features existing side by side with the vestiges of class distinctions. This causes certain difficulties in delineating the generally significant features and perceiving them despite the accepted notion of social types as class types. But habits of perception do not change the essence of the matter, particularly as the new terminology—"new man", "Soviet man"—has become widely and firmly established.

The new man, his needs, interests, views, beliefs, habits and ideals have taken shape on the basis of traditions and stereotypes that have been accumulated in the course of centuries and quite often conflict with the new. Man is not only a social being. He is also a natural being with his own bio-genetic and psycho-genetic qualities, which remain extremely significant components of the life and development of the personality.

One must bear in mind that the socialist ethos does not manifest itself equally in all cases and in relation to all facts and events. When considering how people's qualities manifest themselves one must remember that there are at least three planes of social life: *first,* the fundamental forms of social relations which take shape in the course of revolution, during the transition from one socio-economic formation to another and constitute the basis, the essence of the given

formation. Under socialism these include public ownership
of the means of production, the principle of distribution
according to work, the organisation of social labour and the
forms of exchange, the socialist state and the Marxist-Leninist ideology; *second,* concrete forms in which social relations function and develop and through which people
directly perceive the above-mentioned fundamental forms.
Let us say, the system of economic and political institutions,
laws, regulations, rules, and so on. Concrete forms are far
more mobile and variable because they must respond to the
quickly changing levels of the productive forces and the
needs of social development; *third,* people's current organising activity through which their aims, principles and norms
are realised and which may or may not coincide with the
essence of the dominant social relations, policy, and Party
and state instructions.

This distinction must be made in order to analyse the
various social processes and assess people's behaviour correctly. People's attitude, positive or negative, to the fundamentals of a given system is one thing, while their attitude
to certain concrete institutions, establishments, to the work
or behaviour of certain members of the staff is quite another.
This is what makes the conditions in which the individual
consciousness develops, so complex and contradictory. Hence
it would be naïve to imagine social life under socialism as
something programmed all the way through.

The general, typical attributes of the new personality are
not equally inherent in all people. Several categories of
people continue to retain in some degree or other what we
call the vestiges of capitalism. There are people, though
only very few, who are hostile to society. For such people
the socialist way of life is something alien and external.
They are in ideological and moral conflict with society, and
their own way of life has a disastrous effect on their
children's upbringing. If restrictive measures of a legal and
moral character were relaxed, such phenomena could grow
into a social danger. Consequently, the development of
socialism and the formation of the socialist type of personality is a long and complex process in the course of which the
socialist consciousness develops steadily and widely but
unequally in different groups, and all the more unequally

in separate individuals, because every individual travels a unique path of cognition and experience in the course of his life.

The fact that socialism has its problems—economic, political and moral—is entirely natural. In general there is no such thing as society without problems, or development without problems. The problems of capitalism are problems of escape from the obsolete, decayed conditions of a social system that has outlived its time. The problems of socialism are problems of overcoming the remnants of the old, of seeking ways of achieving concrete economic, political, cultural and moral aims. Increased production, development of socialist democracy, the perfecting of all aspects of social relations, extension of education and improvement of general upbringing—such are the main directions in which the person of communist society is formed.

Thus, although all kinds of problems still exist, there are good grounds for speaking of the purposeful and successful formation of the new personality possessing the attributes of the socialist ethos. This has become possible because socialism has created the corresponding conditions, stimuli and norms of behaviour. A new man has appeared and is developing, and it is he, his convictions and ideals, his behaviour and actions that determine the future of the Land of Soviets, the future of socialism and communism.

CHAPTER FIVE

PROBLEMS OF PERSONALITY TYPING IN SOCIALIST SOCIETY

The formation of an integrated socialist type of personality does not by any means do away with the diversity of types in general. The class structure of society, the differences in people's labour activities and living conditions, in their level of political, moral and cultural development give birth to a whole system of types of personality. The study of this diversity which exists within the framework of the general features of the socialist type is one of the most important tasks of investigating the problems of social development in general and the new man in particular.

Whereas the scientific investigation of all the personal particularities of every individual is impossible in principle, the limitation of research to mere general features, however significant, would make any such inquiry extremely superficial and inadequate. The particular, like the individual, is a form, a means of existence and development of the general. Only by studying the particular in the general, by studying the interconnection and mutual subordination of the general, the particular and the individual, can one capture the rich and complex diversity of tendencies, phenomena and conflicts that makes up the content of social development.

In the works of the founders of scientific communism we find a detailed elaboration of the characteristic features of the social types of their day. Their method of investigating the personality structure of society is a rich legacy that we have still to use to the fullest advantage.

1. SOCIAL TYPES WITHIN THE FRAMEWORK
OF THE SOCIALIST ETHOS

The elimination of the exploiting classes and the formation of the general socialist type of personality not only do not remove differences between classes and within classes, but, on the contrary, for the first time they make differences within classes, which are mainly connected with people's labour activity, increasingly significant. The typical attributes of the personality stemming from the specific nature of its activity and formerly kept in the background by the characteristics of the antagonist classes, now hold the stage and attract more and more attention of researchers. The significance of these attributes is additionally stimulated by scientific and technological progress. New machinery and technological processes along with integration impose a new character of differentiation in the socialist organisation of labour. Moreover, within the framework of the general type there are considerable differences of depth and stability which also constitute definite typical features of the personality and require classification.

Class and Intraclass Types, Character of Work
as the Basis of Typing

The starting point for investigating the type structure of any society, including socialist society, is characterisation of the structural pattern and forms of social life. In this connection the question of the relationship between the processes of development of social homogeneity and the division of labour under socialism needs to be considered in greater detail.

In advocating the establishment of social homogeneity and equality the Communists expressed the ancient desire of the working people to rid themselves of exploitation and oppression. The society of the future was conceived by the founders of scientific communism as a classless society. But the Communists' desire for a classless society springs not merely from moral condemnation of the evil that the exploiting classes bring in their train. It is founded on analysis of the economic development of society. The abolition of the exploiting

classes and ultimately of all division of society into classes is
an inevitable stage in social history and necessary condition
for the further progress of society. As soon as socialist society
mechanises and automates all the production processes, as
soon as it creates an abundance of material goods, it will not
only be able to eliminate the remaining social differences
between the classes and strata of the working people; it will
have to do this owing to the pressure of economic demands.
However, while class differences continue to remain in society
there will also be class types of personality (worker, collective
farmer) moulded by the peculiarities of their classes.

The characteristics of the collective farmer are as follows:
his being engaged in agricultural work; membership of the
collective farm and, consequently, direct interest in its development and the development of co-operative property; the
existence of his own personal subsidiary holding, in view of
which the level of his income also depends on his own personal husbandry and he makes an appearance from time to time
on the market; and finally the level of culture and everyday
life of the general mass of collective farmers being lower than
in town. Although in Soviet society today it is not uncommon
to find members of a collective farm with a higher level of
education and consciousness than is found in the towns, one
must judge by the level of the majority of collective farmers.

Correspondingly, the typical Soviet worker is employed at
a socialist state enterprise and engaged predominantly in
physical labour.[1] The Soviet worker, as a bearer of the features of the class that plays the leading role in socialist society, is distinguished by a high degree of consciousness, initiative at work, discipline and responsibility.

The Soviet intellectual, as a special type differing from
both the worker and the collective farmer, is a person profes-
sionally engaged in mental, intellectual work.

These distinctions of a class nature determine the essential content of socialist relationships and important aspects
of state policy. But alongside the class types there also exist
types whose special features are formed on the basis of

---

[1] Workers at co-operative enterprises who are not members of the
co-operative, and also at enterprises belonging to public organisations,
are no different in this sense from the workers at state enterprises.

distinctions in professional qualifications or skills. In this connection it is appropriate to recall the well-known idea that Marx expressed in a letter to L. Kugelmann on July 11, 1868: "that the masses of products corresponding to the different needs require different and quantitatively determined masses of the total labour of society. That this *necessity* of the *distribution* of social labour in definite proportions cannot possibly be done away by a *particular form* of social production but can only change the *mode* of its appearance, is self-evident"[1]. In other words, society will always require a certain number of workers to put up buildings, to teach, to heal, and so on. Consequently, in the general mass of working people there will always be groups of people who stand out from the rest on account of the work they are performing at the given moment.

There are two standpoints that may be adopted in classifying types according to their occupations. One is the industrial standpoint classifying people as metallurgists, miners, machine builders, weavers, builders, railways workers, communication workers, and so on. The other standpoint entails classification on the basis of skill: high, medium or low. The various forms of activity in socialist society are primarily instrumental in forming sets of living conditions that create or develop certain specific abilities, needs, interests and notions in people.

The specific nature of a particular activity determines the interests of a given group of people and the difference between their interests and those of other groups. Groups of people engaged in producing, let us say, aircraft, in growing grain, in teaching children, and so on, have much in common in experience and the character of their knowledge, and also their specific production features—methods and forms of work, common problems to be solved, common goals, closer interdependence with other people within the given collective, a greater intensity of intercommunication. All this is what gives them their special interests. And even if people are not connected with a particular sphere of work exclusively and for life, while they are thus occupied they are united with their colleagues first and foremost by

---

[1] K. Marx and F. Engels, *Selected Correspondence*, p. 251.

their production interests. These groups, in fulfilling certain functions, performing certain tasks with which they are immediately confronted, take part in the realisation of the general interests. In short, social interest finds its expression in the concrete interests that are formed among people in one or another field of activity—production, socio-political, scientific, artistic activity, and so on. Production interests provide a basis for the development of various kinds of technical, scientific, cultural, sporting and public organisations which are also a form of the realisation of the general and specific interests of these groups of people.

The source of the growing diversity of life and activity is the advance of scientific knowledge. Scientific discoveries provide mankind not only with new sources of energy, materials, instruments of production, but also new forms of activity, new and varied interests, and open up new paths of discovery.

There is also the diversity of the planet itself. Conditions of life in one country differ from those in another; those of steppe dwellers will always differ from those of people in the mountains, those of people who inhabit the taiga from those who live on the sea-coast.

All this goes to show the tremendous variety that is to be found in people's conditions and hence their interests, a variety that continues to exist even in a socially homogeneous society. The significance of social homogeneity, of complete social equality lies precisely in the fact that it provides the best setting for the development and satisfaction of this diversity of interests. Society acquires the opportunity of activating the creative abilities of millions of people who under capitalism would be engaged in compulsory labour or who have no opportunity to work at all, like the millions of unemployed in the so-called "free world".

Bourgeois propagandists do all they can to present socialism and communism as a kind of barracks where everyone lives and acts according to regulations laid down by a single established leadership, where there is no place for initiative and personal individuality.

Yet the founders of scientific communism even in their day always protested sharply against the idea of the future society as a kingdom of asceticism, monotony, standardisation and conformity. In *The Communist Manifesto* Marx and Engels pointed out that socialism could not be built on the basis of asceticism and levelling. Engels subjected Dühring's "radical, levelling socialism" to devastating criticism.

What the Marxists understand by equality is simply the abolition of classes and nothing more. Any attempt to go further than this in interpreting communist equality leads to the vulgarisation of Marxism, and its separation from reality. "...When socialists speak of equality they always mean *social* equality, equality of social status, and not by any means the physical and mental equality of individuals."[1] Communist equality presupposes that "...a *different form* of activity, of labour, does not justify *inequality*, confers no *privileges* in respect of possession and enjoyment"[2]. Equality, therefore, consists in satisfying the reasonable needs of all members of society, and not in making everyone receive the same goods in the same quantity.

The development of social homogeneity and equality, as experience has shown, does not in any way signify the establishment of uniformity of social life and types of personality. On the contrary, society, liberated from class antagonisms and subsequently from class distinctions, acquires new possibilities for developing the individuality of people's talents and inclinations. Social homogeneity is the basis for the development of an incomparably richer diversity in the life of every individual and society as a whole, a diversity that is related primarily to work for the good of society.

Levels and Intensity of the Socialist Ethos

In addition to the diversity that springs from differences in activity, the different levels and intensity of the socialist ethos have a specific significance in type classification.

In the first place, social type classification must be tied in with the characterisation of certain tendencies, patterns of social development. Second, there must be a clear definition of the main foundations of the classification of features, i.e., of those foundations that express what is most essential

---

[1] V. I. Lenin, *Collected Works,* Vol. 20, p. 146.
[2] K. Marx and F. Engels, *The German Ideology,* p. 593.

in social relations. Such foundations are the main spheres of existence: people's attitude to the social system, to socialism as a system (adherence to the communist principle); their attitude to work, the character and content of their own activity; their attitude to the rules of social intercourse, expressed in the level of responsibility and discipline.

It is not enough, however, to point out what spheres of relations provide the foundation for the formation of types; there must also be definite criteria of the development of features, i.e., qualitative characteristics of this or that form of relationship. Such type-forming criteria in respect of adherence to the communist principle may be: complete acceptance and support of communist ideology, a neutral attitude towards it and, in some cases, non-acceptance, hostility, struggle against it. Moreover, adherence to the communist principle may also be expressed in different levels of knowledge and understanding of that ideology, consistency and determination in defending it. Labour activity may also be expressed by various indicators: high level of knowledge, skill and businesslike qualities; medium level of skill and responsible attitude to the task in hand; low level of skill with features of poor discipline and irresponsibility. In the same way one can introduce two or three levels of moral characteristics. Various combinations of particular features or the singling out of one feature as the dominant, allows us to determine what is typical in a personality and characterise the features of that type of personality.

Different people in various circumstances may display certain features and these features may become so strong that they oust or restrict other essential attributes. For instance, a lack of political education may lead to hypertrophy of purely professional features. This type of person is remarkable for his complete indifference or lack of attention to political questions. He is characterised by a comparatively low level of political consciousness and also a narrow cultural horizon. His immediate duties overshadow all his other interests and problems. This disregard of everything that is outside his field of work sometimes takes grotesque forms. Although such people may be useful assistants, they quickly lose their sense of direction in a complex situation, rush to extremes and make serious mistakes.

There is also the moralising type of personality—the kind of individual for whom certain elementary moral norms begin to acquire self-sufficient importance and overshadow more important problems of life. Along with the "moralist" we have the aesthetic type, who buries himself in the world of art, is carried away by certain of its aspects and makes his enthusiasm almost the sole purpose of his life. This list could be continued. But it is not a matter of how many types we enumerate. Our task is to single out the new typical features that reflect the essential processes of the development of socialist society on its path to communism.

In this connection we must point to certain essential directions of development of the socialist personality. An objective need to strengthen adherence to the communist principle among the broad masses of the working people continues to develop. This need is dictated by the tasks of building communist society and the intensity of the struggle with imperialism. As socialism grows stronger and the education and culture of the general mass of members of society increases there is a greater need and opportunity for increasingly wider sections of the people to acquire the scientific world view and the principles of communist morality. On this basis there is developing on a wide scale a type that combines in itself the performance of what could be called "rank-and-file" work (worker, collective farmer, office worker) with a profound mastery not only of the fundamentals but also of many subtleties of the Party ideology and policy. This type already exists and it will grow in quantity and improve in quality.

Yet another tendency consists in the establishment of a more harmonious combination of political consciousness and professional skill. In the context of a politically and ideologically united society the differences between types have largely been transferred to the sphere of work, education, living conditions, and so on. The level of skill, competence, ability to perform the task with which one has been entrusted are acquiring ever greater importance. As we know, in the early years of Soviet power, in the conditions of intense class struggle, it was necessary to give preference to political qualities. Hence the institution of political commissars and the need to send to establishments and offices people who, although not specialists, were able to safeguard the political line, who were devoted to the revolution. Later, in the context of peaceful construction the principle of combining political and business qualities was introduced which is still entirely relevant today.

In conditions of intensified ideological struggle ideological conviction and firmness are essential features for any personnel, particularly those in positions of authority. But since devotion to the ideas of communism and the Party policy have become generally accepted by the overwhelming majority of the people, the significance of business abilities and skills is becoming ever more important. In order to show one's devotion to ideas one must be able to give them practical expression in life. This particularly needs to be stressed in connection with the current scientific and technological revolution and the unprecedented demands that it has placed on the knowledge of personnel at all levels of the national economy. The development of a type combining unconditional dedication to communism, profound knowledge and understanding of the theory and politics of communism with a high professional qualification corresponding to the current level of scientific and technological progress is one of the basic tendencies in the development of the socialist personality.

And yet another aspect of the development of personality. Whereas contempt for personal interests was considered almost the cardinal feature of the new personality in the first years of Soviet power, in present-day conditions society has wider possibilities for satisfying personal interests. At the 24th Party Congress Leonid Brezhnev emphasised: "...Our aims, the greater economic potential and the requirements of economic development make it possible and necessary to steer the economy more fully to resolving the highly diverse tasks relating to the improvement of the people's standard of living".[1]

Concern for the wise blending of social and personal interests, and respect for the individual's personal interests, should be an elementary rule guiding the activity of all Party and state organs, while precedence should, of course,

---

[1] *The 24th Congress of the CPSU*, p. 51.

be given to the social, the public interest in all fundamental matters of social life. Hence the fostering of respect for the dignity of the individual, consideration for personal problems and at the same time an insistence on high standards and the need to foster in every individual a sense of collectivism, responsibility and discipline constitute yet another direction of development of the personality in socialist society.

Although Soviet society has made great advances in producing a new kind of person, people's consciousness is still often a strange mingling of positive and negative qualities, strong and weak aspects of character.

2. TYPES OF ANTI-SOCIAL BEHAVIOUR

Anti-social behaviour does not always fall into the category of the criminal offence by any means. Some actions (instances of bureaucratism, careerism, heartlessness and selfishness, etc.), which clearly testify to a person's anti-social orientation, are not punishable by law. And vice versa, certain misdeeds committed through negligence, carelessness, slackness or moral weakness are punished as criminal offences, although there was no anti-social intent behind them. The policy of the law in punishing offenders, however, though it takes into consideration the motive of the crime, proceeds mainly from the gravity of the immediate damage caused. Only this approach can deal effectively with crime.

Conditions of Preservation and Classification of the Main Types of Anti-Social Behaviour

Professional crime has been liquidated in the Soviet Union. The Soviet Union is free of the organised gangsterism that is corroding the social organism of the capitalist countries, particularly the United States. All that dissappeared together with the ruling classes, as something that they had directly created and that was a permanent feature of their existence.

But in the Soviet Union one still encounters crime and criminals. The fact that they have continued to exist for so long compels us to infer (as science has done) that for such types of behaviour there exist corresponding conditions, corresponding possibilities for their manifestation and, therefore, motives and means appropriate to them. The need is for all-round investigation of the conditions and causes of crime.

Some people are inclined to believe that these causes should be sought in the personality of the criminal; others pay more attention to the environment, to various external circumstances that drive a person to crime. In the present author's view there is nothing to be gained from extremes. If we consider the actual circumstances of any particular crime, it is usually apparent that the criminal himself was to blame as well as certain external conditions that aided and abetted the crime. Thus, we are able to narrow down the task to studying the sets of conditions that provide a fabourable breeding ground for crime and criminal tendencies.

Socialism, having abolished the exploiting classes, did away with the parasitic life style on which the underworld was oriented. Socialism also did away with the poverty and unemployment that forced people to commit crimes because of material want. But socialism cannot immediately establish complete economic equality among people and certain differences, therefore, continue to exist in people's conditions of life. These differences are not as a rule very large. The difference in incomes is determined by the quality and quantity of work which each individual gives to society. This is nothing like the tremendous gaps and glaring contrasts that exist in bourgeois society, where the luxurious and idle life of the rich is viewed with covetous eyes by the criminal world. Nevertheless, the attainment of a higher standard of life (a car, a good flat, elegant clothes, dining out, and so on) may entice people who have neither the desire nor the ability to acquire these things through honest work into making money by unlawful means.

Naturally, this is only a very general background, a background that exists for all members of society but prompts only the person of a certain orientation to resort to crime.

First of all we have the fact of the existence of criminal behaviour, which shows that such behaviour is possible. Although professional crime, as it exists in bourgeois society, disappeared under socialism, it did not disappear at once and not all criminals have disappeared even now. Some of them continue to lead their parasitic, criminal way of life, quite often under the mask of participation in social production and appropriate outward behaviour. Their goal—gain, pleasure at the expense of society, of other people—remains the chief motive of activity of such people, and any methods and means are permissible for its attainment. In 1961, a group of forgers was brought to trial. "What is your aim in life?" the state prosecutor asked one of them, a man named Rokotov. "To buy a three-room flat in Moscow, an out-of-town house near Moscow and a villa in the Crimea. I wanted to experience some gracious living." Another question: "What do you understand by that?" Answer: "Having money and not working anywhere." This man's programme in life and principles were expressed in the clearest possible manner. They are deeply inimical to socialism. It was from such types, concealed kulaks and bandits, that the fascists drew their assistants during the war.

Such people not only manage to survive, but also produce others like themselves, because this is necessary for their own survival. In doing so they rely on the selfish, essentially petty-bourgeois psychology that is to be found among some people. There are families whose watchword, "grab while you've got the chance" or in another version "the main thing is to look after oneself", remains the chief rule of conduct and is passed on to the children if the influence of the school and friends is for some reason not strong enough. Such types are encouraged by pathological parental affection for their children and constant spoiling from early childhood. The child is brought up from the start as a person unable to limit his needs, as a potential breaker of all rules and norms.

The basic conditions for the formation of a purely individualistic, selfish way of thinking bordering on the criminal are created in some families by the cultivation of the principles of putting one's own advantage before the public interest and in others by unlimited pandering to the whims of the growing child. Only a push from outside is needed to give rise to crime and that push often comes from hardened criminal element. It may also be provided by any conducives of set circumstances such as bad management, lack of control, lack of material incentive to look after socialist property, poor law-making and deficiencies in the working of any particular state agency.

In classifying anti-social behaviour the Soviet researcher A. G. Kovalyov takes as his criterion for defining the basic types of criminal the degree to which the personality of the lawbreaker is infected with crime. According to this criterion he calls the first type a *global criminal type,* i.e., totally infected with crime. People belonging to this type cannot conceive life without the crimes which promise them their chief pleasure in life. All their thoughts and feelings are bound up with the idea of committing crimes and they are fully determined in their criminal intent. This type includes several subtypes: the corrupter and rapist, the embezzler, bandit, and so on.

The second type is the *partial type,* i.e., consisting of partially infected criminals. Such people have split personalities in which normal social features and criminal features live side by side. People belonging to this type, for example, show respect for people in authority, have friends, take an interest in the events of social life, keep abreast of news from abroad, go to the theatre, to exhibitions, but at the same time systematically commit crimes in the form of theft of public or personal property.

The third type is the *precriminal type.* These people have moral and psychological qualities that in a certain situation may lead them to commit a crime. These are people with an extremely high degree of emotional excitability and insufficient self-control, which in a given situation may prompt them to commit acts of hooliganism or serious crimes. The second variation of this type is the light-minded idler, who likes enjoying life without giving himself any trouble. This subtype is easily tempted and, when a favourable situation occurs, commits a crime.

A. G. Kovalyov's classification is, undoubtedly, of great interest, particularly from the standpoint of general psychology. However, it is of an extremely general character and contains no socially differentiated material.

The Criminal Code of the RSFSR gives the following classification of crimes: (1) state crimes; (2) crimes against socialist property; (3) crimes against the life, health, freedom and dignity of the individual; (4) crimes against the political and labour rights of citizens; (5) crimes against the personal property of citizens; (6) economic crimes; (7) crimes connected with malfeasance; (8) crimes against justice; (9) crimes against administration; (10) crimes against state security, public order and the health of the population; (11) crimes reflecting survivals of local customs; (12) military crimes.

Here the basis for classification of crimes is provided by the spheres of social life in which laws or legal rules are violated. With this approach the motive of the crime revealing the social nature of the personality involved, though repeated in various sections of the Criminal Code, remains somewhat obscure. If we examine the various types of crime from the point of view of motive and also the means employed, we may single out three basic types of motives: political motives, i.e., disagreement with the principles of the system; desire for gain, self-enrichment, mercenariness; and various aggressive impulses. The means of achieving these aims include: purposeful, conscious actions, political and propagandist, premeditated murder, bodily harm, theft, embezzlement, machinations, blackmail, verbal insult, dereliction of duty, etc.

Working on these lines we can draw up a table of the basic types of anti-social behaviour.

Three types of anti-social behaviour emerge more or less clearly in the political sphere: (1) deliberate group actions; (2) anti-Soviet propaganda; (3) inward dissent expressed in the form of a nihilistic attitude to the values of socialism. Each of these divisions expresses a political, ideological hostility to the socialist nature of the system and, consequently, the counter-revolutionary essence of the types involved.

The means employed by the second group in which the motive is desire for gain and mercenariness run as follows: (1) murder for purposes of robbery; (2) theft at enterprises; (3) bribery; (4) underground private enterprise; (5) profiteering; (6) theft of the property of individual citizens; (7) extortion, blackmail; (8) seeking of particularly lucrative work for purposes of accumulation; (9) nepotism, use of one's position to promote the interests of family, friends, etc., at the expense of the state; (10) avoidance of socially useful work, attempts by various means to live at the expense of others. The degree of hostility to the fundamental principles of the socialist system differs in these cases, and in some of them is altogether absent. But people who behave in this way share the desire to accumulate, acquisitiveness, selfishness, contempt for the interests of society, to which all other motivations in life are subordinated.

In the third group come aggressive forms of behaviour connected with an egoistic attitude to the generally accepted norms of social life: (1) murder for the sake of revenge, jealousy, and so on; (2) insulting behaviour, verbal or physical, towards other citizens, infringement of rules of internal order in public places or places where people live together (hooliganism); (3) criminal indifference to a person in grave distress through selfishness or cowardice; (4) criminal indifference of a person in authority to a person's interests, ignoring of his rights, violation of the dignity and freedom of the individual.

Types of Thieves

In considering the general type of the thief the Soviet researcher V. B. Yastrebov singles out only those who show an ability to conduct active operations in pursuit of their criminal aims. He considers that these attributes are most clearly manifest in the specific nature of non-socialist attitude to social, public property inherent in the various kinds of thieves. The expression of this attitude and its stability may be strong, medium or weak.

The objective situation in which the criminal acts is characterised by Yastrebov according to the degree of difficulty involved in stealing. Accordingly we have (a) extremely favourable, (b) relatively favourable, and (c) unfavourable.

In considering the effect of objective conditions on people, and also the reverse effect of people with anti-social views on conditions with regard to making use of (or creating) conditions for stealing, Yastrebov points out three basic types.

The first type comprises people in whom the non-socialist attitude to social property is expressed to a high degree with a high degree of stability. Thieves of this type make use of a wide range of conditions offering opportunities for stealing. If the situation is unfavourable they try actively to change it to their advantage.

The degree to which the non-socialist attitude is expressed

by thieves of the second type may be defined as medium, with a medium degree of stability. For anti-social views to be realised in a criminal attempt much depends on the situation, i.e., the existence of conditions providing ample opportunities for unrestrained thieving. Use is made chiefly of conditions to which the criminal is accustomed. He does not try actively to create a situation conducive to stealing, but at the same time will not be hindered by minor obstacles.

The characteristic feature of thieves of the third type is weakness of their non-socialist attitude to social, public property. They are indifferent to the protection of public property. In the main these are people who will only steal if something is left "lying about", i.e., unguarded. If the act of stealing entails difficulties, they will, probably, not steal.

Apart from these basic types there is also a distinctive category of people characterised by only a slightly non-socialist attitude to public property. Such people commit crimes out of ideological and psychological weakness. Usually they steal when their personal circumstances are, or seem to them to be, in a bad state, i.e., when the circumstances of life suggest to them the possibility of acquiring some advantage by illegal means and objective conditions offer the chance of doing so without any particular difficulty.

In classifying pilferers one must take into consideration not only the aim and objective conditions but also the methods used, since these express the relationship between aim and objective conditions. Methods of stealing are in this sense a synthesised and objective criterion for classification of types.

Taking into consideration the methods of stealing and also the general orientation of the consciousness and the objective conditions, it is possible to divide thieves into the following types:

(1) those who participate in organised, group stealing, using their position at work for mercenary purposes. Subtypes include the organisers and rank-and-file members who consciously adopt the path of crime;

(2) the thief who also uses his place at work but acts on his own. Subtypes may be classified according to the intensity and scale of the stealing;

(3) thieves performing individual group thefts at enterprises without making use of their official position;

(4) the common thief operating at his own place of work;

(5) the person who is compelled to steal by pressure of
circumstances. Having originally become involved through
weakness, he tries to escape from a situation that weighs on
his conscience.

This classification, while not claiming to be exhaustive,
supplies some fairly definite indications concerning the social
content of the type and the degree of social danger involved
in such crimes.

Types of Politically Hostile Personality

There is no social basis in the Soviet Union for the spreading of bourgeois ideology, i.e., there is no class or social
group of the same type as the bourgeoisie and eager to
accept anti-socialist propaganda. But the Soviet Union is
involved in the system of international relations, whose
condition and development are characterised by intense
struggle between socialism and capitalism. In this struggle
the Soviet people forms one of the forces of international
socialism, of the international working class. Hence the rele-
vance of the analysis and assessment of political, ideological
and also socio-economic phenomena, events and actions from
the class standpoint, from the standpoint of who is served
by a given action or event.

The law emerging from the consolidation of Soviet society
consists in the fact that as socialist principles are strengthened
the intensity of the political and ideological struggle shifts to
the world arena. Within the country it would gradually
disappeare were it not for the capitalist world. In view of
the possibility of imperialist propaganda penetrating into
the socialist countries, particularly under the mask of socialist
ideology, and also in view of the fact that there are still
people in the socialist countries for whom personal gain is
the chief aim in life, it is important to realise that certain
elements may come under the influence of bourgeois propaganda and accept ideological and political precepts hostile
to socialism. One must also remember that in a number of
socialist countries there are still remnants of the former rul-

ing classes. In these conditions there are bound to be panic-mongers, traitors and defectors. Hence the need to make every effort to improve educational work and to foster political vigilance.

In ordinary peaceful circumstances politically hostile types are not easy to discover and rarely are discovered. On the other hand, they show themselves in their true colours at moments of crisis. This was particularly obvious during the war against nazi Germany, and some examples from that war will provide us with the best illustrations of this type of anti-social behaviour.

Let us consider the basic types of traitors according to the character of their ethos and mode of behaviour. On this basis we can distinguish fairly clearly four basic types. People of the first type consciously offered their services to the invaders or became involved with them from purely anti-Soviet, anti-socialist motives, in the hope that the fascists would restore the old prerevolutionary order. Some of them found themselves in punitive forces and the police, others served in other nazi institutions, and still others while engaging in "private enterprise" actively helped the aggressors. Those of the second type were also people who had been hostile to Soviet power and had hopes that the invaders would restore the old order, but adopted a wait-and-see position because they did not particularly trust the fascists and, above all, were uncertain as to the outcome of the war. They had no open contacts with the occupying forces and, if they did help them, did so only in secret. The third type consisted of traitors who found themselves in the enemy camp not on account of any conscious or ideological beliefs or anti-Soviet attitudes, but through lack of willpower and cowardice. However, once in the service of the fascists, such people quite often displayed no less zeal and cruelty than those who had joined the enemy out of conviction, i.e., became out-and-out enemies in the act of committing grave crimes. Finally, in the fourth type we find adaptive people, who have never held any hard-and-fast beliefs, and seen it as their main purpose to have as good life as possible. Many of these either served the invaders or were in close contact with them and, objectively speaking, helped them, although they tried to convince themselves that they had to do so for the sake of a livelihood. In contrast to the first and third types they did not as a rule take a direct part in military or political activities of the occupying forces, and they differed from the second type in that they were openly connected with the fascists.

Thus, we see that types of anti-social behaviour are the product of petty-bourgeois notions and habits that have not yet totally disappeared. They are also the product of imperialist influence in that they more or less consciously orient themselves on the bourgeois way of life.

3. GENERATIONS AND TYPES OF PERSONALITY

The term "generation" is used in different senses.

I. S. Kon in his book *The Sociology of Personality* suggests four meanings. "First, generation means one's contemporaries, people born at approximately the same time, and in this sense we speak of our fathers', grandfathers' generations, etc. Second, anthropologists and lawyers define generation as a stage in descent from a common ancestor; for example, one may say that a grandson is separated from his grandfather by two generations. Third, historians and sociologists use the term to measure the time from the birth of the parents to the birth of their children, reckoned statistically as 30 years, or three generations per century. Finally, in a fourth sense the term generation has a symbolic meaning, stressing not so much the chronological unity of contemporaries as the unity of their life and emotional experience."

The term "generation" is used most often in the last sense. Unity of experience and feeling creates the ideological and psychological image of people living at the same time which is implied in the concept of the generation.

Social conditions place a distinct imprint on the new generations and each new generation brings with it new types of personality. These new types are, naturally, born of specific conditions indicating changes in the historical situation. It is in types and patterns of types that the special features of one or another generation are manifest. It may even be said that outside people's typical features, outside types of personality it is impossible to make any distinction between the generations. If we speak of certain features of a generation there must also exist certain types that personify these special features. When Mikhail Lermontov wrote "Sadly do I look upon our generation, its future is either void or dark," our imagination at once recreates the characters in which this hopelessness, this disillusionment and sense of emptiness, was reflected. This is not to say, however, that different generations may not sometimes produce one and the same social type.

The sequence of generations and types brings us face to face with the steady progression of society, and since this progression is achieved through the struggle of classes, through the overcoming of contradictions, the relationships between the generations also express the social conflicts of society, even if not directly and immediately.

Let us consider the development of the generations in Russia over the past century, beginning approximately from the 1870s. The first generation, if we begin from that time, is the generation whose conscious life was directly bound up with the first Russian revolution, with the Great October Socialist Revolution and the start of socialist construction. This was the Leninist generation of revolutionaries, Bolsheviks, the generation of the October Revolution and the Civil War.

Characteristically, people of this generation are endowed with tremendous sense of purpose, implacability and firmness of political principle in the struggle with the enemy, and also tremendous personal courage. Certain distinctions may be drawn within this generation. It includes professional revolutionaries, organisers, leaders of the type of Yakov Sverdlov; professional revolutionaries of the worker type, such as Ivan Babushkin; worker Bolsheviks, who conducted political education among the masses, mainly on a legal basis, such as the deputies to the State Duma (G. I. Petrovsky and others); Bolsheviks from the intelligentsia, engaged in propagandist and journalistic work, such as Anatoly Lunacharsky. But all of them are people of one generation—revolutionaries of the Leninist mould.

In the second generation come those whose early youth coincided with the revolution and the Civil War. At this time their characters were only just beginning to form and their mature years fall during the period of the New Economic

Policy, the first five-year plans and the building of socialism. They were born in the 1890s and in the first decade of our century. It was the generation of builders of socialism. They also took part in the Civil War and Second World War, but their peak activity was during the period of industrialisation and collectivisation, the period of the revolutionary break-up of the old world and the creation of the new, although some of them are still active today. Their distinguishing feature is political and labour enthusiasm. Their names are linked with the mass development of socialist competition (the first shock-workers, Stakhanovites), and also with the countryside, where the broad masses of the peasant population had begun taking an active part in political life for the first time. There are internal distinctions here too but this generation is united by common feelings and aspirations, common psychological characteristics.

In the third generation one may include people who began their conscious lives during the Soviet years (born between 1910 and 1929). They are united by the events connected primarily with the Great Patriotic War and the postwar reconstruction. Often known as contemporaries of October, they grew up and were educated under Soviet rule. This generation entered life as educated and ideologically convinced citizens and together with their fathers displayed such unprecedented heroism and greatness of spirit that the world was compelled to bow its head before the land of socialism. This generation was the first to display on a wide scale those general features of Soviet people that testified quite definitely to the appearance of a new, socialist type of personality.

The fourth generation comprises people born in the thirties and forties. Their characters were formed in the years when the virgin lands were being brought under cultivation and the first space flights were made. In its formative years this generation went through a difficult period of political changes connected with the criticism of the personality cult and subjectivism. This forced the young people to take a fresh look at history, to review the past with a critical eye and not just accept it as a natural legacy. Understandably, not all of them were able to cope with the task, but taken as a whole this generation has adopted a firm stand on positions of socialism and has brought with it a high degree of education and the desire for deeper understanding of social phenomena.

Now a fifth generation is entering life. These are the young people who have been born since 1950. It is too early yet to talk of them at length, but observation suggests that this will be a generation of active builders of the new society, even more confident of the rightness of its cause and even better educated and full of creative ideas. The young people of the present day are remarkable for their high level of general culture and knowledge and intolerance of shortcomings.

This classification of the generations is based primarily on the special features arising from the significant events of their day. The generations have lived and worked together for a long time. There are direct contacts between them as well as intellectual continuity. It is, therefore, not a matter of the instantaneous replacement of one generation by another, but of a gradual redistribution of tasks and functions.

With the disappearance of class antagonisms the relationships between the generations lose their elements of class conflict. The general tendency to be found in the sequence of the generations in socialist society lies in the development and deepening of the socialist consciousness, in the fact that with every new generation the socialist consciousness adds to its existence its stability in the working people's wider knowledge, in their higher level of culture. Correspondingly, the typological structure of the personality develops in two basic directions: there is a deepening and consolidation of the general socialist features of the personality and development of the diversity of types and individual features as an expression of the integration and freedom of the personality.

Needless to say, socialism still has its problems connected with the accumulation of knowledge, the new technology, the new conditions of life, problems of education and instilling socialist consciousness into new generations that are entering social life, and so on. Noting this fact, Lenin wrote that the young people "must of necessity advance to socialism *in a different way, by other paths, in other forms, in other circumstances* than their fathers".[1]

---

[1] V. I. Lenin, *Collected Works,* Vol. 23, p. 164.

The older generations sometimes find it hard to imagine how far their perception of things differs from that of the young generations. This is particularly true of the political events of the past, which for parents were a reality of their own lives, while for the children they are already history. Every generation takes a different approach in acquiring knowledge and understanding of these events and thus masters life afresh.

The young people as a whole are always more receptive to the new and unexplored. This is their eternal and precious advantage over their elders. On the other hand, their weak spot is lack of experience. But to reproach young people for lack of experience, for their youth is, to say the least, unreasonable. Each generation has had its heroic moments and its weaknesses, its heroes and its traitors. Perceptive study of what the young people are contributing, is the duty and obligation of any society, and particularly a socialist society, in which the struggle for the new is one of the laws of social development.

CHAPTER SIX

SOME PROBLEMS OF THE PURPOSEFUL
DEVELOPMENT OF PERSONALITY

The historical advantage of the communist movement over the old world which is on its way out lies in the fact that the goals and ideals of communism coincide with the objective movement of world history. Here we have the source of the inexhaustible revolutionary optimism of the Marxists-Leninists. But the objective laws of social development materialise only in the process of people's conscious activity, through the posing and solution of problems in various spheres of social life. In other words, the coincidence between the historical process and subjective aspirations imposes on the Communists a definite responsibility for the choice of directions and substantiation of their actions, their co-ordination with the interests of the masses. This fully applies to that part of their activity that is directly connected with the development of the personality in socialist society. Here voluntarist, self-willed decisions and the ignoring of objective demands are just as dangerous as in any other spheres of social life.

The Communist Party, guided by the objective laws and historical advantages of socialism, is working persistently to perfect all the means, forms and methods of communist education of the masses. It proceeds from the fact that the moulding of the all-round personality is a long and complex process, depending on material and cultural conditions, on the depth and scope of ideological educational work.

The growing generations' entry into life, the changes in material and intellectual conditions constantly give rise to new problems and tasks. The comprehension of these problems and tasks, the search for ways of dealing with them, the

elaboration of new forms and methods of education and persistent efforts to put into practice the ideals of communism
constitute the main substance of the diverse and complex
activity by the Party and the state in educating the members
of society.

1. BASIC DIRECTIONS OF DEVELOPMENT
OF SOCIAL RELATIONS AND THE PERSONALITY

The development of social relations and also of the types
of personality, the personality structure of society, may be
considered from two angles: from the angle of society's
transition to communism and from the angle of the specific
practical changes that are constantly taking place and constitute the functioning of social institutions. Although these
forms of change are related to one another, because there can
be no development without functioning systems, just as there
can be no functioning that sooner or later does not lead to
historical change, they, nevertheless, have different significance.

The development of communist social relations presupposes
a further strengthening of the socialist forms of social life
that have already taken shape, although with time there will,
of course, appear some new and extremely important institutions and norms of life that do not at present exist. "Such
gains of socialism," state the CPSU Central Committee's
theses, *Fiftieth Anniversary of the Great October Socialist
Revolution,* "as social ownership, powerful productive forces,
a planned economy and the development of social relations,
freedom from exploitation, the fact that all must work and
have the possibility to do so, socialist democracy, society's
socio-political and ideological unity and the achievements of
science and culture constitute a sound basis for the construction of communism."[1]

The growing of socialist social relations into communist
social relations also presupposes the gradual elimination of
the vestiges of the past, the traces of the society from which
socialism emerged. This means the gradual elimination of

---

[1] *Fiftieth Anniversary of the Great October Socialist Revolution,*
p. 27.

class distinctions, of essential differences between town and country, between people engaged in manual and mental work and the incomplete economic equality which it causes, differences that are responsible for the still incomplete equality of opportunity of personal development among individuals belonging to different groups and strata of the population.

The substance of the main directions of development of social relations may be roughly outlined as follows:

in the sphere of production, economic relations—the development of state and co-operative and collective farm property, their rapprochement and the emergence of a unified form of communist property in the means of production owned by the whole people; transformation of agricultural labour into a variety of industrial labour, the merging of mental and manual work in the process of production; gradual transition from the principle of socialism "From each according to his abilities, to each according to his work" to the principle of communism "From each according to his abilities, to each according to his needs":

in the sphere of social relations—the final overcoming of class distinctions, of essential differences between town and country, between people engaged in mental and manual work, establishment of a socially homogeneous society and of communist equality for all people; further rapprochement of nations on the basis of common economic, political and intellectual interests, fraternal friendship and co-operation, the attainment of the complete unity of nations; the improvement of the everyday living conditions of the family and the elimination of the vestiges of inequality of women in everyday life;

in the sphere of politics and law—the consolidation of the socialist state of the whole people, the further development of socialist democracy, the enhancement of the role of public organisations and, above all, the Communist Party, the gradual development of the state into public communist self-administration;

in the intellectual sphere—the raising of the people's consciousness, the formation of the scientific world view and the establishment of communist morality among all members of society, the elimination of the vestiges of capitalism in people's consciousness and behaviour, progress in science and the arts, the enjoyment by the broad mass of the people of the latest advances in science and technology.

Specific tasks are being carried out in each of the above-mentioned directions of the development of social relations. But as these tasks are accomplished, certain *general* essential features are formed that testify to the development of the communist character of social relations, and at the same time the further strengthening in the masses of the new type of personality. Thus, for example, the further spread of *social homogeneity* and, on this basis, of *communist equality*, will bring a flowering of the talents and abilities of members of society, a new increase in the effectiveness of their work and social activity. In its turn, the spread of social homogeneity and equality, of unity of fundamental interests will still further consolidate *comradely mutual assistance, collectivism, internationalism and fraternity*. As the material and technical basis of communism is built, planning and organisation will become even more widespread in social life, making it possible to guide social processes more effectively. In combination with the abundance of material and spiritual goods this will create conditions for the all-round development of *freedom of the individual and rights of* Soviet citizens. Communism, states the Programme of the CPSU, brings the working people new great rights and opportunities.[1]

The basic processes of development of social relations, thus, predetermine the basic directions of the development of the personality. But there is also a need for purposeful activity in developing the personality's *specific features*. In the course of mankind's long history a huge number of features characterising its various aspects have evolved, and from this enormous diversity we must select the essential, the main features that correspond to the interests of man and society and characterise the communist type of personality.

On the basis of the experience already accumulated the Communist Party Programme defines the attributes that should be developed in people in the course of communist construction and communist education. It states that a high

---

[1] *The Road to Communism*, p. 552.

degree of communist consciousness, diligence and discipline, and dedication to social interests, are indispensable features of the citizen of communist society.[1] At the same time it poses the task of all-round and harmonious development of the human personality, the moulding of a person who harmoniously combines in himself richness of spirit, moral purity and physical perfection.[2]

The posing of the problem of harmonious personal development is not merely the desire of a few humanistically-minded public men, but a strictly scientific conclusion inferred on the basis of analysis of social development. The desire for versatility, the desire to change one's occupation from time to time is a completely natural manifestation of human needs. But changing of occupations and hence the all-round personal development at a certain stage in history becomes a social problem requiring its own specific solution. History in general knows of many gifted and versatile people who left their mark in many spheres of activity, particularly in science and art. These people provide a practical illustration of the tremendous potential of the human personality, the beauty and effectiveness of the wholly developed person. But when the Marxists pose the question of a person's all-round development in communist society, they are tackling a problem of a different nature—the development not of separate, even if numerous, individuals, but of *all* members of society.

The Marxists regard the idea of change of occupation, the idea of all-round development of the personality not as fantasy but as the natural, predetermined consequence of the development of production, which becomes possible only in the conditions of communism. Already modern production demands that the single-skill worker should be replaced by the fully developed individual "...to whom the different social functions he performs, are but so many modes of giving free scope to his own natural and acquired powers".[3]

The scientific conception of all-round development of the personality has nothing in common with the idea that the person in communist society will with the greatest of ease be

[1] *The Road to Communism,* p. 509.

[2] Ibid., pp. 566-67.

[3] K. Marx, *Capital,* Vol. I, p. 488.

able to transfer from one job to another. Today he makes steel, tomorrow bakes bread, the next day builds a mine and the day after takes a ship out to sea or simultaneously weaves cloth and makes machinery. The combination of such diverse professions is usually impossible today and will be even in the future because of the amount of complex knowledge to be acquired and also because society will always need a more or less stable force of workers in the various branches of production in order to ensure continuity of the production process.

The all-round development of the worker has real possibilities, first, in the mastering of the allied skills that go to make up a certain specialisation; second, in the combination of occupations which, although they demand specialised knowledge and experience, possess certain features that make for combination. An agronomist, for instance, who specialises in growing grain may at the same time become a stock-breeder, an actor, or an artist, depending on his abilities and inclinations. The metallurgical engineer may become a literary critic, a musician and philosopher at the same time, and so on.

The main thing in getting rid of the old division of labour lies in the fact that automation and raising of the general educational and cultural level of the working people lead to the emergence of forms of activity in which mental and manual work become organically united. Automation makes use mainly of similar mechanical, hydraulic, pneumatic and electrical devices. The worker in automated production, therefore, requires less individual skill with his hands and more scientific and specialised technical knowledge, more understanding of the mechanical, physical and chemical laws of the technological cycle of which he is in charge. This in turn creates opportunities for the worker to obtain a greater variety of work within his own branch of production and also in other related and more specialised spheres of production.

The disappearance of the situation in which certain functions are assigned for life to a category of people mainly engaged in physical labour, while other functions are assigned to the intelligentsia, as a special stratum of society, will create conditions for the development of all working people's versatility. The society where this special stratum, the intelligentsia, no longer exists, will, in effect, be a society of universal intellectual work.

Yet another change that is coming about in the sphere of labour is the combination of physical work in production with work in the field of management of production and the affairs of society, the combination of physical work with technical and artistic creativity, etc. This change is also affecting increasingly significant groups of the population, the decisive factor being the increase in leisure. As Marx predicted, the power of the productive forces and the wealth of the future society will be felt above all in the amount of leisure time at people's disposal. Marx's dictum that "the measure of wealth will be no longer labour time but free time" fully applies to developed communist society. As we approach communism the growth of free time, the creation of possibilities for its rational use will be an important condition of the best possible satisfaction of the ever growing and varied requirements of the builders of communist society.

Millions of working people take part in the Soviet system of representation. Concurrently with this system a system of direct participation of the masses, of manual workers in the management of production, culture, public affairs, etc., is also developing. Production meetings at enterprises, commissions of the Soviets of Working People's Deputies operating as a public service, voluntary public order squads, comradely courts, tenants' committees for apartment blocks, neighbourhoods and microdistricts, old-age pensioners' councils are only some of the components that go to make up the system of social self-administration and at the same time open up for millions of people engaged in physical labour the path to mental and intellectual accomplishment.

The same possibilities are created by the various forms of technical and artistic creativity of the working people—social design bureaus, the rationaliser and inventor movements, the people's universities, theatres, studios, clubs, and so on. Creative activity in technology, literature and arts is ceasing to be the exclusive province of the professional and is becoming the second profession of the millions.

Thus, socialism, having transformed the economic, political and cultural environment of the individual, creates opportunities for diversified occupations for the broad masses of the working people, creates a type of educated, skilled worker who combines a number of trades and is concerned not only with his own basic form of activity but also takes part in the management of public affairs. In working to further development of the personality in socialist society the Communist Party takes its stand on what has already been achieved, proceeds from the fact that man's collectivist nature develops successfully given suitable circumstances, and that consequently the task lies in continuing to strengthen and develop the socialist principles and norms of community life. Marxism-Leninism, based on the idea of the revolutionary transformation of conditions of existence, develops the reasonable, collectivist principles in man and builds the process of education accordingly.

The already available experience also clearly reveals the futility of attempts to mould a new person without a revolutionary transition from capitalism to socialism. A substantiation of such fantastic plans is to be found in the psycho-pedagogical conception of Erich Fromm. Fromm speaks of capitalist society as an irrational, neurotic, sick society which must be healed by the same therapeutic means that are used in the psychoanalytical treatment of individuals. He sees the main factor of social transformation not in historical forces but in "humanistic psychoanalysis". The medium is the psychoanalyst (a representative of the reformed school of psychoanalysis) on whom rests the whole responsibility for social change, for the transformation of capitalism into socialism, etc. As an ever increasing number of individuals are cured of their neuroses the new society will spread ever wider and eventually replace the capitalist order. One day with the help of psychoanalysis all mankind will be cured and socialism will become the universal form of life on earth.

Fromm believes that "the only constructive solution is that of socialism". And he goes on: "...it aims at a fundamental reorganisation of our economic and social system in the direction of freeing man from being used as a means for purposes outside himself, of creating a social order in which human solidarity, reason and productiveness are furthered rather than hobbled."[1]

[1] Harry K. Wells, *The Failure of Psychoanalysis*, New York, 1963, p. 130.

This conception of psychoanalysis is strongly reminiscent of various idealistic utopian teachings whose advocates saw the key to salvation from all ills in re-education or, as in the given case, in the treating of separate individuals. The objective implication of such doctrines was and still is repudiation of the only realistic path of liberation and all-round development of man—the path of socialist revolution.

It is true that people living under capitalism and entering socialism are infected with egoism, individualism and they include quite a few neurotics with various obsessions. But a successful educational process, bringing desirable changes in people's psychology, can occur only in a context of radical social change. The experience of socialist society in the USSR and other socialist countries offers sufficiently clear testimony to this fact.

Of course, the education of the new man is a complex and contradictory process. Unsatisfied desires and unrealised hopes, embittered and disappointed people exist in socialist society too. A person may be dissatisfied with the work he has to do, or the payment he receives for doing it, or dissatisfied with his flat, or with the management's attitude to some proposal of his that strikes him as exceptionally important; he may have failed to be selected for a certain post. It may happen in exceptional circumstances that a family finds itself in temporary financial difficulties and has to put up with certain hardships. But such individual cases do not provide the key to the situation. The essential condition of exerting a purposeful influence on the development of the personality is elucidation of the nature of the contradictions involved in its formation.

Personal development under socialism proceeds in the form of an accretion of a socialist diversity of thoughts, feelings, aspirations and social activity on the basis of the spread of social homogeneity and equality, on the basis of collectivism, internationalism and fraternity in human relations, freedom of the individual and growth of organisation and planning in social relations. But each of these tendencies encounters a certain opposition and runs into objective and subjective difficulties. The development of diversity and social activity, for instance, certainly does not mean that society can permit any kind of diversity, including that which is an expression

of bourgeois ideas and moods. The development of collectivism, internationalism and fraternity is not infrequently
hindered by instances of selfishness, nationalism and bureaucracy. The development of social organisation and freedom
of the individual are also potentially contradictory tendencies. Social organisation is, undoubtedly, essential to
individual freedom but it also restricts freedom that contradicts the interests of society, while individual freedom,
understood in the anarchical sense, may cause harm to
society and other people.

Or let us take another aspect. The basic directions of the
development of social relations that were discussed earlier
are prepared by constant improvement of the concrete forms
of organisation of social relations. By this we mean the
proportions between the various branches of the national
economy and form of labour, prices, wage rates, work quotas,
forms of enterprise management, structure of the organs of
power, the electoral system, judiciary bodies, i.e., everything
that forms the concrete living embodiment of social property,
the principle of distribution according to work, political
organisation of society, and so on, the totality of social
relations in all its diversity.

Once created, the forms of organisation of social life
acquire a definite stability. They are instituted in legislation,
instructions, rules, and so on and also in customs, traditions
and habits. As a result of scientific and technological progress these forms gradually become obsolete and have to
be changed. Situations of conflict arise that require solution
through the improvement of concrete organisational forms
and search for new ones. But all such collisions involve
human interests. Thus, it follows that analysis of social
processes entails not only elucidation of the social phenomena, and forms that hinder progress, but also indication
of people's interests, as well as indication of the social types
of personality that represent them and that must be subjected
to educational and sometimes even coercive action.

If we take as our basis for classifying the contradictions
in the development of social relations, of the new personality,
the differences in people's motives of behaviour, which lead
to situations of conflict, we obtain the following kinds of
contradictions:

(1) *Contradictions of search.* The construction of socialism and communism is a new and complex undertaking. It demands constant search and practical testing of the most effective forms of organisation of social life. Here, even where people have common interests, duels are fought between innovation and conservatism, creativity and dogmatism, knowledge and ignorance, the desire to discover the truth by means of argument, by discussion and rigidity, the fear of making a mistake. Even when guided by social interests, people sometimes display weakness of character and are hindered by ignorance, obstinacy and set habits.

(2) *Contradictions of group interests.* In various ways people come into conflict when defending the interests of the group to which they belong. "Group" is to be understood here in the broad sense of working collective, office department, territorial unit. Here we have the struggle of departmental interests, the so-called localism, and also instances of some of the contradictions between town and country, between workers by hand and brain.

(3) *Contradictions involving personal egoistic motivations.* These are also extremely diverse in character and sphere of action, but here the basis of the conflict lies in the fact that some people give first place to their selfish interests through desire for gain and refusal to consider the interests of others, through cowardice, laziness, careerist considerations, and so on. Here, too, we have conflicts connected with hooliganism and drunkenness, since they have their roots in blatant contempt for the interests of other people.

(4) *Contradictions of unrealised expectations.* The influence of this type of contradiction on people's mood, thinking and behaviour is as broad as the amount of theoretical attention paid to it is small. Incidentally, here we are concerned with one of the contradictions that will always exist.

(5) *Contradictions of a political nature.* These have to do with the influences of the bourgeois world, with individual defections to the enemy camp, with traitors and deserters, with the principled struggle for the purity of our ideology.

These groups of contradictions are naturally the specific expression of the general character of contradictions under socialism. With the exception of the last group they are not antagonistic in character and are eliminated in the process of the everyday practical activity of the organs of administration and all members of society.

2. DEVELOPMENT OF THE INDIVIDUAL AS A WORKER IN SOCIALIST PRODUCTION

The further development of the socialist type of personality, its shaping primarily as that of a worker, entails the transformation of production relations. Specialised knowledge, a high degree of professional training and general culture become in their turn an essential condition of successful work for ever wider sections of working people, become a need for the development of production.[1]

The improvement of production relations influences the development of the personality, first, directly—in the process of change of the character of labour, the forms and methods of distribution, which mould the individual both as a worker and consumer; second, indirectly—through change of the class structure, of political, legal and moral relationships.

Educating People to Regard Work as the Primary Need in Life

The period of the construction of communism raises the task of educating in all members of society an attitude to work as the primary need in life. For society to be able to distribute goods without calculating the quantity and quality of each person's labour, people must learn to work without considering the reward, out of sheer interest in the work itself, out of a feeling of the need to work.

One sometimes encounters the notion that the need for work is something like the need for air, for food, etc. Such an understanding oversimplifies the essence of the problem and at the same time blocks its solution since the need to work cannot be considered analogous to such needs. The need for air is a physiological need. Needs for food, housing, clothing, although they develop under the influence of social production, are at the same time an elementary condition for

---

[1] *The 24th Congress of the CPSU*, p. 51.

the existence of the organism. The need to work, on the other hand, is a social, a moral need. The shaping of such a need among the broad sections of the people is bound to be a long and complex process depending on many factors.

Understanding the need to work is closely connected with how we understand the differences between socialist and communist work. People sometimes ask whether we should not give up the idea of "socialist competition" now that there is a movement for communist work. Other people suggest that it may be too early yet to organise a movement for a communist attitude to work. To prove their point, they argue that communist work (bearing in mind Lenin's well-known proposition[1]) is work given free of charge for the good of society, that communist work is inconceivable, outside the worker's concern for the common good (referring to Lenin again[2]), and that such work is creative, highly skilled work. But under socialism, they argue, there is still heavy unskilled work and, hence, categories of workers with low qualifications and low wages. There are some people who see wages as the sole aim of work, and there are also some who avoid socially useful work.

A third view is that all these features exist to some extent under socialism and, therefore, the movement for a communist attitude to work is perfectly legitimate as something towards which the mass of the people are clearly striving. One cannot but agree with this view. Socialist competition became possible even before socialism had been built, and it played a tremendous part in building it. The situation is exactly the same with the movement for a communist attitude to work, particularly if one regards it as a higher form of socialist competition. The Central Committee's Report to the 24th Congress of the CPSU stated that "the Party saw that its task was to support the movement for a communist attitude to work, and to give every encouragement to the creative initiative of Soviet people."[3]

The problem of the development of a communist attitude to work consists in the all-round solution of a number of

---

[1] V. I. Lenin, *Collected Works*, Vol. 30, p. 517.
[2] Ibid.
[3] *The 24th Congress of the CPSU*, p. 100.

tasks that may be summed up as follows: to eliminate heavy physical labour through mechanisation and automation and thus create possibilities of interesting work for all; to raise the productivity of labour and create an abundance of material and spiritual goods for the all-round development of the needs and abilities of all members of society. Another condition for making work a primary need in life is the bringing up of highly educated and communistically conscious people who are able to place the interests of society first.

The experience of socialist construction convincingly shows that as far as education is concerned the decisive thing was and still is to establish in people's minds an understanding of the social significance of their work, the link between their everyday efforts and the socio-political goals of the whole people. This task continues to be at all stages of the development of socialist society the basic task of labour education.

The assumption of the need to mould the consciousness as the dominant aspect of labour education in no way violates the principle of the materialist approach to the formation of the personality, because in the given case the objective basis is supplied by the socialist system, above all socialist property and socialist production. Besides, such an attitude to the problem presupposes the further development of the material conditions of labour—its mechanisation and automation, and material stimulation. What is more, once the working people's general social activity is ensured the further development of a communist attitude to work largely depends on the rate and character of the mechanisation and automation of production. Changes in equipment and technology alter the content of labour operations, the proportion between the worker's physical and mental efforts, the character of the demands placed on him by technical progress, the level of his skill and education and, hence, his attitude to the work he performs.

Thus, every effort must be made to improve educational work, stressing the social value of labour. At the 24th Congress of the CPSU this task was treated as a matter of primary importance. Satisfaction from work proceeds not only from the actual process of work but also from the attainment of the goal a person pursues in performing it, and from the atmosphere that exists in one or another working collective.

At the 24th Congress of the CPSU much attention was paid to the development of the worker's social activity. It was emphasised that the working people's participation in economic management is not confined to reaching economic targets. The point is that Party and state policy is dictated by the basic interests of the working people, is evolved by representatives of the working people in elected bodies, and that the working people take an active part in controlling the execution of these decisions.[1]

At the same time scientists and practical workers are hard at work on the tasks of wide development of professional orientation and professional selection, the study of professional inclinations and the active shaping of these inclinations during school life. It has been suggested that there should be a comprehensive assessment of the working activity of personnel as a means of improving the organisation of labour and socialist competition. The point is that attention is paid to only one index—fulfilment of output norms, while a number of other extremely important characteristics are ignored, such as degree of responsibility shown at work, amount of initiative, self-dependence, culture, production know-how, discipline and other moral qualities.

The development and all-round encouragement of a highly conscious, disciplined creative attitude to work, the support and propaganda of positive examples, the general inculcation of this example—such is the basic idea of all educational efforts in this field. Communist work can triumph completely and undividedly throughout the system of social production only as a conscious movement on the part of the masses themselves.

Stimulation of Individual Labour Activity

The sphere of distribution, which lies between production and consumption, emerges as the direct condition for the formation and development of material and spiritual needs

---

[1] *The 24th Congress of the CPSU*, pp. 84-86.

and at the same time as a sphere in which the features of the personality are manifested.

The social essence of distribution is always connected with the *sources* of distribution. Are they private or public, individual or collective, legal or illegal? Do wages coincide with the qualitative-quantitative characteristics of labour or are they at variance? These indices exercise a definite influence on a person's moral features, his social aspirations and level of activity.

The socialist principle "From each according to his abilities, to each according to his work", while expressing the social, socialist nature of production, is addressed to each individual worker, defining his share in the social income. Distribution and consumption act as a means for the development and varied manifestation of a person's active essence.

Distribution according to work is conditioned by the current level of the productive forces and plays a progressive role in the social and moral development of the personality.

It promotes the growth of social production, which is the decisive prerequisite of communist abundance. It fosters respect for work as the first and sacred obligation of every citizen, and creates a personal material incentive for workers in improving their skills and raising labour productivity. And this develops people's abilities and gives them the habit of working "according to their abilities". Only as the differences between skilled and unskilled labour are eliminated will the gap between low-paid and highly-paid workers disappear. Only through the consistent application and improvement of the principle of material incentive can we approach general and complete equality. The consistent realisation of the law of distribution according to work opens the road to a situation in which "equality is achieved for all members of society *in relation* to ownership of the means of production, that is, equality of labour and wages, humanity will inevitably be confronted with the question of advancing farther, from formal equality to actual equality, i.e., to the operation of the rule 'From each according to his abilities, to each according to his needs' ".[1]

Why, however, is communist distribution connected in our

---

[1] V. I. Lenin, *Collected Works*, Vol. 25, p. 472.

minds with everything being free of charge? Although this question has no wide practical application, it is of theoretical interest because its interpretation exerts a definite educational effect, particularly as it involves a point that is not clear. It is obvious that in the total assortment of all the goods produced there will always be some that owing to their scarcity cannot be distributed "according to need". It must be assumed that for such goods some principle of regulation resembling the present distribution according to work will remain in force. This exception must already be borne in mind and theoretical allowance made for it.

As we know, payments out of social, public funds are not yet a communist form of distribution, since this form of distribution is influenced by class differences (different level and system of payment for collective farmers as compared with workers), and by the principle of distribution according to work. But all the same a somewhat different approach to the satisfaction of the needs of the working people is made through social, public funds than through distribution according to work.

By providing education, including higher education, free of charge, by organising free medical service, by allocating large subsidies for social insurance payments in the form of pensions, student grants and by maintaining the world's lowest apartment rents, socialist society effectively deals with three cardinal problems: first, society takes care of such vitally important needs as are connected with the development of people's abilities, maintenance of their health, i.e., the most sensitive sides of human life; second, and this is directly connected with the first point, society effectively solves the problem of selecting from the whole mass of the people the individuals who possess the required abilities and talents; third, despite the differences in the amounts paid out of social funds, they cannot by their very nature promote a revival of private property, individualistic inclinations and habits because they directly link up personal interest with social interest and reveal this connection in all its clarity. Such a system of satisfying needs makes it possible to level up the incomes of different families, since the amount of income received from social funds depends on the number of members a family has. It is larger in

families where there are children attending kindergar-
tens, crèches and schools, where there are students, old-age
pensioners, etc. Distribution from social funds develops
among members of society a collectivist psychology and
makes for complete overcoming of private property individualism.

The transition to distribution according to need is not
an act of will. It is inevitable because in conditions when an
abundance of consumer goods has been achieved, and when
work becomes a vital need, it will be superfluous to make the
satisfaction of person's needs proportionate to the quantity
and quality of his work. Under communism a person will
be eager to work not because he needs to earn a livelihood;
all his wants will be provided for by the high level of social
production and the abundance of material and spiritual
goods. In such circumstances personal material incentive as
a stimulus to work will give way to concern for the satisfaction of the material and spiritual needs of the entire society.
To put it more exactly, a high consciousness of one's social
duty, the desire to achieve a creative solution of production,
technical, scientific and other problems—these incentives to
work show that man has an inner need to work voluntarily
and according to his inclinations for the good of society.

Engels, dealing with this aspect of the problem, wrote
that distribution, in so far as it is governed by purely
economic considerations will be regulated by the interests
of production, and that production is most encouraged by a
mode of distribution which allows *all* members of society to
develop, maintain and exercise their capacities with maximum universality.[1] Only as the material and technical base
of communism develops and social wealth increases can
society expand the range of needs that it is more expedient
to satisfy out of social, public funds.

Following the slogan "All in the name of man and for the
good of man," the Communist Party is pursuing a policy of
constant raising of the people's standards of living.

The 24th Congress of the CPSU defined the raising of
the people's living standards as the main task of the Ninth
Five-Year Plan and as the long-term orientation of the

[1] F. Engels, *Anti-Dühring*, p. 239.

national economy. Soviet people see this as an essential condition of the growing of socialism into communism. The ideologists of imperialism, on the other hand, try to present the raising of the Soviet people's standards of living as something that will lead—to the collapse of socialism. They assert that the further development of the socialist economy will increasingly reveal the "conflict between communism and the rising standard of life in the USSR" with the result that "communism will fade away in the age of high mass consumption".

Communism, however, is not merely things, but a definite system of social relationships, as incidentally is capitalism. It is this definite system of social relations that determines a corresponding attitude to things and gives them their place in the life of man.

In complete conformity with its class interests the imperialist bourgeoisie tries to foster among the masses a consumer ideology and psychology corresponding to the type of personality known as the consumer man. It tries to direct the energies of the working people towards the acquisition of things, towards the struggle for things, to channel these energies into a campaign of acquisitiveness and divert them from the political struggle against the prevailing system.

The needs of the Soviet person, in contrast to those of the petty-bourgeois, the Soviet educationist Makarenko stressed, are "a manifestation of the interest not of a consumer of social goods but an active member of socialist society, a creator of these goods".[1] The behaviour of the overwhelming majority of Soviet people testifies to the fact that in our attitude to things they see a manifestation of the socialist ethos, i.e., interest not only in the material or prestige aspects of things but above all interest in them as spiritual values.

Interesting evidence of this attitude is to be found in an inquiry conducted by Soviet sociologists L. N. Zhilina and N. T. Frolova into the attitude towards things in socialist society. On the basis of a questionnaire addressed to 1,740 working-class, engineers' and teachers' families they reach the conclusion that the characteristic tendency of all groups

---

[1] A. S. Makarenko, *Works,* Vol. IV, p. 40 (in Russian).

is to prefer things that satisfy their spiritual, cultural requirements (books, TV sets, radios). "We have no intention
of claiming that all the individuals in the USSR act the
same, according to the demands of a system of preference of
social values. We only want to say that despite the assertions
of bourgeois ideologists concerning the ability of increasing
prosperity to automatically and mechanically destroy the socialist system of ideological orientation created by all historical experience, a system in which spiritual values play the
leading role, this system also works in the context of the steadily increasing well-being of Soviet people, and that it also
manifests itself in such a fact as the acquisition of things."[1]
Characteristically, the interest in spiritual values rises in
groups with greater material welfare and education.[2]

Despite the growth of the social consumption funds, the
money wage remains the basic form of distribution of material goods at the current stage. This line has been confirmed
by the 24th Congress of the CPSU. Improvement of the
forms and methods of distribution according to work is the
chief means of materially influencing the labour activity of
the individual and his social activity in general.

The role of distribution according to work in raising
labour productivity and education of the builders of communism becomes all the more significant, as the forms of its
applications are improved. Scientific and technological progress creates new branches of production and forms of labour
which replace the old and reduce their role in the national
economy. In this connection the social significance of various
forms of work, i.e., what is generally known as the quality
of work, changes, and this makes it necessary to constantly
improve the system of payment. The essence of the problem
is to make the level and forms of payment reflect as precisely
as possible the qualitative diversity of the various forms of
social labour and ensure as effectively as possible a material
incentive in the growth of socialist production as a means
of raising the living standards of the working people.

The improvement of payment according to work, the
raising of material incentives is not so much a matter of

---

[1] L. N. Zhilina and N. T. Frolova, *Problems of Consumption and
the Education of the Personality,* Moscow, 1969, p. 58 (in Russian).

[2] Ibid., p. 61.

paying more (the most general, though essential condition), but of paying more wisely—how much, to whom, when and for what. All the same, material stimulation must be on a mass scale and take in a large number of people on whom the growth of labour productivity and other production indices depend, so that many people have real possibilities of receiving additional reward for good work. The system of encouragement must work automatically upon attainment of certain prearranged targets that must be stable and widely known, so that people can be guided by them, and due notice should be given of any change that they may undergo. "It is wrong to think that ... distribution is only a matter of fairness. We must bear in mind that it is a method, an instrument, and a means of increasing output."[1]

In the USSR, until the September Plenary Meeting of the Central Committee of the CPSU in 1965, the link between worker and society operated directly. For a certain quality of work he was guaranteed a certain payment. Under this system, however, the link with the interest of the enterprise where the worker is employed, the actual results of his activity, is not clearly enough revealed to him. The enterprise may be working well or badly, producing needed or unneeded goods, and this may be of no concern to its workers. The dependence was only felt in extreme cases, when the enterprise was chronically underfulfilling its plan, and so on. The September Plenum's decision to distribute part of the enterprise's profits among members of the staff introduced collective material incentive.

Lenin stressed the prime importance of the direct link between the workers' wages and the economic showing made by the enterprise in question. The labour of the individual worker has significance for society only when embodied in the final product put out by the enterprise and, therefore, payment will correspond more accurately to the social significance of each person's work if it takes into account the general economic effect of the enterprise. Making rewards dependent on the level of productive activity of the enterprise, the shop or the work-team promotes each person's interest in the results of the work of the whole collective,

---

[1] V. I. Lenin, *Collected Works*, Vol. 32, p. 448.

promotes collectivism and enhances the workers' activity in production management.

Collective material interest helps to strengthen the collectivism of socialist social relations. It creates an economic foundation for the worker's direct interest in managing the production and social affairs of the collective. In the new conditions each worker has an interest in seeing to it that his comrades work better, enhance their skills and improve the quality of their output.

Moral stimulation is of great importance in developing an active personality.

Moral stimulus is sometimes understood as encouragement not connected with wages or bonuses (the awarding of certificates, official messages of thanks, etc.). All this is, of course, addressed to people's moral consciousness. That is true enough. But it is also true that moral stimuli are rooted deeply in the nature of the system, in the nature of social progress. The socialist revolution and the subsequent socialist construction have created a permanent and tremendous stimulus to the enthusiasm of the broadest masses of the working people, because the revolution and socialism have brought the people the solution to age-old problems of social development. The revolutionary abolition of oppression and exploitation, the just social system, the just interconnections and interrelations between people based on the principles of socialism—these are the basic moral stimulus of the political and production activity of all members of society. The essence of moral stimulation lies in encouraging the very qualities and behaviour of the personality that show its socialist orientation.

The moral incentives that promote the communist education of the personality include also strict adherence to the principles of distribution. In the context of the present day Lenin's idea of accounting and control signifies that society must see to it that all its members work in accordance with the demands of the Constitution; that the only source of income of members of society is their labour (with the exception of the right of inheritance and making gifts); that the level of wages corresponds to the quantity and quality of the work done. (The latter is ensured both by solving the problem of putting the right man in the right job and also by perfecting the system of wage rates). All this, taken together, along with the means of ideological influence, are essential conditions for the rapid development of production and success of the communist education of the working people.

3. PROPAGANDA OF MARXISM-LENINISM IS THE FUNDAMENTAL MEANS OF GIVING PEOPLE STRONG COMMUNIST PRINCIPLES

Success in moulding the new personality certainly does not remove the necessity for persistent and systematic work in fostering communist consciousness among all members of society. This is made imperative by a number of circumstances, including the fact that new generations are setting forth in life who must always receive an elementary introduction to the spiritual values of socialism, and the fact that imperialism is conducting a constant campaign of subversion against socialism and striving to exploit for its own interests the backward and unstable elements in the socialist countries; and finally the fact that in the very system of socialist relations itself new problems are always arising that need to be understood and solved and, therefore, demand broader knowledge, a deeper mastering of the fundamentals of the scientific world view and the strengthening of the principles of communist morality.

The 24th Congress of the CPSU in its resolution on the Central Committee's Report emphasised that "the formation in the working people of the Marxist-Leninist world view, high ideological and political qualities and standards of communist morality continues to remain the central aim of the ideological work of the Party organisations.

"In the Party's ideological work the main emphasis should be on the propagation of the ideas of Marxism-Leninism and on mounting a relentless offensive against bourgeois and revisionist ideology."[1]

The Class and Party Character of Educational Tasks

The scientific world view is based on knowledge of nature and of society and cannot, of course, be acquired without an

---

[1] *The 24th Congress of the CPSU*, p. 229.

all-round education. A person goes on adding to and developing his scientific world view practically all his life, although most people acquire the fundamentals, the essential ideological positions quite rapidly in youth, during the years of family and school upbringing, and at college. Moreover, it is decisively important that a person should acquire the key knowledge and ideas that are most clearly and firmly related to the position and interests of the community to which he belongs. Such key knowledge and ideas are expressed in people's socio-political views. They include questions related to the sphere of the class struggle, the socialist revolution, the dictatorship of the proletariat, the ways and methods of building socialism and communism. In other words, it is mainly a matter of shaping the political sphere of the consciousness, the individual's political awareness as the most important task of education at all stages in the history of the new society and at all periods in a person's life.

The fostering of political awareness is the main direction of the whole process of formation of the scientific world view and communist morality. In so far as realisation of the ideals and principles of communism comes about through the medium of politics, it is through being drawn into political activity that the masses most effectively absorb the fundamentals of the Marxist-Leninist world view and communist morality, because "... the political line of Marxism is inseparably bound up with its philosophical principles".[1] The introduction of politics into the system of education and upbringing, into cultural life in general, has been and remains to be a vital feature of social life under socialism. The fostering of political awareness in present-day conditions entails, as it did before, the fostering of class, Party consciousness, the ability to assess social phenomena and processes from class, from Party positions.

From the *internal* point of view the problem lies in correctly defining the ideological content of the social interest. The differences between the classes that still remain in Soviet society do not affect their fundamental interests, and these are not what is meant when we talk about the necessity for

---

[1] V. I. Lenin, *Collected Works,* Vol. 15, p. 405.

class, for Party assessments. As the peasants and the intelligentsia adopt the positions of the working class and the Soviet people emerges as a new socio-historical unit, the whole people becomes a vehicle of socialist consciousness, the promoter of the fundamental interests of society. Hence to approach any question from class positions in the conditions of the USSR is to approach it from the standpoint of the general interests of the people, of the Soviet state. Such an approach is called a class approach because the social content, the ideological orientation of the Soviet people's interests is derived from the working class and the working class remains the leading force of society. From this standpoint the social content of such crimes as, say, the stealing of socialist property, has a definite anti-socialist character. In assessing the social nature of anti-social behaviour, the Central Committee of the CPSU considers that "a class, political appraisal of anti-social phenomena profoundly alien to socialism, such as the plundering of socialist property, money-grubbing and violation of labour discipline and public order, and the struggle against these negative phenomena are an important function of the socialist state, of the entire public, the civic duty of every Soviet person."[1]

One sometimes encounters another view, the view that infringements of the law, crimes and amoral actions may be attributed to people's selfishness, to their natural instincts. There is no doubt that natural instincts and needs determine man's actions and behaviour in many ways. But the fact he possesses natural instincts and needs does not deprive him of the possibility and indeed the necessity of choosing the motives of his actions according to the bourgeois scale of individualism or according to the socialist scale of collectivism. In a world divided into classes, split up into diametrically opposed world systems, in a world of opposed moral systems these motives must inevitably bear a class character. The type of the pilferer of socialist property, the confirmed criminal, the money-grubber, the profiteer, the deliberate hooligan, and so on, has an orientation of an anti-socialist, class character.

---

[1] *Lenin's Ideas and Cause Are Immortal*, Moscow, 1970, pp. 59-60.

From the *external, international* standpoint the problem lies in the influence exerted upon the internal life of the USSR by the intense ideological and political contest that is being fought out on the world stage by the forces of socialism and capitalism. Mastering the ideas of Marxism-Leninism means above all an understanding of the fact that the development of the new world, of new relations between people is taking place in the context of an intense and implacable struggle between socialism and capitalism, between new, progressive ideas and moral principles, and the old ideas and moral principles. Formulating the task of educational work, Lenin said: "We must inculcate in the working people the realisation that it is impossible and inexcusable to stand aside in the proletariat's struggle, which is now spreading more and more to all capitalist countries in the world, and to stand aside in international politics."[1]

The class enemy is trying to penetrate into the socialist countries. Various devices and forces are being used against socialism. Sharp anti-socialist, openly hostile propaganda is combined with allegedly objective reporting of facts and events, is supplemented with "positive" attempts to improve socialism and to counterpose certain "ideals" and "humanised" conceptions of socialism to the socialist society that actually exists. The aim, the purpose, more or less concealed, of any anti-communist trend lies mainly in trying to overthrow the socialist society that actually exists, i.e., the force that opposes world imperialism. This was particularly obvious in the bourgeois propagandist campaigns conducted in connection with the 50th anniversary of the Great October Socialist Revolution and the Lenin centenary.

The anti-socialist forces use for their own ends the various wavering elements in the countries of socialism that are infected with the private-property psychology, nationalist prejudices and apolitical attitudes. These prejudices, religion and much else are used by bourgeois propaganda to keep people under their influence.

In the Central Committee's report to the 23rd Congress of the CPSU Leonid Brezhnev spoke of how "the giant imperialist propaganda machine corrupts the individual and

---

[1] V. I. Lenin, *Collected Works*, Vol. 31, p. 366.

attempts to distract the people from politics. In all circumstances, the struggle against bourgeois ideology must be uncompromising, because it is a class struggle, a struggle for man, for his dignity and freedom, a struggle to invigorate the positions of socialism and communism, in the interests of the international working class."[1]

Thus, Lenin's proposition that the fundamental demand of class and Party spirit is that whenever one is appraising events one should directly and openly adopt the standpoint of a definite social group,[2] the standpoint of socialism, retains its significance in contemporary Soviet society. The CPSU Central Committee's Theses on the Centenary of the Birth of V. I. Lenin point out the necessity for ". . .a consistent class policy in matters concerning education, . . .clarity and preciseness in ideological positions, the further raising of revolutionary vigilance, a consistent struggle against indifference to politics, against survivals of the private property, petty-bourgeois mentality, against manifestations of a nihilistic attitude towards the gains of socialism, and the penetrations of bourgeois and revisionist views."[3]

One of the major general criteria of the individual's socialist orientation should be the ability when examining any important phenomena of social life to look at things from the standpoint of the interests of the whole people, regardless of what class, group or nationality the particular individual belongs to. In so far as the Communist Party is the concentrated expression of the interests of the people as a whole, and also of socio-class groups and nations, the practical expression of the individual's class consciousness is his understanding of the Party's policy and ability to support and carry out that policy.

Hence the tasks of Party propaganda, its role in developing the consciousness of the individual and the people as a whole. In contrast to the conceptions of some bourgeois "theorists", according to whom propaganda like commercial advertising is based on lies and devoted to the task of

---

[1] *The 23rd Congress of the Communist Party of the Soviet Union,* pp. 145-46.

[2] V. I. Lenin, *Collected Works,* Vol. 1, p. 401.

[3] *On the Centenary of the Birth of V. I. Lenin,* Moscow, pp. 60-61.

shaping the mass consciousness accordingly, the Marxist-Leninist understanding of the purpose of propaganda is that it should help to develop the masses' political and moral consciousness, to enhance their knowledge so that they can better appreciate their position and their revolutionary tasks. This is where radical difference lies between the whole information and propagandist activities of the socialist and the bourgeois states.

With the help of subversive ideological operations the class enemy seeks to sow doubt, wavering and uncertainty among the members of socialist society, to find supporters and to build up some sort of base out of them.

"The Czechoslovak events were a fresh reminder that in the countries which have taken the path of socialist construction the internal anti-socialist forces, whatever remained of them, may, in certain conditions, become active and even mount direct counter-revolutionary action in the hope of support from outside, from imperialism, which, for its part, is always prepared to form blocs with such forces."[1]

All this means that educational work must be centered on important questions and that they should be appraised from class positions. It is essential to give constant attention to the questions and problems that arise in the consciousness of the mass of the working people, to study the practice of propaganda work from the standpoint of its content.

Current Questions of Ideological and Political Education

The strengthening and further development of the individual's socialist consciousness is out of the question unless the people, every individual, has knowledge and profound understanding of the fundamental problems of the ideological and political struggle. "...Politics," Lenin said, "should be the business of the people, the business of the proletariat."[2]

At every stage of historical development the Communist Party, guided by scientific analysis of the disposition of class forces, the needs of communist construction and the interests

[1] *The 24th Congress of the CPSU*, p. 17.
[2] V. I. Lenin, *Collected Works*, Vol. 31, p. 371.

of the international communist movement, singles out the most important questions constituting the main target of political activity and, hence, of educational work. Profound understanding of these basic questions by the broad masses is an essential condition of the ideological stability of society, the successful solution of its various problems, developing the socialist personality and making it more active.

In present-day conditions these problems have been thoroughly and clearly elucidated in a whole series of Party documents: the CPSU Central Committee's theses *On the Centenary of the Birth of V. I. Lenin,* Leonid Brezhnev's report *Lenin's Cause Lives on and Triumphs,* the materials of the International Meeting of the Communist and Workers' Parties in Moscow (1969) and the materials and decisions of the 24th Congress of the CPSU.

The Central Committee's Report to the 24th Congress is a remarkable political and theoretical document. In a highly compressed form it generalises the whole experience of the USSR, the world socialist system and the international communist movement. The systematic propaganda of the Congress materials and decisions forms the basis of all ideological and educational work among the masses.

In the Central Committee's report to the Congress Leonid Brezhnev stressed that the Party attached serious importance to the correct, objective recounting of the history of the Soviet state. It is essential to the success of communist education that all Soviet people, particularly the young people, should acquire a good knowledge of the history of the revolutionary struggle and socialist construction, a deep understanding of the necessity and correctness of the socialist transformations that have been achieved, and a sense of pride in the great accomplishments of the builders of communism.

Fearing the influence of the example set by the Soviet Union and the other socialist countries, the anti-Communists seek to present the history of the revolutionary struggle and socialist construction as a long series of mistakes and accidents. With this end in view they spread the idea that the October Revolution occurred by accident, and that the victory in the Civil War was no less an accident; they assert that the sacrifices made by Soviet people in the course of the revolution and the construction of socialism outweigh the benefits achieved; the heroism of the Soviet people in defeating nazi Germany is consistently played down or passed over in silence; the mistakes connected with the cult of Stalin's personality are boosted.

In view of this situation all educational institutions are confronted with the task of giving a clear and convincing account of the mass character of the revolutionary struggle and the need for socialist transformations. It is impossible to bring up true sons of the Motherland, steadfast ideological fighters, without fostering respect for the history of their own people, their own culture. It is essential that every Soviet person should understand that the socialism built in his country according to Lenin's plan acts as the most powerful, effective and humane force which along with the other socialist countries today stands in opposition to imperialism. All Soviet people must fully understand that no mistakes committed in the process of building socialism, no problems of the present day can remove the historic significance of the building of socialism or diminish its achievements.

Fostering communist firmness of principle means establishing in people's consciousness the correct, scientific, Marxist-Leninist conception of the essence of socialism, the need to strengthen and develop all its basic principles and institutions.

While not, of course, abandoning its political provocations against socialism, the imperialist bourgeoisie, unable to stop the advance of socialism by force, is widely circulating the ideas of various pseudosocialisms as a counterweight to the actually existing socialist society. Christian, Labour Party, Swedish, Israeli "socialisms" and others fall into this category.[1]

---

[1] The appearance of varieties of petty-bourgeois socialism is due to the growth in the prestige and influence of socialism. In the wake of the working class and alongside gigantic peasant masses, the urban petty-bourgeoisie and the intelligentsia are being drawn into the world revolutionary process. The hirelings of imperialism seek to use this fact for their own mercenary purposes. Back in the days of the First World War, Lenin noted that "socialism in general, as an aim, as the opposite of capitalism (or imperialism), is accepted now not only by the Kautsky crowd and the social-chauvinists, but by many bourgeois social politicians. However, it is no longer a matter of contrasting two social systems, but of formulating the *concrete* aim of the *concrete* 'revolutionary mass

The efforts of the Rightists in Czechoslovakia, who were steering a course towards liquidation of the leading role of the Communist Party and social ownership of the means of production, was an attempt to replace genuine socialism by its bourgeois imitation. Objectively the military bureaucratic interpretation of socialism by the Peking propagandists plays an anti-socialist role.

The Central Committee of the CPSU, guided by Lenin's works, having generalised the experience of the building and development of socialism in the USSR and in other countries of the socialist system has published a number of political and theoretical documents elaborating the contemporary Marxist-Leninist conception of socialism. In generalised form this conception is expounded in Leonid Brezhnev's report *Lenin's Cause Lives on and Triumphs.*

The question of the basic features of the socialism that has already been built, said Comrade Brezhnev, is clear to Communists. "It is clear to us today not only from the theoretical propositions of Marxist teaching but also from the experience of development gained by the socialist countries. What are these features? They are the power of the working people with the vanguard role exercised by the working class and the leadership of social development provided by the Marxist-Leninist Party; public ownership of the means of production and, on its basis, the planned development of the national economy on the highest technological level for the benefit of the whole people; the implementation of the principle 'From each according to his abilities, to each according to his work'; the education of the whole people in the spirit of the ideology of scientific communism, in a spirit of friendship with the peoples of the fraternal socialist countries and the working people of the whole world; and lastly, a foreign policy founded on the principles of proletarian, socialist internationalism.

"All these general, basic elements of socialism are of decisive significance."[1]

---

struggle' against a *concrete* evil...." (V. I. Lenin, *Collected Works,* Vol. 23, pp. 153-54.) Even in those days Lenin drew attention to the fact that it is not a matter of the concept itself but of the meaning that is put into that concept.

[1] L. I. Brezhnev, *Following Lenin's Course,* Moscow, 1972, pp. 291-92.

Each one of these features of social relations in the consciousness of Soviet people is firmly connected with socialism. This is the great achievement of the Party's ideological and educational work. The task now lies in further strengthening just such an understanding of socialism, consciousness of the fact that each of these features is vitally important for the development of socialism, that only their unity can create socialism as a whole, that attempts to "combine" socialism with ideological-political "pluralism", with the bourgeois-liberal "freedoms" or with a military bureaucratic dictatorship, attempts to make it an instrument for the realisation of nationalist goals are in profound contradiction to the very nature of this system. Firm defence of the general principles of socialism, understanding of and respect for the special ways of realising these general principles in the conditions of various countries are an inseparable feature of the socialist orientation of the personality, to the establishment of which all means of educational influence should be directed.

The fostering of communist adherence to principle also entails exposing the class essence of the strategic tasks and tactical devices of anti-communist propaganda, elucidation of the class, mercenary nature of ideas of "neutralism", nonpartisanship and "deideologising" of social life, which have now become almost the chief subversive weapon of imperialism.

Despite their absurdity and lack of historical background, these ideas have exerted and continue to exert a definite influence on the understanding and behaviour of a certain section of the scientific and artistic intelligentsia, who for various reasons seek to avoid the complexity of life, to avoid class conflicts, the problems of war and peace and political struggle and to shut themselves up in the circle of their professional or personal interests. To some extent these bourgeois influences have an effect on some intellectuals in the socialist countries. The influence of "neutralist" illusions in the Soviet setting took the form in some cases of a one-sided interpretation of peaceful coexistence, when coexistence was extended to the ideological sphere as well, and of non-class understanding of the problems of democracy and freedom of the individual. This was further manifested in the attempts of certain scientists to cultivate the idea of setting up "non-class sociology", a kind of human engineering outside the influence of ideology and the Party. In fictional writing this was expressed in the efforts of certain writers to portray the lives of their characters outside any concrete, historical framework, as people without social or political class interests and aspirations.

The Party organisations and ideological bodies have in recent years concentrated their efforts on showing why bourgeois propaganda has been compelled to raise against socialism the slogans of democracy and freedom, on showing the true meaning of these slogans, and this has been of great importance in giving Soviet people the correct orientation in these complex and important questions, which are of both ideological and theoretical nature. The imperialist bourgeoisie, hard-pressed by the forces of socialism, has recourse to the slogans of democracy and freedom in order to divert the masses from the political struggle and gives these concepts a twist that will help to defend their own interests: democracy for the capitalists, freedom to own the instruments of production and exploit the working people, freedom to spread anti-human ideas and to confuse the masses. Every Soviet person must thoroughly understand the historical paradox which lies in the fact that imperialism, although deeply hostile to freedom for the mass of the working people, although it exists by crushing and limiting that freedom, and is the most formidable obstacle in the path of its attainment, appeals for a freedom that may help to continue its existence. Imperialism seeks to present bourgeois freedom as freedom for all and in doing so labels itself the "free world".

But the task cannot be confined to exposing the stratagems of bourgeois propaganda around the problems of freedom and democracy. The strength of ideological positions lies in the correct understanding of the essence of socialist democracy, the fact that it is opposite in all respects to bourgeois democracy, and the advantages, compared with the latter, of having the Communist Party play the leading role. This question, as was pointed out at the 24th Party Congress, has become the key point in the struggle between the Marxists-Leninists and the representatives of the various forms of revisionism. The experience of the ideological and political struggle in recent years clearly shows that the working class, the working people possess no other, stronger means of unity, of struggle for the realisation of their ideas than organisation in a Marxist-Leninist party. This truth runs right through all educational work and, undoubtedly, helps to develop correct conceptions of the Party and its place in socialist society.

The CPSU views the task of fostering internationalism among Soviet people from class positions. Nationalism disunites and splits up the international working class, the working people, whereas internationalism is a most important prerequisite for rallying all the revolutionary forces for a further offensive against imperialism. The Communist Party is irreconcilably opposed to any manifestations of nationalism and chauvinism and educates the working people in a spirit of love for their socialist Motherland and the fraternity of free peoples.

Fostering the adherence to communist principles means endowing the personality with such features, as the ability to see the achievements of socialism and its problems correctly, the desire to constantly improve the state of affairs in society, in the collective and eagerness to increase one's own contribution to the common cause, to improve one's knowledge and skills.

Successful communist education is possible only through the correct combination of instruction by positive example and of making people profoundly and realistically aware of the problems that face them. Teaching by drawing attention to the achievements of socialism, by positive example, is one of the basic principles of education in Soviet society. This deeply humanistic and extremely effective principle is fully realisable only under socialism. The Communist Party, while guiding the propaganda media, ideological and artistic education, in such a way that the broad masses of the working people comprehend the historic advantages of socialism and its humane ideology, at the same time fosters a sober understanding of existing problems. For the masses to have a correct understanding of these problems is the first condition of their having a correct attitude towards them.

Clear thinking and realism were highly characteristic of Lenin's approach to the construction of the new society. He always took a sceptical view of those who expected an ideal system, free of all contradictions and difficulties, to appear overnight. All Soviet people should remember Lenin's warning that the building of communism is a very complicated, long and difficult process.

Interest in social problems is implanted in Soviet people from an early age. They become deeply imbued with the ideas of equality and freedom and a sense of participation in the common cause of building communism. This gives them high ideals and makes them socially active. But the task of education consists not only in helping people to acquire ideals and goals but also in training their ability to fight for them.

To instill firmness and determination one must give people a clear realisation of the fact that in Soviet society along with great achievements there are also problems that are waiting to be solved; one must give them a realistic notion of the stage of socialism that society has reached at present. Otherwise it is impossible to train the young generation ideologically and morally for active participation in the building of communism.

Ideological and political education in socialist conditions is unthinkable unless all educational and propaganda work is tied in with the practical socio-political and production activity of every individual and society as a whole.

Lenin said that business matters are the politics that interest us most.[1] Actually this proposition is fundamental to the organisation of educational work in a socialist context, because a person's attitude to work for the good of society, to social property is, in fact, the most essential expression of his socialist consciousness.

Everyone is concerned not only with his machine, his tools, the instruments of labour; he is also involved in relations with other people. And here a person's behaviour depends not on the level of his professional skill, but on his moral and political qualities. On whether he understands the main issues affecting the life of his collective, whether he under-

---

[1] V. I. Lenin, *Collected Works*, Vol. 32, p. 430.

stands the internal and international position of his country, on whether he is ready under any circumstances to defend the truth of communist ideals, the interests of society, or whether he gives up at the first difficulties, at the first encounter with a bureaucrat or a hooligan. These features have great moral and political significance. They also have a direct effect in production because only a strong, healthy collective with a well-organised system of educational work can deal successfully with production targets.

The political approach always implies a need to take into account the interests of the people, of collectives, of separate individuals and to bring them into correct alignment. The managers of any branch of the economy must fully understand that when dealing with this or that question of production, scientific or cultural activity, they cannot (even if they want to) avoid the questions of ideological and political education. It is impossible to cope with production and organisational problems (so-called business matters) without touching in some way upon the interests of society, the collective and individuals, and this has always involved questions of an ideological and political nature.

". . .Our Party," L. I. Brezhnev said at the 24th Congress of the CPSU, "constantly stresses the need for an organic link between managerial and educational work. It demands that leading cadres should constantly think of the educational effects of the economic and administrative decisions adopted by them."[1]

It is impossible nowadays to fulfil the aims of ideological and political education of the working people without reference to the problems of scientific and technological progress. The CPSU has set up a task of historic importance—to combine organically the achievements of the scientific and technological revolution with the advantages of socialism. Its realisation confronts propaganda with a number of fundamentally new problems, above all the problem of training personnel, of mastering the latest achievements of science and technology, the latest know-how. What is today known only to a narrow group of scientists and experts, projects that are only on the drawing board or being calculated in specialised

---

[1] *The 24th Congress of the CPSU*, p. 120.

laboratories, must tomorrow find their way into production. But the recommendations of science cannot become a reality of production until they are mastered by the masses of the workers, technicians and engineers.

All Party organisations, state and economic agencies are urgently confronted with the problem of propaganding economic knowledge, the achievements of science and technology and advanced production know-how. It is essential that people in all the leading trades should have the minimum of general scientific knowledge that enable personnel to cope successfully with their functions in the context of scientific and technical progress. Only if this is so can one count on creative activity on the part of workers, collective farmers and professional people, and, consequently, on the moral growth and social activity of the personality. The problem of the close connection between purely technical matters and social problems, between the tasks of production and those of ideological education, cries out for attention.

Taking into Account the General, the Particular and the Individual in the Organisation of Ideological Propaganda Work

Although the actual content, what one is trying to say, is the decisive factor in the success of propaganda, no effective propaganda can be achieved without organisation. The more people there are to absorb certain ideas, the more important it is to have a proper system of propaganda work, to select the right forms and methods of propaganda.

In the literal sense "propaganda" means the oral and written spreading of ideas, doctrines, opinions and political theories. Organisational work in the sphere of propaganda is the linking of sources of information with the masses. Considered in more detail, propaganda is the purposeful, differentiated conveying of ideas and knowledge of various levels and in various forms to this or that section of the population, taking into consideration its emotional impact and in accordance with certain political precepts. In other words, the organisation of propaganda is also activity in selecting and planning the material and constant analysis of whether it corresponds to the demands of the moment. In addition, it is also the building up of the organisational forms by means of which propaganda is put into effect, selection and training of personnel and study of the effectiveness of propaganda efforts.

In organising ideological and political education the Communist Party has at its disposal Lenin's teaching on the organisation of Party propaganda and immense practical experience. Lenin fully elaborated such problems of propaganda as the necessity for instilling socialist consciousness among the masses, the role of advanced theory in the revolutionary struggle, the correlation of theoretical activity and propaganda, politics and propaganda. Lenin always saw to it that the Party's ideas, expressed in concrete tasks and slogans, were propaganded as widely as possible, so that they would rally and stir the masses into activity. He paid enormous attention to the organisation, forms and methods of propaganda and the training of propagandists.

The organisational structure of communist propaganda has been subordinated from the very start to the profoundly humanistic task of uniting people on the basis of progressive ideas while paying maximum attention to the special features that characterise the position of different groups. On this subject Lenin wrote: "We must learn to approach the masses with particular patience and caution, so as to be able to understand the distinctive features in the mentality of each stratum, calling, etc., of these masses."[1]

The general interests in the organisation of ideological and political education are ensured by the fact that the media of ideological influence—preschool, school and university-level education, the press, radio and television, the cinema, theatre, literature and art, and ideological training in the work collectives—give the working people the possibility of assimilating the basic ideological and moral tenets of socialism, the goals and aims of the policy of the Communist Party and the Soviet state.

The general interests of all members of society are ensured by a unified system of political, economic and cultural information, which supplies people with reliable knowledge on all the most important questions of internal and international

---

[1] V. I. Lenin, *Collected Works,* Vol. 31, p. 192.

life. Moreover, the Communist Party, realising the tremendous effect of information on people's consciousness, has always held that material for political information should be selected from class, Party positions.

The anti-Communists are particularly bitter in their opposition to the principle of Party commitment in the field of propaganda, which they present as contrary to freedom of the individual, as violation of the personality. Thus, Georges Friedmann, for instance, asserts that only free competition in the field of mass media and the possibility of reporting information from different sources provide a certain guarantee against the loss of personal individuality. What he means by competition is the right of certain owners of the information media to defend the general interests of the capitalists at their own risk. (Incidentally, this right is being constantly narrowed down by the rapid monopolisation of the information media, and also by the ideological and political pressure exerted by the imperialist states.) In countries where there are no "principles of competition" in ideology (meaning the socialist countries), complete degradation of the personality through "mass persuasion" is, Friedmann maintains, almost inevitable.

How do such assertions look when compared with the actual reality?

First, if these "different" sources actually guaranteed the preservation of "individuality" among the people, in the United States and other capitalist countries where such "competitive principles" exist, one would not observe any standardisation of thinking and behaviour. The facts reveal quite a different situation, however. The crux of the matter, therefore, lies in the content of the material that the mass media transmit to the mass consciousness.

Second, no matter how they try, the advocates of "free" information cannot conceal the inevitability of selection of information, which is bound to occur because of the amount of information available. The so-called information explosion means that modern technology has made it possible to inform the whole world of practically all significant events, facts, phenomena, scientific discovery, and so on. This has enormously increased the amount of information at society's disposal. And yet every individual's ability to make use of information is limited by the time factor, by individual and group abilities.

In such a situation the problem of selection of information and determining the criteria of its usefulness becomes exceptionally acute. On the one hand, it is an organisational and technical problem—efficiency, quality, etc. On the other hand, the selection of information, particularly concerning social life, is a political problem because it implies a certain standpoint. The selection of information and its transmission to a certain audience, consequently, always involves problems of organisation and problems of ideological and political education. This fact is always taken into consideration by every state, even if the selection is carried out in different ways.

Third, it is inevitable that the information will be appraised from a class standpoint because "...no living person *can help taking the side* of one class or another..., can help rejoicing at the successes of that class and being disappointed by its failures, can help being angered by those who are hostile to that class, who hamper its development by disseminating backward views, and so on and so forth"[1]. It follows that selection of information from the class and Party standpoint is a key principle in the organisation of all ideological-educational work, including political information.

The Communists openly admit the class character of information, organise it in accordance with the interests of the working class and the working people with the aim of all-round development of the working man's personality.

The differentiation of political propaganda according to the peculiarities of the social strata and professional interests serves the same aim of developing the working man's consciousness to the maximum. Every branch of information has long since acquired its organisational forms. Oral information is transmitted in talks by agitators and political spokesmen, reports and lectures, political classes, theoretical seminars and conferences; in the newspapers and magazines it takes the form of special publications and pages; on the radio and television, a huge variety of specially devised programmes—for the rural areas, for soldiers, for builders, for women, for young people, etc. The present-day schools of communist

---

[1] V. I. Lenin, *Collected Works,* Vol. 2, p. 531.

work have become an effective form of propaganda of production experience and political education.

One of the most important features of the differentiation of propaganda is the existence of a special system of Marxist-Leninist training of Communists (and Komsomol members) and the development of the system of mass propaganda and agitation aimed at the broad masses of the working people. The general aim—the study of theory, Party history and policy—is the same in both cases, of course, but the methods and volume of training differ. The system of Party education entails consistent study of all the components of Marxism-Leninism and Party policy, mainly by Communists, whereas mass propaganda explains the Party's ideology and policy to the broad masses of the working people.

At the present time there is an effective system of Party education covering more than 16 million people. This system was highly appraised in the Central Committee's Report to the 24th Congress. The structure of the system of Party education provides for continuity, consistency and fullness. The three stages—primary, secondary and higher—give students over a number of years a sufficient knowledge of all the components of Marxism-Leninism—philosophy, political economy and scientific communism, and also Party history and current questions of Party policy. The system of Party education has its study plans and programmes, study aids and textbooks. All this, taken together, creates generally favourable conditions for the Marxist-Leninist training of Communists and of non-Party activists, and ideological training of Communists is an essential condition for raising the fighting capacity of the Party's ranks and enhancing its vanguard role.

The Communist Party aims at stepping up the activity of those who study under its educational system. It is constantly stressed that the chief method of training is the method of independent study of the questions of theory and policy; importance is attached to the principle of voluntary choice of form of study and the need for making wider use of the practical knowledge of individual students. Thus, the personal inclinations acquire suitable conditions for development.

In present-day conditions the question of the effectiveness of propaganda emerges in a new light. The correctness of the

Communist Party's ideas and policy, its great organisational efforts, always ensure the success of its policy. But as the ideological struggle in the world grows more intense and technical means of the mutual ideological penetration of the opposing camps improve and multiply, a general notion of the favourable results of propaganda becomes an inadequate criterion of propaganda activity. We must now have a precise assessment of the results of all major propaganda operations, i.e., we must know exactly how much was learned of what the source intended to inform its audience, and by what circle of people, how various categories of people react to information (positively, negatively or neutrally), what they expect in the future, and so on. It is quite natural that Party committees, newspapers, magazines, radio and television more and more often have recourse to sociological research.

4. DEVELOPMENT OF THE FREEDOM AND RESPONSIBILITY OF THE INDIVIDUAL

The general proposition that freedom is the product of social development applies entirely to freedom in conditions of socialism. The growth of the social productive forces, the maturity of social relations under socialism, the development of the scientific consciousness, create favourable conditions for people's life, for improving their abilities and talents, and thus widen the limits of freedom. On the other hand, the fostering of a sense of responsibility is also an essential condition of the development of freedom and one of the Party's most important tasks in communist construction.

Freedom of the individual never has been and never can be unlimited. The achieved level of the productive forces and the amount of material wealth available to society determine the economic and other material possibilities for the development of the members of society, and also their spiritual, intellectual opportunities. The growth of production and the consequent obliteration of the still surviving social differences, the further development of democracy, the upsurge of education and culture, the fostering of communist consciousness are all essential conditions without which any growth of the freedom and strengthening of responsibility among members of society is unthinkable.

The anti-Communists present the elimination of class distinctions and the consolidation of social unity as the path to the destruction of individuality. They create an antithesis between unity of ideological views and the development of personal freedom. According to them, the education of the working people in the spirit of the unified communist ideology "coerces" the personality and contradicts its "nature", inasmuch as the individual is deprived of spiritual freedom, becomes enslaved and thus loses the possibility of making a free choice of his spiritual orientation. Some anti-Communists declare that the Soviet person is left without any of the spiritual alternatives that in general make possible and nourish the creative process of thinking. They often write that the Communist Party's plan to mould the "new man" may become an instrument of a new terror, because it involves "superhuman criteria".

Arguments of this kind are in crying contradiction to the whole experience of history, and the practice of socialism above all. History has shown that unity of opinions, common ground on the fundamental issues could not stop creative search for the solution of new problems, but unity inevitably arises where there is common interest. It is another matter that before socialism was established there was never such a thing as community of fundamental interests on the scale of the whole of society.

Socialist practice shows that along with a general unity of basic principles there exists an enormous diversity of ideas and activity. While seeking to establish fundamental unity in the ideological and political sphere, socialist society is no less eager to develop a diversity of abilities, inclinations and talents, because only this can ensure successful search for solutions to current problems. Diversity of the individual's abilities, activity and character are, in fact, essential manifestations of personal freedom. Consequently, the richer and more varied these manifestations, the fuller freedom will be.

Freedom is not merely a good thing for the individual. It is an essential condition of the further progress of socialist society and of its growing into a communist society. The growth of production, the solution of social problems, the level of scientific and artistic creativity are directly dependent on the initiative, skill and ideological orientation of workers in all parts of the social organism. In other words, the posing and solution of current problems, the intensity and level of creativity depend on conditions of work and rights, on the degree of freedom of thought and action of individuals. Without creative discussion of scientific and practical problems, without criticism and self-criticism there can be no advance.

An important factor in the development of freedom in socialist society is the engendering of a high sense of personal responsibility and a high degree of consciousness. Awareness on the part of the individual that his interests coincide with those of society is of great importance in enabling him to perceive necessary action as free action. A highly conscious person treats activity for the good of the people as free activity; he sees in it his own fundamental interest and the chief content of his life. If, on the other hand, despite favourable external circumstances, a person has no conscious aim or formulates it incorrectly, guided by narrow selfish interests that he himself has misunderstood, wastes his energy and leisure on drinking, hooliganism and so on, his conduct becomes a threat to society and to the person himself.

Socialist society is not guaranteed against attempts by individuals to attack certain of its members or the interests of society as a whole. And society cannot remain indifferent to such attacks. The use of coercion in such cases is a necessary condition of the freedom of society, a manifestation of concern for the freedom of its members. Society, naturally, has a system of social prohibitions designed to protect the gains of socialism. Anti-Soviet subversive activity, high treason, anti-socialist propaganda, war propaganda and the like are punished as serious crimes. These prohibitions also have the aim of protecting the liberties of the citizens of the socialist state.

Under socialism the moral demands that are sanctioned by society coincide with the laws and legal norms. Supported by the state apparatus of coercion, these legal norms ensure the rights and freedom of the individual. The further socialism develops, the more complete this coincidence will be.

"The whole system of government and social organisations," states the Programme of the CPSU, "educates the people in a spirit of voluntary and conscientious fulfilment of their duties and leads to a natural fusion of rights and duties to form single standards of communist behaviour."[1]

As society advances towards communism, as equality and social homogeneity become more complete, as the survivals of the past are removed and communist morality becomes fully established, society will become less and less concerned with coercion and more and more with voluntary observation of the rules of community life. And this leads to a further extension of the rights of the individual.

Being responsible means considering the consequences of one's actions in relation to the standards prevailing in society. Here we have two aspects of responsibility, its purely organisation-technical side and its moral political aspect. In the first case, it is a question of being qualified to make a decision and capable of carrying it out. In the second, one has in addition to weigh the moral and political consequences of one's behaviour and this depends on one's ideological and moral convictions. Whatever job a man has, whether he makes machinery, builds homes, or runs a factory, he is involved in a system of political and moral relations with other people. His actions cannot fail to be important in some degree to his collective, to society.

Politico-moral responsibility has a special significance for Communists. The socio-political and ideological consolidation of Soviet society must not for a moment be allowed to hide the fact that an intense struggle is being waged in the world and the USSR is taking an extremely active part in it.

Fostering of adherence to the communist principle and a high sense of political responsibility on the part of every member of society has been and remains to be the most important task of the Party, the state, the Komsomol, the school and the family.

In the first years of Soviet power Lenin, returning again and again to the problem of making the new man, pointed out the need to foster an understanding of the ordinary person's part in solving problems of general importance to the state.

---

[1] *The Road to Communism*, p. 553.

He spoke of the need of "...every politically conscious worker feeling that he is not only the master of his own factory
but that he is also a representative of the country, of his
feeling his responsibility."[1] He urged that the young people
should strive in their daily work to cope with the general
tasks of building the new life. Lenin stressed the importance
of labour heroism in the daily work of the masses. He demanded we should free ourselves of people who find such
work "dull", "uninteresting" or "unintelligible", who turn
up their noses or fall into a panic or become intoxicated with
their own declamations about the absence of the "previous
elation", the "previous enthusiasm", etc.[2]

The two factors of a practical nature that play the most
important part in forming the individual's social activity,
responsibility and competence are (1) attracting people to
take a practical part in managing public affairs and (2) social
control.

The CPSU Programme defines as the main direction of
the development of the socialist state in the period of the
building of communism an all-round extension and perfection of socialist democracy, active participation of all citizens in the administration of the state, in the management of
economic and cultural development, improvement of the
government apparatus and increased control over its activity.[3] In its resolution on the Central Committee's Report the
24th Party Congress also pointed out that bringing the masses
into the management of production remains one of the central
tasks.

Why is the question put in this particular way?

Because practical participation in the administration of
public affairs strengthens ideological and moral precepts in
people's consciousness. Participation in self-administration
helps people to develop a wider outlook, a deeper understanding of the situation, of the general goals and means of
achieving them, teaches people to respect generally accepted
rules and norms of behaviour and to combine personal
wishes and the public interest. People derive satisfaction

---

[1] V. I. Lenin, *Collected Works*, Vol. 27, p. 403.
[2] Ibid., Vol. 33, pp. 28-29.
[3] *The Road to Communism*, p. 548.

from seeing certain ideas become reality through their participation. Hence the creative activity of the masses, confidence
in the rightness of the ideals of communism and firmness in
dealing with the problems of communist construction.

Guided by its Programme and the Directives of its 24th
Congress, the Communist Party of the Soviet Union is
following the line of bringing the working people into the
discussion and solving of the practical problems of social life
on a wide scale. In the work of the permanent commissions
of the Soviets, in the trade unions and other public organisations, at production meetings and workers' conferences millions of workers, collective farmers, office workers and professional people systematically discuss and solve problems of
social, public administration. There are more than 20 different public organisations that take part in state administration.

But it would be wrong to close one's eyes to the fact that
at many enterprises, collective and state farms and institutions there is a fairly significant number of people
who have been "on the passive list" for years. And it
is among this section of the population, which as a rule is
badly informed, that various foolish notions and persistent
prejudices are to be found. This environment quite often
provides recruits for criminal activities and various infringements of public order. Bringing the broad masses into the
building of the new life also means ensuring successful economic construction and more effective education of the people.

The current economic reform is a new and signficant step
in developing freedom and enhancing the responsibility of
the individual and the working collective for the future of
socialist production and society as a whole. The changed system of planning and economic incentives gives the collective
a greater interest in increasing production and raising mutual demands within the collective, because unproductive
spending and carelessness will come under the fire of criticism from the whole collective, which has a material stake
in the general results of the work. In other words, the economic reform widens the material conditions for the further
development of socialist democracy.

The development of active social initiative and participation, the inclusion of every person in the life of the working
collective form the basic condition for fostering a high sense

of personal responsibility. If it is true that there can be no freedom without responsibility, it is equally true that there can be no responsibility without rights.

The organisation of systematic political, economic and cultural information for the working people is highly relevant to developing freedom and fostering people's sense of responsibility. The better people are informed, the more freely can they weigh up a situation and more responsible is their attitude to their work. The more a man knows and understands about the job he is doing, the better his general orientation, the more free he feels himself and the bolder he is in taking on responsibility. Lenin emphasised that the state "is strong when the people know everything, can form an opinion of everything and do everything consciously."[1]

The Communist Party is making persistent efforts to improve the system of getting political information across to the working people. In accordance with the instruction of the 23rd Party Congress that all political agitation should be built on the basis of widely and systematically organised informing of the public about the political, economic and cultural life of the country and the international situation, the Party organisations have done quite a lot to improve information at all levels. Greater speed is being achieved in supplying press, radio and television news. A system of political informants has been set up that keeps all workers' collectives supplied with regular and reliable information.

Even now, however, the information service in some work collectives still depends wholly on the goodwill of this or that administrator. If the person in charge understands the needs of the collective and thinks of its unity, he will see to it that the collective is systematically supplied with information about its own activity and that of the enterprise of which it is a part; if not, a situation is created in which people are better informed about international affairs than about the work of their own enterprise, town or village.

The Party believes it necessary to encourage the practice of heads of enterprises and amalgamations and also top-level officials of ministries regularly accounting for their work directly to the workers.[2]

---

[1] V. I. Lenin, *Collected Works*, Vol. 26, p. 256.
[2] *The 24th Congress of the CPSU*, p. 85.

The interests of building communist society demand that keeping the workers informed in general and about the effect of their critical remarks should not depend on the goodwill of a particular local leader, but should become standard practice in every collective, that all political agitation should be based on widely organised and systematic provision of information on current political, economic and cultural questions.

Publicity and information are essential to the development of criticism and self-criticism as a means of raising officeholders' sense of public responsibility and improving the work of all departments of administration. Soviet people must know what is going on around them, how the administrative bodies they have elected work, and how the people in whom they have placed their trust are living up to their obligations.

Regular reports by the heads of workshops, work-teams and departments, by the heads of municipal and cultural services on their work, on the fulfilment of requests and proposals, on their response to criticisms coming from the working people must be as regular as Party meetings and sessions of the Soviets. This will be in the people's interests and help to overcome instances of red-tapism and improve the work of the administration.

Regular reports on the fulfilment of voters' demands are an important form of publicity in the functioning of the Soviets. A great deal of work goes into fulfilling these demands. At meetings with their constituents, in the press and on the radio, the executive committees of the Soviets and the Soviet deputies report back systematically on their work.

Propaganda measures and attempts to bring the masses into the administration of public affairs must be supplemented by social control and the application of certain sanctions, in other words, by compulsion. Even the most humane ideas and principles cannot be carried out, cannot be translated into reality if they are not backed up by compulsory measures to be applied to people who put their own selfish interests first, who oppose society, the general interests with their own slackness, lack of discipline, and so on. In this respect the organs of people's control have a great part to play.

The Party insists that all its organisations, all Commu-

nists must develop criticism and self-criticism, improve the
work of the organs of people's control and the organs of
Party control, set higher standards for their personnel and
be quite uncompromising in cases when a member refuses to
listen to criticism and systematically violates Party and state
discipline. The perfecting of Soviet legislation has a big
part to play in consolidating the legal system and legality,
and hence the legal education of the working people.

An implacably critical attitude to various shortcomings,
to bad work, indifference, slackness, bureaucratic distortions,
to people who try to suppress criticism and those who brush
aside the proposals and demands of the working people is
essential to the development of activity and responsibility
in the collective.

Thus, the development of personal freedom and development of ideological and moral features are two aspects of
the one general problem of the development of the whole
personality. The Communist Party is constantly improving
the methods of communist education of the working people,
pointing out the increased possibilities of producing a new
kind of person who harmoniously combines a richness of
mind, moral purity and physical perfection. *"The transition
to communism,"* states the Party Programme, *"means the
fullest extension of personal freedom and the rights of Soviet
citizens.* Socialism has brought the working people the broadest guaranteed rights and freedoms. Communism will bring
the working people further great rights and opportunities."[1]

*   *   *

The level of social activity of the masses that has been
achieved and the features of the new personality while in
general providing convincing proof of the possibility of educating the masses in the spirit of collectivism, at the same
time reveal the complexity of the tasks involved in producing
the new kind of person. This complexity lies in the need
to overcome age-old individualistic habits and inertia, the
need to raise labour activity and skills, to equip people for
coping with sophisticated social demands.

---

[1] *The Road to Communism,* p. 552.

A whole complex of conditions, material, political and psychological, have to be created for dealing successfully with the basic tasks of forming the personality.

The CPSU links the further development of the personality with the transformation of socialist relationships into communist relationships, and at the same time introduces consistent measures in the field of upbringing and education, measures to improve the work of the secondary and higher schools, propaganda and political information, the development of literature and art. Though in itself a subjective sphere, education emerges as an objective demand of the process of transition to communism.

Development of the system of communist education presupposes that everyone must receive certain general knowledge and ideas about the world, the principles and norms of the new society, and at the same time, on the basis of this general knowledge and these conceptions, be able to develop his individual abilities and talents. Although the solution of the problem of achieving such a combination of personal and social interests is an extremely broad and intricate task, socialist social relations create a favourable objective basis for its fulfilment.

By uniting social and personal interests socialism for the first time in history makes personal freedom adequate to personal activity for the good of society and thus enormously increases the possibility of social activity on the part of the masses. Freedom becomes a law of social development and at the same time a law of the development of the individual. The problem of the further extension of freedom lies in creating the most effective organisation for guiding social processes at each stage of historical development.

CONCLUSION

The emergence of the socialist type of personality has come about in accordance with the laws of social development and is the natural result of a whole complex of socio-historical causes. It was prepared, *first*, by the history of Russian society that preceded the October Revolution, particularly the history of the liberation movement and the founding and building up of the Bolshevik Party as the vanguard of the revolutionary proletariat; *second*, by the dissemination among revolutionary fighters of the Marxist-Leninist teaching on socialism and communism (including the Marxist-Leninist conception of personality), which has guided the Communist Party and the socialist state in all their varied practical work of transforming the socio-economic, political and other conditions of life and educating the working people; *third*, by the creation and consolidation in the process of the working people's revolutionary transforming activity of a new system of socialist social relations—a new social environment for the individual.

The question of the inevitability of the appearance of the new personality, the legitimacy and viability of its basic features essentially coincides with the questions of the inevitability of the socialist revolution, the building and development of socialist society. Only on the basis of the theory of scientific socialism was the proletariat able to counterpose its interests to those of the capitalists, to seize power and set about building socialism. Only by taking up conscious struggle for the realisation of socialism and communism is the proletarian able to become an individual of the new socialist type. The proletarian type of personality, the type of the proletarian revolutionary thus expresses the demands, interests and ideals of his class, and at the same time the demands of the historical development of all working people, of contemporary society as a whole.

The revolution, the victory of socialism sets as the moral standards of the new personality the models of behaviour inherent in proletarian revolutionaries. And although the process of the establishment of these standards in mass behaviour is a long, complicated and contradictory process, it is, nevertheless, on the whole being carried out successfully. Besides abolishing the exploitation of man by man socialism does away with the situation where the individual's status depends on social origin or nationality; socialism invests all material and spiritual wealth in the development of the working man, and work itself becomes something infinitely more important than a mere means of livelihood, namely, service to the community, to the common good. Socialism makes people's spiritual unity the basic principle of community life and gives them a profoundly inspiring aim—the building of communist society. Socialism, Lenin wrote, provides for the first time the opportunity "for actually drawing the majority of working people into a field of labour in which they can display their abilities, develop the capacities, and reveal those talents, so abundant among the people"[1].

Social relations under socialism are such that the interests of society objectively become the interests of the individual, and the individual—the bearer of social interests, that is to say, the socio-historical demands of society's advance towards socialism and communism, having been expressed in real social forms and institutions, in ideological and moral values, become the demands, interests, ideals and, consequently, the motives of the behaviour of separate individuals. Of people of this type it is quite justifiable to say that communism becomes for them their own personal concern. Here ideological motivations are so basic and stable that they become constant stimulators of mass behaviour. This prompts the conclusion that the socialist type of personality becomes under socialism a universal phenomenon.

Trying to belittle the significance of this fact and damp

---

[1] V. I. Lenin, *Collected Works*, Vol. 26, p. 404.

down the struggle between the two world systems, bourgeois ideologists present relations between the individual and society as an everlasting conflict between the collective in general and the individual in general. Bourgeois ideologists seek to make it appear that the struggle is being waged between those who put human freedom above everything else, who consider the individual the highest value (these, of course, are the bourgeois ideologists themselves), and those who are ready to sacrifice human freedom for the sake of ultimate political aims, who subordinate the individual to the state (these, of course, are the Communists).

But this is a crude falsification of the essence of the problem. Man is a social being and he develops as an individual, a personality, only in society, and in no other way. The dilemma between collectivity and individuality is meaningless. These borderlines of human existence have always existed and will always continue to exist. There is no life without the collective and hence without collectivity, just as society without individuals and hence without individuality is also an absurdity. The only way of looking at the question is that there is both the individual and society, both collectivity and individuality. Each specific society resolves the problem of the individual in its own particular way. The true essence of this problem lies in deciding which social system—capitalism or socialism—offers an effective solution of the question of the freedom and all-round development of the masses of the working people.

The Marxists have emerged onto the world stage with their own special conception of the emancipation of the working man. This is where they have a tremendous advantage. But practice always turns out to be far richer, far more complicated than any theoretical assumptions. One cannot fail to see that there are considerable difficulties on the road of development of the socialist personality. Any forecasting, and particularly social forecasting, while extremely effective in some ways inevitably involves losses. When speaking of the formation of the new man in socialist society we cannot, therefore, underestimate the negative phenomena that continue to exist in Soviet society. Further advance on the road to communism depends on the realistic appraisal of successes and failures.

The development of the new personality proceeds on the basis of the achievements of previous history and the accumulated material of the past, in conditions of acute ideological and political struggle with the enemy camp. Comparison with the past, and also with the opposing, hostile camp of imperialism is as essential as comparison of the results achieved with the ideal. This enables us to see clearly enough the achievements and the unsolved problems, the complexity of the current processes and the true significance of what has been accomplished. If a person in bourgeois, class society is always a representative, a member primarily of his own class, capitalist, say, or proletarian, the Soviet person, the socialist man is a representative primarily of the whole Soviet people, and only after that may he, and should he, be characterised as a member of one or another class, or social group.

This fact, naturally, confronts the investigator with a specific task. To characterise the new personality that is taking shape on the scale of the whole of society one must reveal the fundamental changes in the basic spheres of social existence, in the sphere of property, activity and mutual relationships between people. Only by so doing can one avoid the temptation to make use of the normative method in describing the type of personality. The normative approach always involves the danger of departure from reality, and such departures are the more likely to occur the broader the type we seek to characterise.

Only on the basis of singling out the features of the new personality from actually existing and most significant features of people's positions, and activity, only by revealing the key characteristics of the socialist ethos, which lies in the acceptance of the fundamental material and spiritual values of socialism, can one investigate the depth, stability and consistency of the qualities that make up the features of the various subtypes within the framework of the overall socialist personality.

The question of classification into types is fundamental to the problem of personality because it involves the further development of the theory and practice of education. The study of the foundations of classification of the features of various types of personality indicates the tremendous diversity of the typical features that concern contemporary Soviet man and that need to be systematised and classified. This work becomes all the more important and significant the more profoundly it reveals the movement of the social organism, because the typical in personality is the personified expression of social laws or patterns. Such an approach allows us to remain on the grounds of reality because it takes into consideration only the content of the changes that have been brought about, the level of development of the productive forces and social relations. Though it has fundamentally changed people's lives, socialism does not rigidly predetermine their behaviour or their personal qualities but leaves a wide field for the emergence of diverse interests, aspirations and discoveries. An orientation on the objective foundations while identifying personal qualities gives the investigator real criteria and puts the theory of the mutual relations between society and the individual on the plane of investigation of objective processes.

Given this approach, the progress of the personality is seen as part of the general advance of society. The degree of development of the personality in society cannot be defined by characterising the qualities of separate individuals or even groups of individuals. It is determined by the content, the intensity of the relations between all groups, all sections of society. Referring to the progress of the personality, Karl Marx pointed out that one must judge the power of human nature not by the power of separate individuals but by the power of society.[1]

The progress of the personality under socialism has expressed itself in the development of the scientific world view, the improvement of morality and the growth of education; progress has also meant development of personal freedom and its self-awareness. The personality is an entity comprising species essence, biological and social, with social essence as its main aspect. Therefore, the degree of development of the personality is determined by the depth and breadth of its social relations with other personalities, i.e., with its socialisation.

Whereas socialisation of the personality lies in the indi-

---

[1] K. Marx and F. Engels, *The Holy Family*, p. 176.

vidual's absorbing general and unifying features, the qualitative leap in personal development under socialism consists
in bringing the mass of individuals into intensive social life
proceeding on the basis of socialist relations and Marxist-
Leninist ideology. It is in the general that the strength of
the human race lies. Already under socialism the social function becomes the essential side of the individual's life and
activity for the majority of the members of society. The
higher level of social organisation under socialism has not
only drawn the masses of the working people into active social life but has also made it possible to endow this activity
with a varied humanist content, has raised the general level of
the individual's social content. "...*Only* socialism will be the
beginning of a rapid, genuine, truly mass forward movement, embracing first the *majority* and then the whole of
the population, in all spheres of public and private life."[1]

The main thing is that, despite all the difficulties, socialism has created conditions, stimuli, norms and goals that
have brought about a new type of mass human behaviour, a
new type of individual. Its essence lies in an active attitude
towards social life, in its deeply rooted interest in the establishment of socialism and communism.

The new man has appeared and is developing, and it is
he, his views, his beliefs and ideals, his deeds that determine the future of the Land of Soviets, the future of socialism
and communism.

The historic significance of the experience of the Soviet
Union in moulding the new man consists, *first*, in the fact
that for the first time in history, it has been proved on the
basis of the experience of a large country with typical conditions that a person's character can be formed on collectivist principles, so that he chooses service of public interest
and the common good as his goal in life.

At the same time the development of the new personality
is a requirement of socialist and communist construction and
of the inner organisation of the future society. Dealing with
great and complicated tasks and overcoming difficulties
demand tremendous creative efforts, mobilisation of the talents and abilities of the working masses. Moreover, it is in

---

[1] V. I. Lenin, *Collected Works,* Vol. 25, p. 472.

the actual process of building already that the builders of communism must become members of communist society, because without a high level of consciousness, without a definite intellectual and moral level it will be impossible to realise the principles and rules of communist community life. Only as communist forms of social organisation are created will communist principles become firmly established in life, in labour, in the relations between people, will people acquire the ability to make use of the benefits of communism.

As a result of the creation of social conditions and a gigantic leap forward in the growth of the productive forces the individual and the whole of society will move from the realm of necessity to the realm of freedom, where it is really possible for the vocation, destiny and task of man to become the all-round development of all his abilities.[1]

Second, the appearance of the socialist type of personality clearly confirms the viability and correctness of the Marxist-Leninist proposition that man's essence is the totality of social relations, that the problems of the individual can be solved along with the emancipation of all the working masses, that the way to change man's conditions of life and re-educate him lies through socialist revolution and the building of socialism and communism.

It is coming true, as the founders of Marxism predicted, that "only conscious organisation of social production, in which production and distribution are carried on in a planned way, can lift manking above the rest of the animal world as regards the social aspect, in the same way that production in general has done this for mankind in the specifically biological aspect."[2]

No other social theory has done so much for the analysis of the real social forms in which the working man's life and work are carried on. Marxism-Leninism is addressed to the people and expresses the interests of the people. It is not surprising, therefore, that this unique feature of Marxism-Leninism should have been chosen by its opponents as a pretext for claiming that the Marxists ignore the personality.

---

[1] K. Marx and F. Engels, *The German Ideology,* pp. 322-23.
[2] F. Engels, *Dialectics of Nature,* Moscow, 1954, p. 49.

Third, the Soviet Union's experience, the behaviour and way of life of the new man exercise a tremendous influence on the consciousness of all mankind. Contemporary man has acquired an attractive ideological, moral and cultural image, a model has been created for solving the problems of man's humanisation. This experience proves that socialist society has the material as well as the spiritual capacity for producing new people. The historical significance of the victory of socialism in the USSR, state the Theses of the Central Committee of the CPSU on the *50th Anniversary of the Great October Socialist Revolution,* lies in the fact that "the peoples of our country have shown the world the practical ways of resolving the cardinal contradictions of the contemporary epoch. Over the decades, vast experience has been accumulated in the construction of socialism and the application on a mass scale of socialist principles and rules of the human way of life, experience which is creatively adopted by other nations."[1]

For the Soviet Union itself this experience has the further significance that it creates the conditions, the confidence for further advance towards communism.

Fourth, the appearance and development of the new, Soviet person further intensifies the profound crisis of the social and spiritual values held by the bourgeoisie. Life has forced many bourgeois ideologists and politicians to acknowledge the successes of Soviet society in educating a new kind of person. They are unable to deny that Soviet people believe in the justice of the principles of socialism, share the Marxist-Leninist ideas of the transition to communism and support the policy of the Communist Party. It is clear to the world at large that the Soviet Union's oustanding economic and cultural achievements are backed by a definite social system—socialism.

The attitude abroad towards Soviet people has shown the historic significance of the socialist way of life, the socialist type of personality. Socialist practice, socialism's solution of the problem of the personality have deepened the antagonistic contradictions between the working people and the ruling

---

[1] *50th Anniversary of the Great October Socialist Revolution,* Moscow, p. 26.

classes in the bourgeois world and evoked a split in the bourgeois consciousness, while stimulating the growth and unity of the forces fighting for socialism. This constitutes one of the most important laws of the struggle between the two world systems—socialism and capitalism. The 20th century is the century of expanding socialist practice, of its steadily increasing influence on world development, on social consciousness.

The anti-Communists seek to counterpoise the complexities and conflicts of reality to the ideals of scientific communism, and to produce various twisted arguments to assert the idea that it is unrealisable, that its basic suppositions lack credibility. The socialism that actually exists is contrasted with various "humanised" models of socialism, the meaning of which is to remove the most essential things from the concept of socialism, i.e., the leading role of the Marxist-Leninist party, of public ownership and democratic centralism; national prejudice is exploited in every possible way; the forms and principles of socialist democracy are attacked and falsified with particular zeal because it is the political organisation of socialism that forms the greatest barrier to the penetration of bourgeois ideology; attempts are also made to set the various generations of the working people of the socialist countries at odds with each other.

The ideological struggle between socialism and capitalism reached a new pitch of intensity over the celebration of the 50th anniversary of the Great October Socialist Revolution and the centenary of Lenin's birth. The huge machine of imperialist propaganda worked at frantic speed, roping in and bribing anyone it could for anti-Soviet propaganda.

But to no avail. The whole world was once again convinced of the colossal historical achievements of socialism, and Soviet people emerged victorious from yet another series of ideological battles with imperialism. Even communism's ideological opponents and the anti-communist press were compelled to admit most reluctantly that the anti-Soviet campaign that had been carried on everywhere on an enormous scale had not produced the desired results. The various intimidating forecasts made by the enemy on the eve of the 24th Congress of the CPSU also suffered fiasco.

The difference between the attitude of friends and that of the class enemy towards Soviet people helps to reveal to the whole world the socialist, humanist nature of the new way of life and new type of personality that are taking shape. By comparing the various similar and diametrically opposed points of view we see that the support of friends, on the one hand, and the forced acknowledgements coming from the bourgeois environment, its intensely hostile criticism, on the other, bear out the fact that the Soviet man is really remaking life in the interests of the working people, that the Soviet man is not a myth but reality, not propaganda but the sum total of the social and political changes that have taken place in the USSR.

The drive to bring about socialist transformations is an insuperable force. The world is in a state of ferment, the world demands changes, the world is seeking a way out of the narrow confines of bourgeois society. The socialist countries' solution of the problems of social development, the problems of moulding the personality provide a great and inspiring example for all the forces working for the triumph of democracy, freedom and social justice.

In our day the argument between the Marxists-Leninists and the bourgeois sociologists on the future of Man and Mankind has been carried into the field of socio-revolutionary practice. While the exploitative systems were alone and all-embracing, this argument remained largely hypothetical. The Soviet Union's half century of development and the quarter of a century of the other socialist countries supplies irrefutable arguments in favour of Marxism-Leninism, in favour of the communist movement. The world is going through a transition from humanist ideals to humanist practice, from the intellectual creativity of the élite to the intellectual upsurge of the mass of the working people.

Bourgeois sociologists quite often refer to the Soviet experience as a great experiment. One could agree with this if it were only a matter of the speed and unusualness of what is happening. Indeed, the socio-economic and political structure of socialism so firmly rejects the previously existing structure that even the avowed anti-Communists cannot fail to recognise this fact. And it has taken not centuries but years to bring about these profound changes.

And yet, even so this is not an experiment, but a natural historical turn that is opening up a new age in human history. In a comparatively short historical period communism, conceived as an ideological-theoretical system, has become embodied in the real social forms of the life of millions of people, has become a powerful socio-political movement in nearly all countries of the world. Soviet people, the working people of the socialist countries, the millions of workers and peasants of the capitalist countries are showing profound dedication to the ideas of communism and the policy of the Communist parties.

Socialism, followed by communism, emerges as the essential form that is capable of absorbing and further developing the achievements of material and spiritual culture, as the form in which, consequently, human society is destined to continue its development. Marx described the future society as "the complete return of man to himself as a *social* (i.e., human) being—a return become conscious, and accomplished within the entire wealth of previous development"[1].

The 20th century has provided numerous proofs of the intensification of social life due to the acceleration of scientific and technological progress and the increase in the world's population. In this context the significance of the consolidating, unifying effect of socialism, of the communist ideology, should considerably increase in the next few decades. The population growth, the speedup of communications, the demand for greater organisation and coherence not only within separate societies but also in the world as a whole will compel the world's progressive forces to fight more energetically for adoption of the socialist system. The experience of the formation of the socialist personality offers invaluable arguments in favour of socialism.

The social system that socialism establishes and hence man's position in society, his moral personality are the product of History and Revolution, and because socialist transformations are carried out according to a scientific plan of revolutionary action, it may be said that Soviet man is in a quite definite sense the product of History, Revolution and Science.

---

[1] K. Marx, *Economic and Philosophic Manuscripts of 1844*, p. 102.

REQUEST TO READERS

Progress Publishers would be glad to have your opinion of this book, its translation and design and any suggestions you may have for future publications. Please send them to 21, Zubovsky Boulevard, Moscow, USSR.

Progress Publishers, Moscow offer readers four series of books dealing with various social and economic aspects of the modern world.

PROGRESS. SOCIALISM TODAY

Internal and Foreign Policy of the CPSU and the Soviet Government; Problems of the Development of Socialist Society and the Building of Communism in the USSR

Progress Publishers put out recently in this series:

BUZLYAKOV N. *Welfare—the Basic Task* (Five-Year Plan, 1971-1975). "Progress. Socialism Today"

This book examines the 9th Five-Year Plan's projects for raising the people's living standards, such as increasing real incomes, better housing, improved social and medical services, and a higher level of cultural development.

PROGRESS. CURRENT PROBLEMS

*Problems of the World Communist,
Working-Class and National Liberation
Movement; Current International Problems;
Competition Between the Two World
Systems; Growth of the Influence of the
World Socialist System; Analysis of New
Phenomena of Modern Imperialism*

*Soon to be published
in this series:*

International Communist Movement.
"Progress. Current Problems"

This book is about the fundamentals of the Marxist-Leninist revolutionary theory and of the strategy and tactics of the communist movement. It shows the characteristic features of the contemporary working-class movement and the reasons for its split, the co-operation between the Communists and Socialists in various countries, the Communist Parties' policies towards the peasantry, the youth, the middle urban strata of the intelligentsia and religious believers, and the struggle for national liberation and democracy. The authors reveal the substance of both Right-wing and "Left" opportunism and the ways in which they manifest themselves, and they show the damage opportunism is doing to the struggle for social progress.

PROGRESS. THEORIES
AND CRITICAL STUDIES

*Critical Studies of Bourgeois and Revisionist
Theories of Social Development*

Soon to be published in this series:

BOGOMOLOVA N. *The Doctrine of Human Relations—the Monopolies' Ideological Weapon.* "Progress. Theories and Critical Studies"

This is a critical study of the doctrine of "human relations" which is disseminated in the USA and other capitalist countries as a means of shaping the thinking of the working people. The book traces the development of this doctrine, the signs of its crisis in 1960s and its present evolution.

PROGRESS. PROBLEMS OF THE THIRD WORLD

Soon to be published in this series:

SHIROKOV G. *The Industrialisation of India.* "Progress. Problems of
the Third World"

India, one of the developing countries, is currently making great
strides towards industrialisation. In Marxist economic terminology
"industrialisation" means accomplishing an industrial revolution in the
entire national economy and its transfer to industrial methods of
production. Drawing extensively on factual material the author examines
the methods and scale of India's industrialisation, the changing structure in various industries, the effectiveness of production, and also the
interaction of large and small-scale industries.